MW01625452

LI KUNG-LIN'S *Classic of Filial Piety*

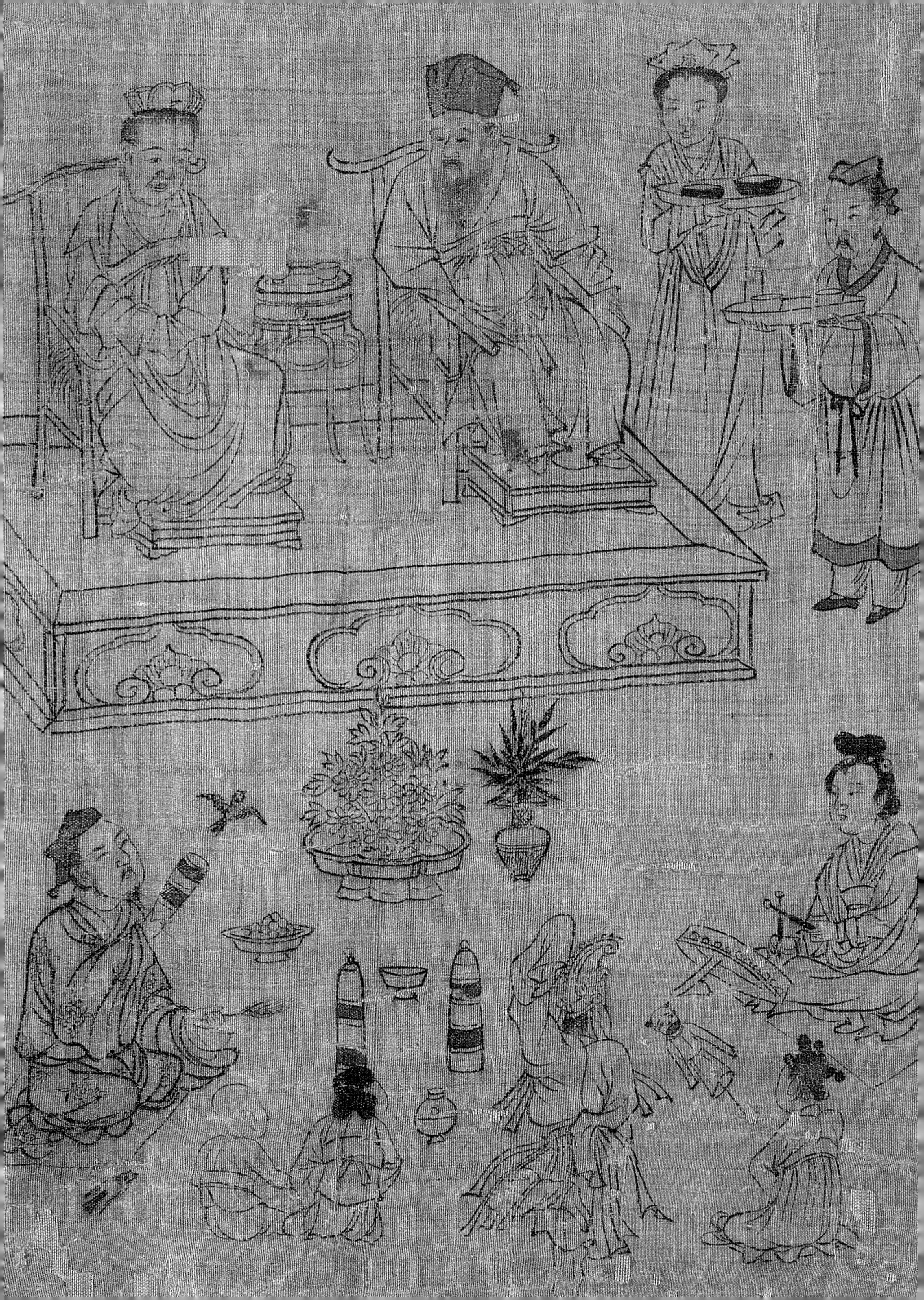

LI KUNG-LIN'S *Classic of Filial Piety*

Richard M. Barnhart

with essays by Robert E. Harrist, Jr.,
and Hui-liang J. Chu

THE METROPOLITAN MUSEUM OF ART
NEW YORK

The publication is made possible with the help of the Tang Fund of New York.

Published by The Metropolitan Museum of Art, New York

John P. O'Neill, Editor in Chief
Emily Walter, Editor
Malcolm Grear Designers, Inc., Designers
Rachel M. Ruben, Production

Color photography by Malcolm Varon
Type set in Palatino by The Sarabande Press, New York
Printed on Warren's LOE dull, 150 gsm
Color separations by Professional Graphics, Rockford, Illinois
Printing by Mercantile Printing Company, Worcester, Massachusetts
Bound by Acme Bookbinding Company, Charlestown, Massachusetts

Library of Congress Cataloging-in-Publication Data

Barnhart, Richard M., 1934–
Li Kung-lin's Classic of filial piety / Richard M. Barnhart ; with
essays by Robert E. Harrist, Jr., and Hui-liang J. Chu.
p. cm.
Contains a reproduction of Li Kung-lin's handscroll Classic of filial piety.

ISBN 0-87099-679-7

1. Li, Kung-lin, ca. 1041–1106. Classic of filial piety. 2. Li, Kung-lin, ca. 1041–1106—
Criticism and interpretation. 3. Scrolls, Chinese—Sung-Yüan dynasties, 960–1368.
4. Scrolls, Chinese—New York (N.Y.) 5. Metropolitan Museum of Art
(New York, N.Y.) I. Li, Kung-lin, ca. 1041–1106. II. Harrist, Jr., Robert E.
III. Chu, Hui-liang. IV. Title. ND1457.C56L5325 1993

759.951—dc20 93-17578
CIP

Jacket illustration
Li Kung-lin (ca. 1041–1106), detail from chapter 12 of the *Classic of Filial Piety* (pl. 9)

Frontispiece
Li Kung-lin (ca. 1041–1106), detail from chapter 10 of the *Classic of Filial Piety* (pl. 7)

CONTENTS

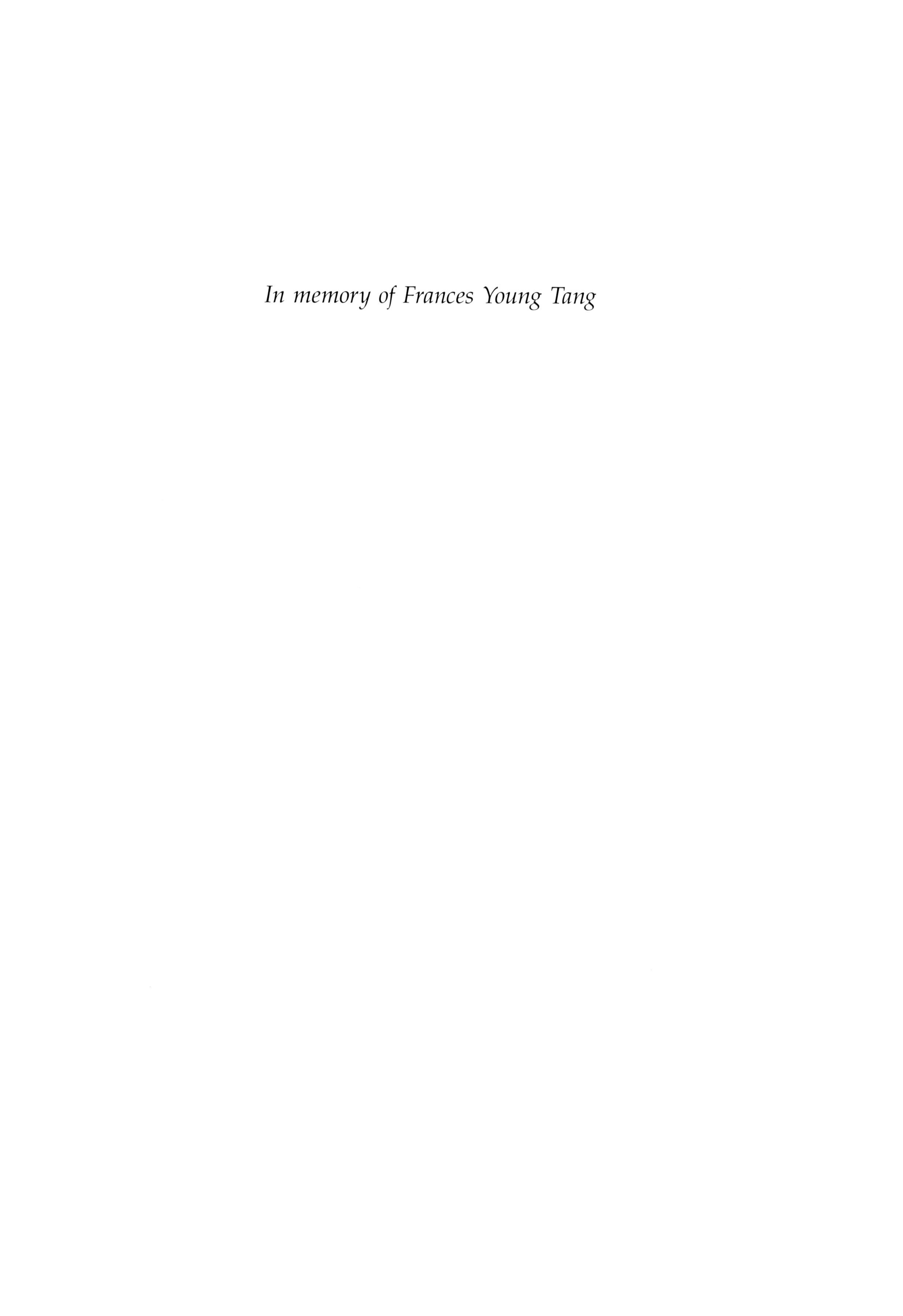

In memory of Frances Young Tang

FOREWORD

The *Classic of Filial Piety*, by the eleventh-century figure painter Li Kung-lin, is one of the preeminent monuments of Chinese art history. This publication, with contributions by three leading Li Kung-lin scholars, Professors Richard M. Barnhart of Yale University and Robert E. Harrist, Jr., of Oberlin College, and Dr. Hui-liang J. Chu of the National Palace Museum, Taipei, analyzes the painting and calligraphy of Li Kung-lin and elucidates the significance of the handscroll in the context of Chinese culture. It also commemorates the promised gift of this important work to the Metropolitan Museum as part of a group of paintings donated and promised as gifts to the Museum from Oscar L. Tang, Jack C. Tang, and Wen Fong and Constance Tang Fong. The Tang family gifts significantly augment the Museum's growing collection of Chinese painting and calligraphy. In addition to Li Kung-lin's handscroll, the gifts include three rare fourteenth-century Yüan paintings by Wang Meng, Hsia Yung, and Teng Yü; a monumental hanging scroll by the fifteenth-century Ming court painter Chung Li; two gemlike albums by the seventeenth-century Individualist masters Shih-t'ao (Tao-chi) and Kung Hsien; a lavish oversize handscroll by the late-seventeenth-century Yangchow professional painter Yüan Chiang; and a magnificent four-panel painting of bamboo by the eighteenth-century Yangchow "eccentric" painter Ching Hsieh.

The gifts of the Tang family paintings reflect the recent surge of interest in Asian art in this country and the continued commitment to Chinese painting and calligraphy at the Metropolitan signaled by the opening of the Astor Garden Court and the Douglas Dillon Galleries in June 1981. This publication is made possible with the help of the Tang Fund of New York. I would also like to express my thanks to the following members of the Museum staff: Mr. Takemitsu Oba, C. V. Starr Conservator, and Sondra Castile, Assistant Conservator, worked for many years to bring the scroll to its present state of rejuvenation, and for this volume they have written a most interesting and valuable account of its conservation and mounting; Dr. Maxwell K. Hearn, Curator in the Department of Asian Art, devoted meticulous attention to the preparation of the publication; and Emily Walter, Senior Editor, lent her wonderful skills to editing the manuscript.

PHILIPPE DE MONTEBELLO
Director
The Metropolitan Museum of Art

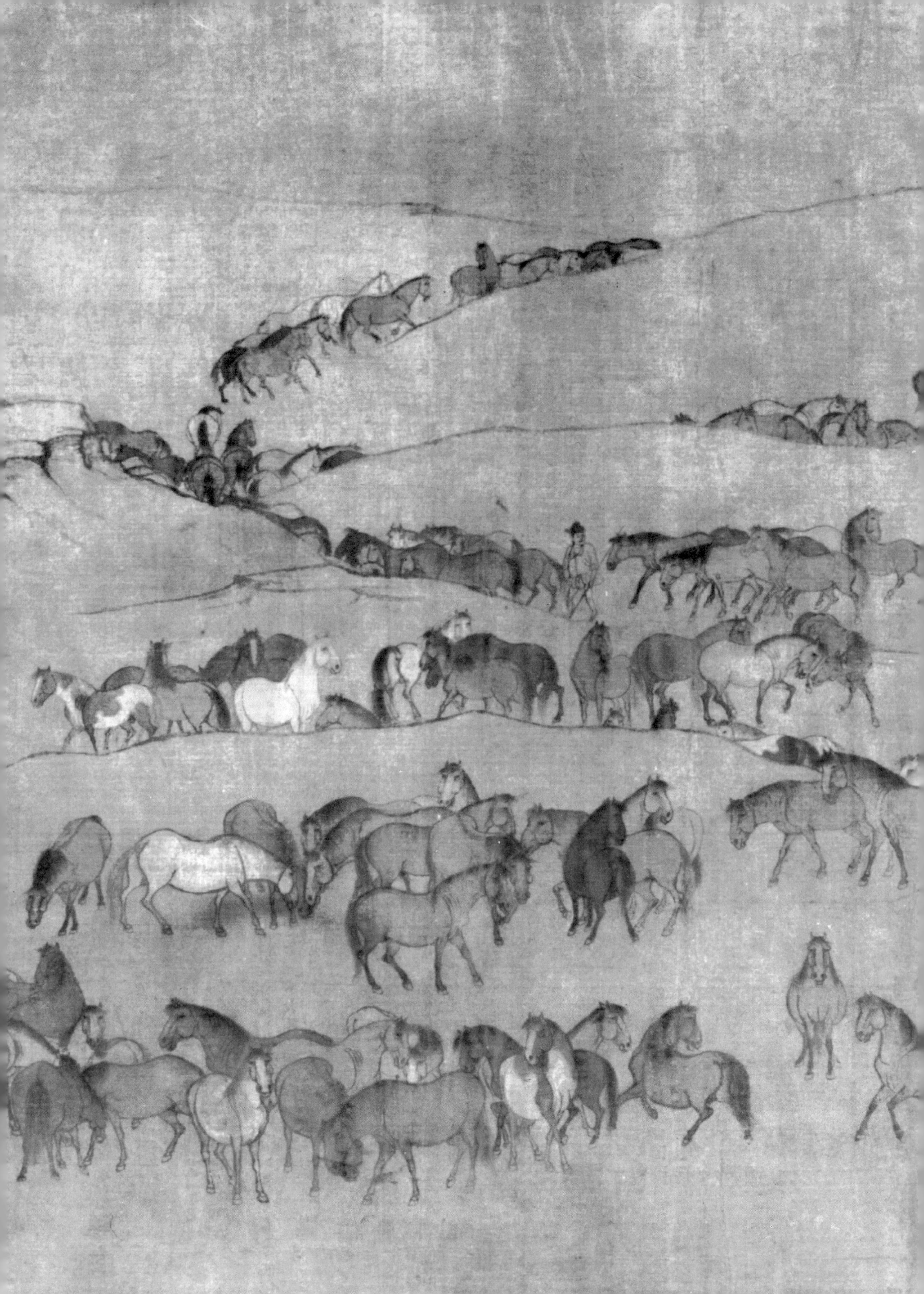

LI KUNG-LIN AND THE ART OF PAINTING

Richard M. Barnhart

If today we are less interested than we once were in systems of critical and historical evaluation of the kind that would identify Li Kung-lin (ca. 1041–1106) as "the greatest painter of the Sung dynasty," we might nonetheless still find it appropriate to examine Li as one of the central figures among those whose art defined what Sung painting became in the eyes of later historians. In this regard, Li stands at the precise historical point at which the systemic bases of the earlier imperial tradition were just beginning to be undermined by proponents of a new gentry style and philosophy of painting that would eventually dominate the later periods of Chinese history. China itself, during this same period, was being transformed from a society ruled by a hereditary aristocracy into one effectively governed by a new class of scholar-gentry-bureaucrat. Li's own life is, in fact, an embodiment of this change, since he was born into one of the great aristocratic families of Chiang-nan, the Li clan of Nanking, which founded and ruled the small Southern T'ang kingdom of Chin-ling in the tenth century. His ancestral family lost its status with the establishment of the Sung state, however, and Li spent much of his life as an official serving in the lowest levels of the government bureaucracy.

Before Li's time, the art of painting was a public and imperial art, sponsored by the imperial courts, the powerful hereditary families, and the great temples, and was required to convey the images, ideals, values, and propaganda of those institutions. It was by and large a colorful, handsome, and dramatic art, glorifying the political, religious, and economic rulers of China and narrowly serving their purposes. This pattern did not by any means end with the Sung dynasty, and in fact remained the central tradition of art until the end of the Chinese empire. In the hands of Li and a few others, however, painting began to take on

Figure 1. Li Kung-lin, *Imperial Horses at Pasture*, after Wei Yen, detail of figure 2

a new role and transform itself into a formal mode of expression, like poetry, that could serve to convey the mind of the individual artist as well as the emblems of those who controlled his life.

Art, in other words, acquired the capacity to criticize, reject, exhort, and subvert, as well as to flatter and glorify the powerful. It was only when it was seen and understood to have this capability that painting began systematically to attract the most intelligent and highly educated of men to its ranks. Such later masters as Chao Meng-fu, Shen Chou, Wen Cheng-ming, Tung Chi-ch'ang, Pa-ta Shan-jen, and Shih-t'ao might never have become painters had not Li developed the potential of painting to convey the nuances of the individual life through its forms.

A few years after Li's death, the great government catalogue of the imperial collection of paintings recorded 107 of his works.[1] Many others are mentioned in later historical sources, but only three of them exist today. This reduction by time and fate of an oeuvre originally numbering perhaps several hundred down to three is, of course, a crippling loss. Even allowing for the fact that copies of varying degrees of reliability permit us to reconstruct something of what is lost, it might be argued that we can no longer truly understand the art of Li Kung-lin, so little has survived. Some might argue the opposite, that even one fragmentary original work allows us true art-historical understanding; but, in any case, the three extant works by Li are such extraordinary and beautiful works that they not only richly embody his own art but also reflect upon and interact with the art of his time in such a way as to convey the nature of Sung painting and indeed the very processes by which it was formed.

All three works are handscrolls, a matter of some interest, since Li certainly worked in other formats. Possibly because handscrolls are slightly more easily preserved than other formats, more of them have survived. (They are certainly more easily carried or stored than large hanging scrolls; in Sung times, however, handscrolls and hanging scrolls were about the same size, generally speaking, and albums, fans, and album leaves were as easily carried or hidden as handscrolls.) But it appears more likely that the majority of Li's works were handscrolls. In his time, they were used primarily for narrative and didactic works serving a small, focused audience, since there was almost no way to display a handscroll publicly in traditional China.

Why this may be of interest is the possibility that Li himself did a great deal to contribute to the growing popularity of the handscroll format. All three of his extant paintings were done originally as handscrolls and could have had no other intended function than to be seen, read, and understood by one particular patron. One of them was made at the order of the emperor himself—or the imperial court—and therefore fits the earlier imperial practice. Another, however, was made for a scholar named Yang, and the third may have been painted directly for one of Li's friends, a scholar and poet named Chang Hsün. Before Li, it is unlikely that the artist in China painted primarily for specific and often private patrons in this way. Since it would seem that his friends Mi Fu, Wang Shen, Su Shih, and others also painted more for individual friends, colleagues, and patrons, it is clear that what is emerging in China at this historical moment is the birth of a new relationship between the artist and his patrons.[2]

Li's three handscrolls represent something considerably more than simply three works. Their combined length is over thirty-six feet. One of them contains five separate paintings; another, twelve; and the third includes over a thousand horses and a hundred men, so that we have in the surviving oeuvre a total of hundreds of men, animals, buildings, and pieces of furniture, as well as countless other miscellaneous elements. If we wish to see how Li painted bamboo or landscape or architecture, we can do so. How did he paint in color on silk, as opposed to working in ink on paper? How did he "copy" ancient works? What are the principles of his compositional structure? Which classical masters did he emulate and study, and how did he use their characteristics? If we must deeply regret the loss of so much of his art, at least we can take some satisfaction from the fact that so rich and diverse an array of his art as we have remains in the three handscrolls now extant. Their range is interesting for other reasons. One work is a copy of a T'ang-dynasty composition; one is a series of portraits (of both horses and men); and the last is an imaginative and rich visualization of social, philosophical, and moral ideals. Three primary elements of the Northern Sung are thus embedded in Li's art. In one he studies and copies the classical masters. In another he sketches from life. And in the third he isolates intangible moral properties and seeks a way to give them form. Studied separately, they shed much light on the nature of Sung art. As a group, they separate and put into focus the strands of his art as we have it today, and they define the unique contribution Li made to both the substance of Sung art itself and the historical remaking of earlier art that was also the contribution of only a few such men.

According to the artist's inscription and signature, *Imperial Horses at Pasture* (figs. 1, 2) was copied by Li at the order of the imperial court from an original painting by the T'ang horse painter Wei Yen.[3] Although we cannot be certain when Li painted it, it is quite clear from the array of seals and the very physical materials of the scroll itself that it was mounted and registered during the reign of Emperor Hui-tsung (r. 1100–1126). Li had already retired from official service by this time, but his reputation was at an early zenith, Hui-tsung having elevated Li and the landscape painter Li Ch'eng (d. 967) to the highest pantheon of the art of painting, judging from their biographies in the imperial catalogue, *Hsüan-ho hua-p'u*.[4] It is interesting that both men were of aristocratic descent, Li Ch'eng from the T'ang imperial family and Li Kung-lin from the royal Li clan of Chin-ling.

The imperial catalogue records twenty-seven paintings by Wei Yen, several of which could have been Li's model.[5] None of Wei's works exists today, but it is

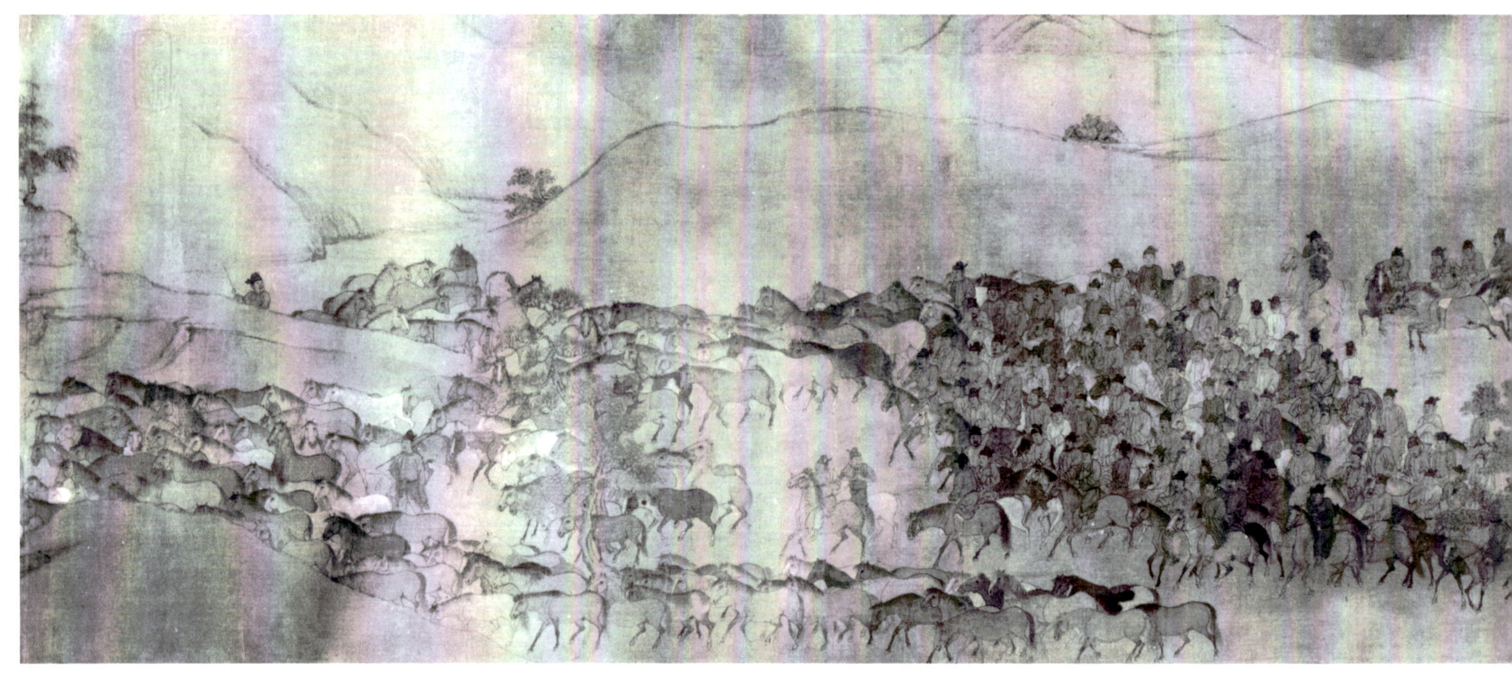

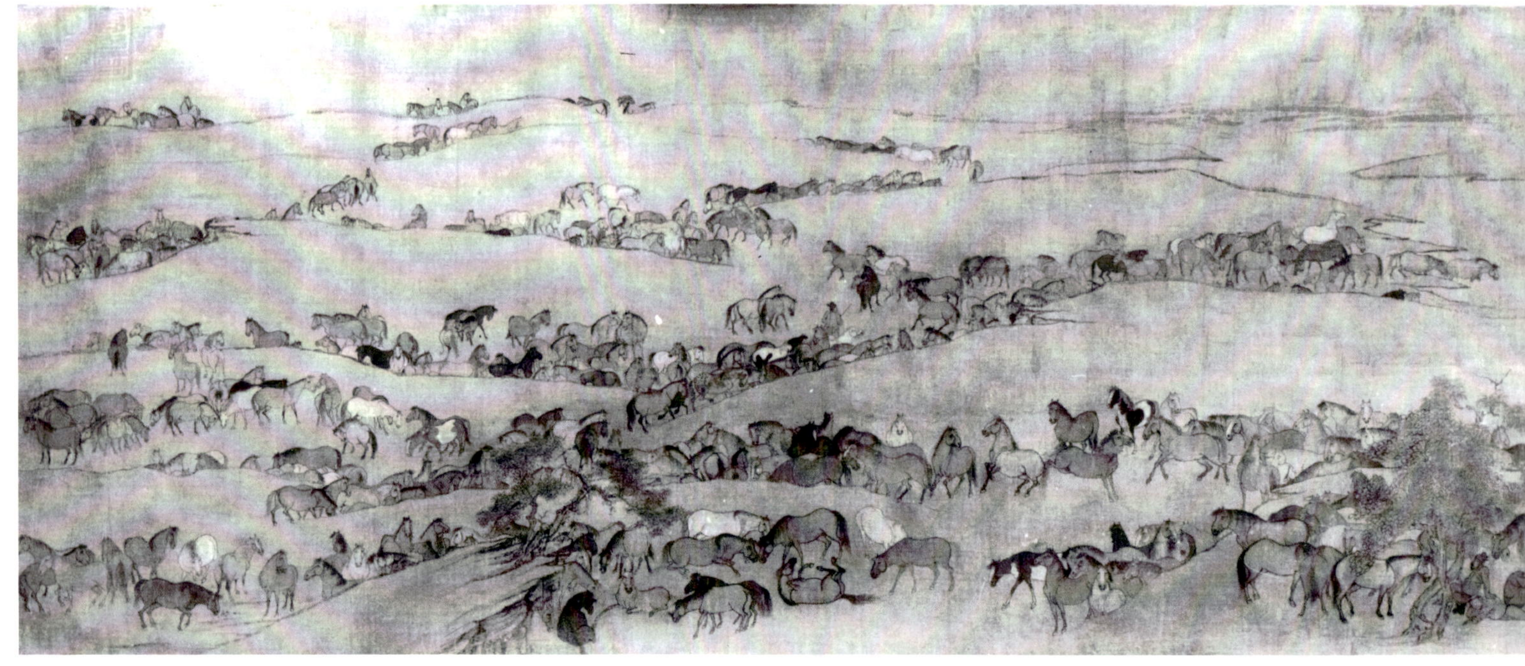

Figure 2. Li Kung-lin, *Imperial Horses at Pasture*, after Wei Yen. Handscroll, ink and color on silk, 18 × 168⅝ in. (45.7 × 428.2 cm). Palace Museum, Beijing

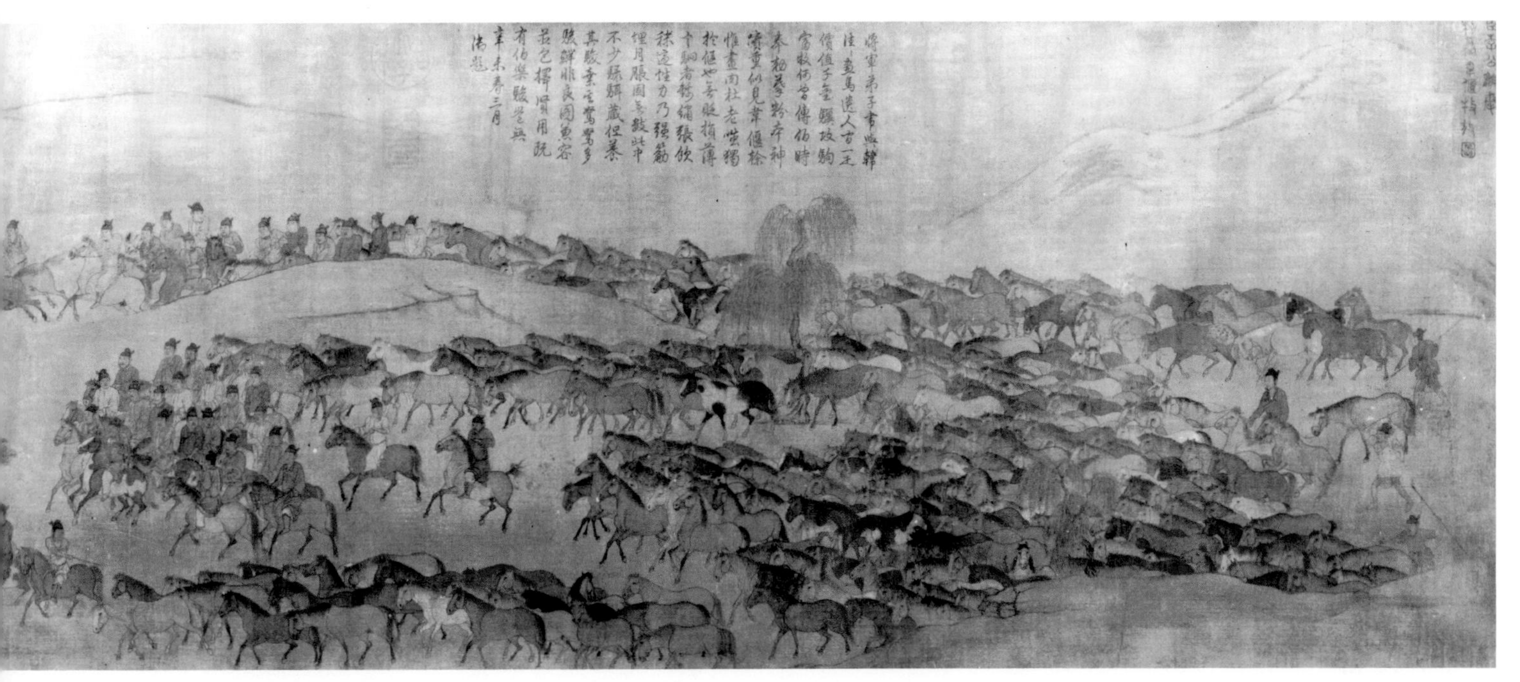

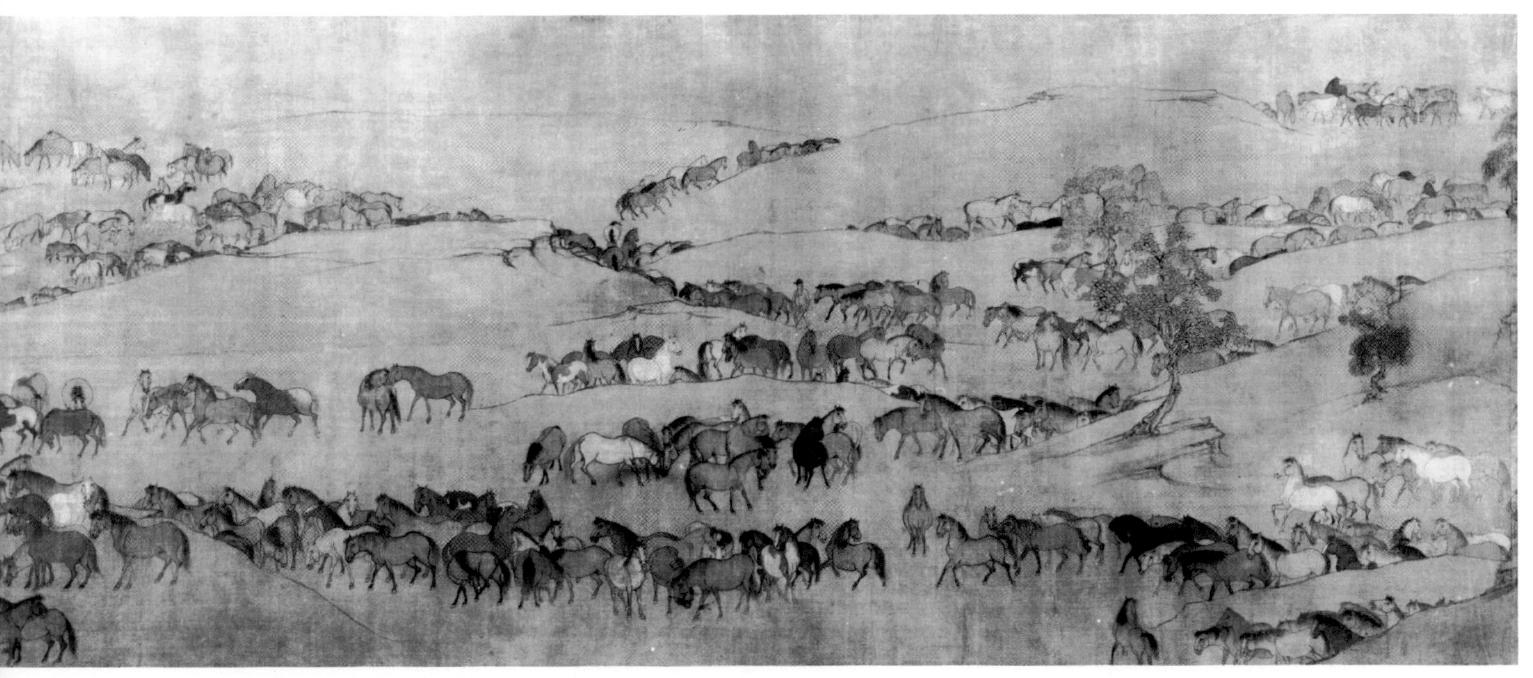

possible to see something very close to his art through the medium of the anonymous wall paintings from the T'ang imperial tombs, especially those in the tomb of Prince Chang-huai (Li Hsien; 654–684).[6] The galloping polo players, mounted hunters, and other massed horses and horsemen constitute a major theme of the tomb and surely reflect the passion for horses and equestrian activities that typified the T'ang imperial family, as it did nearly every later imperial court. All of the earliest classical masters of horse painting—Ts'ao Pa, Han Kan, and Wei Yen—were T'ang artists, and *Imperial Horses at Pasture* is only one of the many copies and studies of their work that Li made.[7] Our only knowledge of the otherwise lost early works is in fact preserved in such copies, so that we begin to sense the degree to which the Sung period reconstructed its own past.

Nonetheless, it is also clear that Li's passion for horses preceded his study of earlier paintings of the subject, and that his long practice of collecting, copying, and studying older paintings of horses was but an element in his lifelong fascination with the animal. His love for horses seemed to some of his contemporaries an unnatural and potentially harmful excess: Buddhist friends warned that he was in danger of becoming a horse in another incarnation, and in his late years he is said to have given up the subject of horses to paint only Buddhist and Taoist images.[8] If the latter is true, however, it is more likely to have happened simply because Li became quite ill and partially incapacitated in his final years, and could no longer visit the imperial stud as he once had done habitually. Confined to his bed much of the time, he could, according to one account, do little more than draw his fingers over the cover as if tracing old lines and shapes from mind pictures.[9]

According to Li's nephew, the master once painted a picture of the early Buddhist scholar Chih-tun judging horses. Chih-tun, when criticized for his passion for horses by Buddhist colleagues, had replied, "I love to gaze upon their lively spirit and fire."[10] We may suppose that in choosing to paint Chih-tun, Li was answering his own critics in the same way. We might even imagine that when, late in life, he lay incapacitated in his bed, it was, among other images, those of horses that he traced on his bedcover.

In any case, in the catalogue of Li's paintings compiled by T. Y. Leo for Agnes Meyer in 1923, thirty-six paintings of horses are recorded. These include horses pasturing in the imperial stud, tribute horses from the various foreign kingdoms, horses being trained in both civil and military exercises, horses at foal, rolling in the dirt, and galloping in springtime, the judging of fine horses by skilled connoisseurs, famous horses from earlier dynasties, and copies of classical early paintings of horses. There is no doubt that Li admired, studied, sketched, and depicted horses throughout his lifetime with a purposefulness which surpassed that of most men, and which led to his rank among the greatest masters of the subject who have ever lived in China.

Imperial Horses at Pasture is a realistic depiction of more than twelve hundred horses and nearly one hundred fifty men in a broad sweep of fields through which the imperial horses are driven by officials, keepers, and herdsmen. In the sheer number of details and the broad, heroic scale of its vision, the painting is comparable to another monument of imperial art from the period, Chang Tse-tuan's (11th–12th century) *Spring Festival on the River* (see fig. 9).[11] Just as this work portraying bustling city life in the Sung capital depicts scenes known well to Li, so also does the scroll of galloping horses at the imperial stud. It has been pointed out that Li's composition resembles that evoked by the T'ang poet Tu Fu's description in his "Sandy Stud Park," a poem that may have been related to Wei Yen's original paintings on the subject which now became the model for the Sung painter.[12] Tu Fu's description of the imperial stud was a warning against the rebellious schemes of the usurper An Lu-shan, and it is likely that in Li's time as well a pictorial composition of pasturing horses recalled both imperial power and predatory dangers. Tu Fu's poem has been translated by William Hung:

> *Have you not seen in the P'ing-i Prefecture white sands as white as water,*
> *Surrounded by a wall forty miles in length?*
> *In ancient times imperial steeds were reared by the waters of Wo-wa,*
> *Now the blooded breeds are offered from here.*
> *Graze on the fresh, green grass that flourishes even in winter.*
> *Such well-fed, strong horses are not found even in the West Regions;*
> *The colts foaled here each year excel those of the frontiers.*
> *His Majesty has a brave officer in charge of the stud,*
> *Within which the Imperial stables are grouped like thick clouds.*
> *A snow-white courser alone is chosen for His Majesty;*
> *Twice in the year, spring and autumn, he goes to Court.*
> *Of the hundreds of thousands in the stables or pastures*
> *Of the Empire, which one can compare with him?*
> *As the fleetest of foot he is already peerless,*
> *Not to speak of his heroic loyalty and resourcefulness.*
> *I see horses dash among sandy mounds,*
> *I see them jumping and leaping across the streams.*
> *Entering the woods, they play and wrestle with wild deer;*
> *Floating on the ponds, they disturb the turtles and water-lizards. Beware!*
> *There appears a giant fish as big as a man.*
> *It has golden scales and a vermilion tail.*
> *Has monstrosity anything in common with righteousness?*
> *It is frightening, though it is not really a dragon.*[13]

While we may continue to think of the Sung dynasty as a long age of peace, the fact is that rebellion, revolt, and insurrection were never far from the seat of power in imperial China. From the beginning of the Sung, founded through warfare and military power, until its end at the hands of invincible Mongol forces, the dynasty was beset both from without and from within by constant threats to its existence.

Li's friendship with the chief officer of the imperial stud allowed him easy and frequent access to the kind of scene portrayed in his painting, and it is likely that he observed sweeping panoramas like this one more than once. He enjoyed watching the imperial guard in its military exercises and training, and perhaps it was during these activities that he met the brilliant young officer Wang Shen, whose later landscapes of exile are a counterpart to Li's images of disaffected officialdom.[14] Li's position in the bureaucracy was, however, an ambiguous one, since his own family had been among the victims of the Sung conquest and his father had been disgraced by the Sung government. He clearly avoided bureaucratic service as long as he could, and he retired at the age of barely fifty, after having avoided even the slightest bureaucratic accomplishment for twenty years.

There can be little doubt that Li intended his composition as an allegory. It begins with massed horses herded into dense groups by attendants and outriders. Stick-bearing herdsmen bring up the rear, a well-controlled pack of animals running before them. This tightly reined community extends through exactly the first half of the composition. Thereafter, among the hundreds of horses that wander freely throughout the broad pastures and fields there are only five men; three of them sleep under a tree, and two others wander idly and alone among the grazing horses. As control slackens freedom grows, until we see the animals spread freely across the entire range of vision (the end of the scroll appears to have been cut, so we may no longer see the original end of the composition, but the general direction is clear). Of course, if Tu Fu's forty miles of walls correspond to an equivalent Sung boundary, then there were no truly wild, free animals, only some that were relatively unrestrained within those final, uncrossable boundaries.

Imperial Horses at Pasture is a painting about control, for all the beauty of its depiction. Men with sticks and power create order out of chaos, and horses that would otherwise graze by distant streams are herded into conformity and obedience. Throughout the obviously troubled years, during which he held one minor office after another and saw his friends imprisoned, banished, retire early, or die prematurely, Li came to know well the results of such control, and he depicted this disturbing aspect of the imperial system more than once, as we shall see.

Here, the system of central control beloved by Chinese rulers from their earliest appearance in history—and much in favor even today—is cast into an almost musically enchanting form, orchestrated by the artist with sensitivity to the slightest interplay of opening and closing forms and movement. The tight herd of horses we see at the beginning is contained both by men and by the hills that rise beyond, holding it inside as if framed; gradually, as control slackens, we see a wider and broader setting, as one hill becomes another and yet another, while, by contrast, the stunting limits of control that we saw at the beginning are made more dramatic.

Within that slowly changing structure, the artist attends lovingly to his images. The knowledge of horses—how they look, move, rest, and interact—that lies behind such representation is unmistakable, and in seeing it, we recall the artist haunting the imperial stables, giving his paintings to stable boys and handlers in return for access, and sketching what he saw until, in consternation at his devotion, his Buddhist friends warned him that he was going to turn into a horse. Li loved horses. He loved them for their spirit, courage, and strength, and for their individuality, just as if they were people. As he depicts them here he reveals an unerring certainty as to their every variety, every mannerism, pose, and movement, the fruit of those long hours of study and reflection, when perhaps he even wandered among the grazing animals, just as the two isolated men toward the end of his scroll do, just like one of them.

In other words, no matter what the original painting by Wei Yen may have looked like, what Li reveals to us is his own reflective and highly trained skill and the daily, habitual study of life that was unmistakably his practice. With masterly assuredness, he presents his pageant of horses and men in a perfectly calibrated landscape setting in which the challenging problem of perspective is made to seem incidental: from near to far, a gradual diminution of scale prevails. A hundred horses in a hundred poses fill a square foot, each of them lively and vivid. Only when we have arrived at the end, however, and see them in their variety and freedom, can we look back at the beginning and realize that there, docile and tightly controlled, they all have the same head-down, submissive, sheeplike sameness. At the end they playfully fight with and nuzzle each other, idly drink from a stream, or wander back into the ravines. In a state of Taoist freedom—protected, of course, by those final, invisible boundaries somewhere far off—their handlers can sleep easily beneath the trees, and the horses may live at ease, without either tight control or chaos.

I believe that in such paintings Li quite consciously conveys to us this particular aspect of his view of life. Even his earliest biographers, the compilers of the imperial catalogue *Hsüan-ho hua-p'u,* for example, acknowledge that his paintings "usually convey some subtle admonition, in the same way that Yen Chun-p'ing reformed people by telling their fortunes."[15] Surely those who controlled men's lives also would have read such a message.

Li Kung-lin was a skilled portrait painter, and the purpose of his portraits was to reveal and convey those qualities of place, class, character, and personality that distinguish human lives one from another.[16] In other words, he drew careful distinctions, describing things as they are—within the conventions and limitations of his time and place. His admirers, in any case, regarded him as the greatest realist painter of his day, esteeming precisely that attention to detail which distinguished one personality or social class from another.[17] If today all

Sung painting seems relatively realistic in comparison with everything that followed in the later history of Chinese art, it is valuable to know that in an age of realists, Li stood out. This is particularly important in looking at the subtleties of his great masterpiece of *pai-miao*, or plain-ink drawing, the *Five Tribute Horses* (figs. 3a–e), believed to exist still in a private Japanese collection (but reportedly destroyed during the Second World War).[18] The five horses and five grooms depicted here are the only overt portraits by Li that have survived—though we should not regard ourselves as greatly deprived, since there are at least these portraits of five horses and five men. Ten portraits by the greatest portrait master of the eleventh century are in fact a feast of portraits.

Li did not invent the technique of painting in black ink, but he elevated to an art the earlier practice of sketching and making preliminary drafts in ink alone.[19] The technique consists of painting directly on a paper or silk surface without preliminary underdrawing (except for the kind of swift, pale line visible in some *pai-miao* paintings of the Sung and Yüan periods, indicating that a loose, sketchy underdrawing was sometimes done to provide guidelines for the ineradicable black-ink lines that followed) and without color, except for occasional vermilion accents and, of course, ink wash, both as tone and as a modeling device.

While few portraits remain from the eleventh century, one with which we can compare Li Kung-lin's is owned by the Kōzanji Temple in Kyoto, a portrait of an unknown Ch'an, or Zen, master (fig. 4). Painted in brilliant colors and rich decorative patterns of silk and brocade, the unidentified teacher is depicted in strict formal style (Japanese *chinzo*, Chinese *ting-hsiang*), seated in a high-backed chair with his feet drawn up under him. The face is done with subtle attention to nuances of curving cheek, nostril, and eyelid, conveying the personality of a fleshy, broad-chested man whose calm, expressionless face does not altogether conceal an impression of great authority and intelligence.[20] Among such men Li was a familiar figure, for he was a devoted Buddhist and numbered among his friends some of the most learned Ch'an teachers of the time.

Li's first groom (fig. 3a) is another broad-chested, calm-eyed man of apparent wisdom and experience. Drawn relatively quickly with pale ink and a few darker accents in the pupils of the eyes, the face is remarkably vivid and realistic. In place of the rich color and design of the Ch'an portrait, Li's drapery is drawn swiftly and surely in plain ink, without shading or texture. The ink lines themselves have a rhythmic, harmonious quality, radiating across the paper surface like slow waves. All that matters representationally about the body itself is its strong physical presence and attitude of reverent subservience. This reduction of all the painterly elements of portraiture to ink lines and sparse ink wash, without traditionally decorative qualities, is a transformation something like the one that characterizes the change from a colorful, richly decorative, and realistic late-medieval style to the quiet, shadowed monumentality of Masaccio. It is a fundamental art-historical change that harbors deeply significant associations, since such change does not occur superficially, as a merely aesthetic exploration.

To critics of the time, Li's *pai-miao* painting was an assertion of the philosophy and the aesthetic of the scholar over those of the professional painter; this could be interpreted as a class statement as well, in which the scholar-bureaucrat establishes superiority over mere professionalism. Professionalism, of course, is another of the evils that some critics would have seen Li's *pai-miao* aesthetic triumphing over, just as the scholar's lack of interest in technical or professional expertise puts itself in the service of a higher, more intelligent order, unencumbered by mere technical skill or specific knowledge. In fact, Li's *pai-miao* is yet another rejection of the imposed conditions of servitude that Li reacted against throughout his lifetime. If those at court expected colors and decoration on silk, then he would paint on paper with ink alone. There was no reduction in the skill required for this style; if anything, even greater skill was required, since nothing could be covered up. In exposing every risk taken, every failure encountered, every bold stroke achieved, it was akin to the art of calligraphy.

But Li's *pai-miao* was not calligraphy; it was painting reduced to its linear essence—ink lines without color, and with only the merest suggestion of tonality. With this new medium Li painted his most personal and intimate works, such works as *Five Tribute Horses*, which seem to address a handful of friends and colleagues rather than any larger audience, friends like the poet and calligrapher Huang T'ing-chien (1045–1105), who inscribed a brief identification and description next to each horse and added a colophon praising both the painter and another common friend's writing style. Even this mutually congratulatory flavor may have been more than Li expected. The painting itself seems to be closer to private observation—a reflection on the nature of man and the horse—than to anything possible through verbal description. Huang T'ing-chien's inscriptions thus became curiously trivial and unnecessary. Here, for example, is the inscription beside the first horse: "To the right is the horse, Phoenix Head Piebald, eight years old, five feet four inches high, given as tribute by the Yü-chen kingdom, and received by the Left Unicorn stud on the sixteenth day of the twelfth month of the first year of Yüan-yu [1086]."

In the past, judging from such copies and descriptions of earlier works as we have today, paintings of tribute horses (which were popular and very common) were done as though they were colorful public processions.[21] Foreign tribute to the Chinese throne, after all, was as much a public act as any other necessary ceremony of state authority; if no one saw it, it had no effect. The audience, of course, may have been composed only of court officials, which is what Li was, but the audience for both the occasion itself and depictions of it needed to be impressed by the drama of the ritual and entertained by the sight of exotic foreign objects and people. Such processions certainly were something to mar-

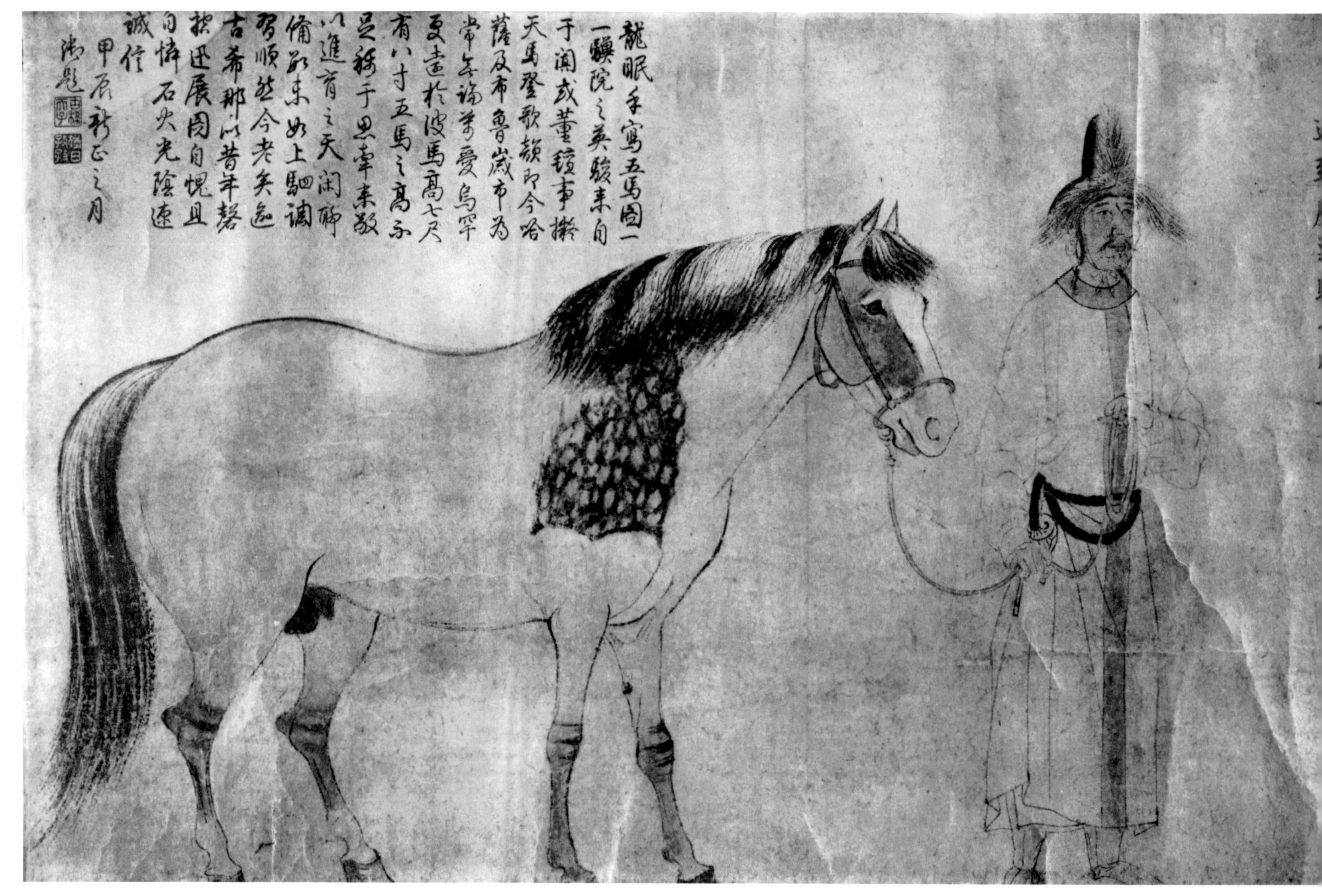

b

Figure 3a–e. Li Kung-lin, *Five Tribute Horses*, datable to 1090. Handscroll, ink on paper. Present location unknown; formerly in Kikuchi and Yamamoto Teijiro collections, Japan

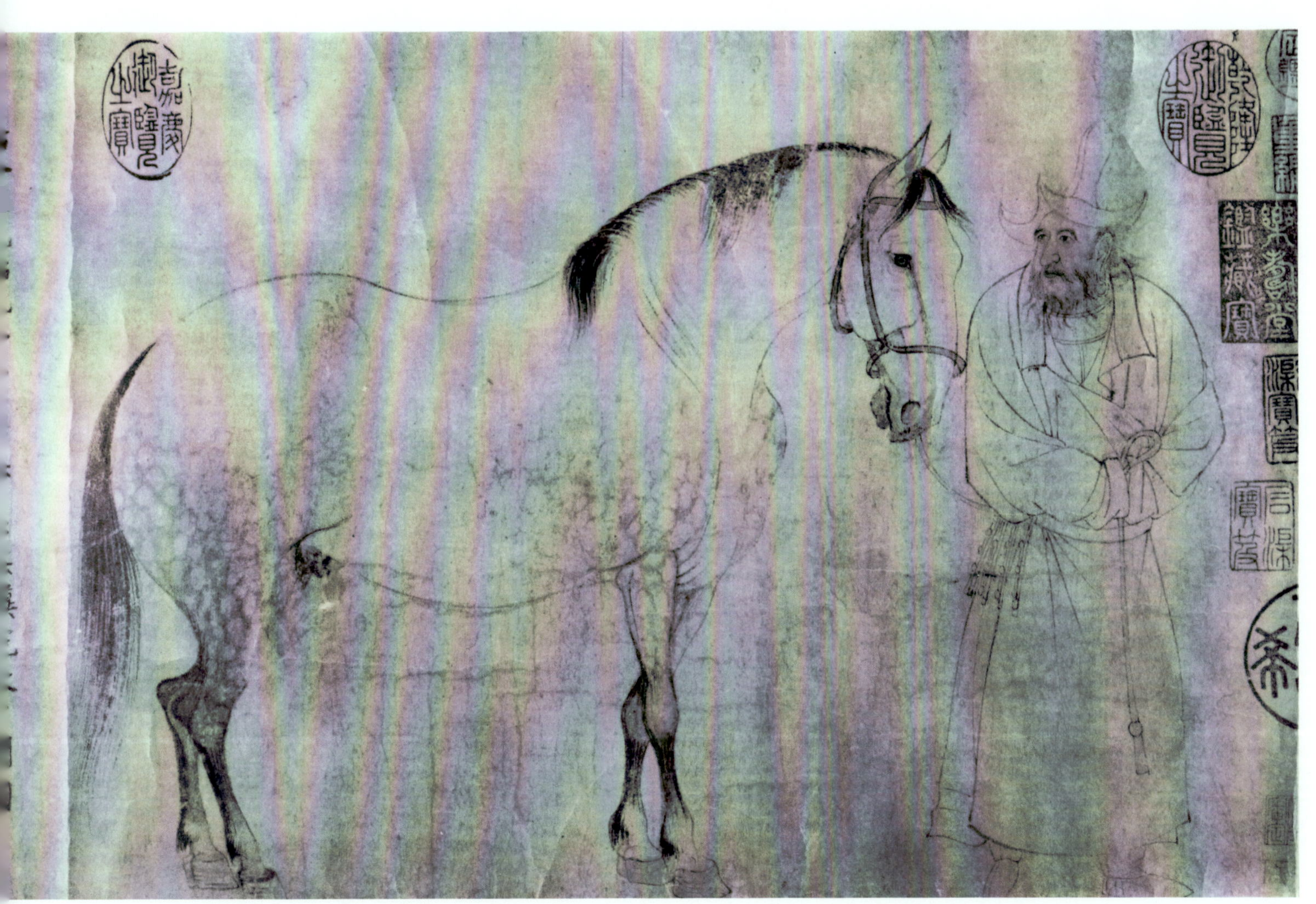

a

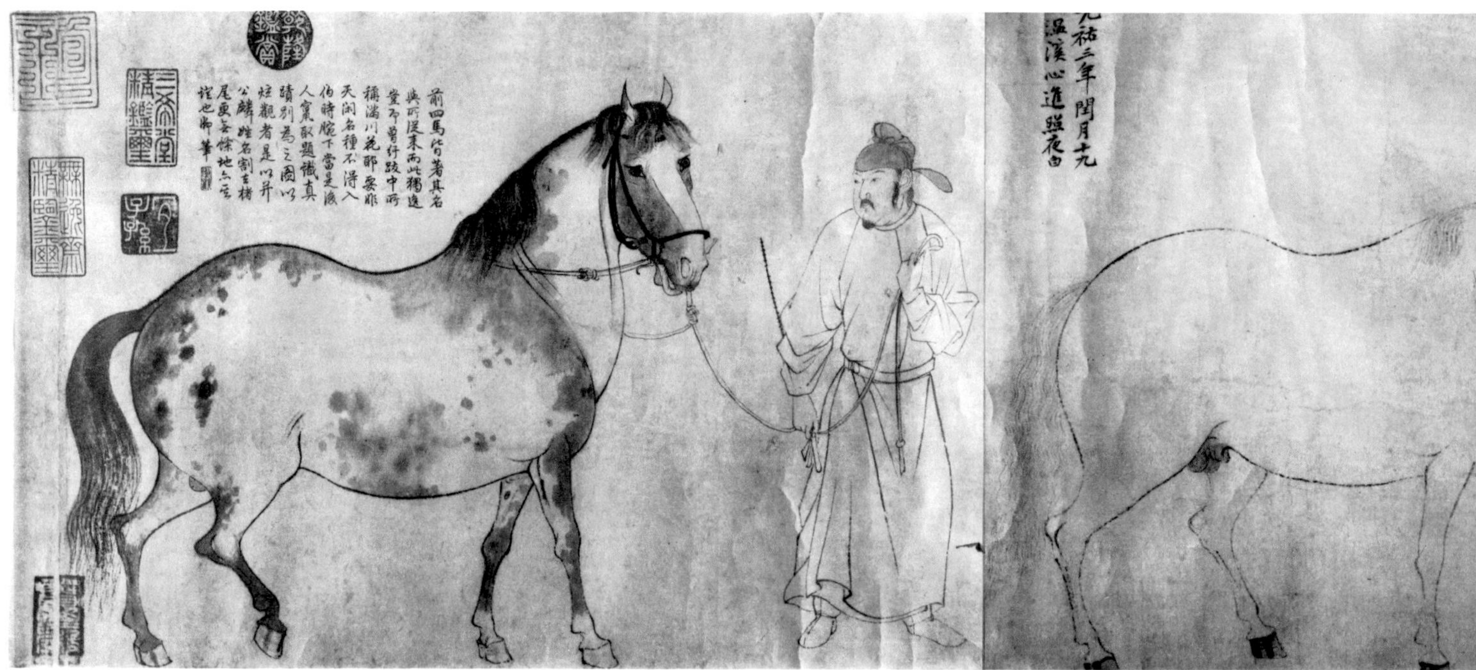

e

Figure 3a–e. Li Kung-lin, *Five Tribute Horses*

vel at, though the audience could still congratulate themselves on being Chinese, residents of the central kingdom of the universe.

Li gives his audience no color, no drama, no pageant, nothing at all to inspire self-congratulation. His horses are prisoners; his grooms, servants. Despite this reality, each animal and each man is presented as an individual, as keenly and sympathetically observed and depicted as if he were an intimate friend or close relative of the artist. This was a small and subtle heresy, a slap in the face of arrogance and power.

Li looks so closely at his objects that he sees what others may not: how each groom resembles the horse he has cared for, how the posture or stance of each echoes the other, how physical attributes are similar in horse and man, and how these two different worlds of man and beast are held together by a short piece of rope and a long bond of mutual trust.[22]

As portraits alone they are the very measure of achievement in a great age of portrait painting. Perhaps only George Stubbs and Giuseppe Castiglione would have appreciated Li's attention to the individuality of each horse. Feng-t'ou-ts'ung, Phoenix Head Piebald (fig. 3a), is a horse of great strength with a large, intelligent head. His visible eye is like the eyes of his attendant, open wide, calm, and unafraid. Brocade Shoulder Piebald (fig. 3b) has the youthful, eager look of a Shetland pony and a long, curly mane like a mat, or like the straw hat worn by his groom; and he too has a faithful, smiling face. Good Head Red (fig. 3c) is more introverted, his shadowed eye like the eyes of his groom, sunk deep into his skull; both horse and man stand awkwardly. White Shining in the Night

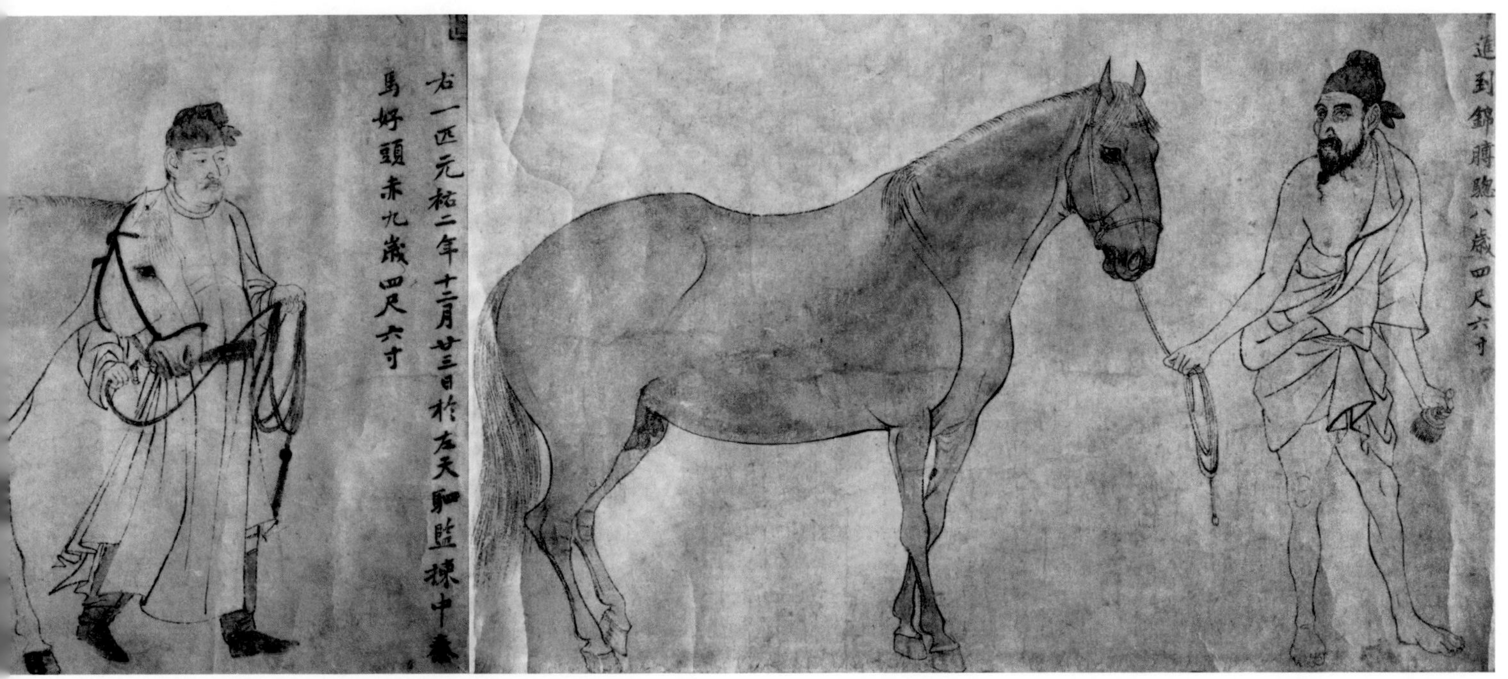

d

c

(fig. 3d) is as calm and placid as the moon his name evokes. And the last horse, Flowers Fill the Stream (fig. 3e), a beautifully dappled stallion, is proud and spirited, evidently the least broken and domesticated of the five, despite the whip carried by his handsome attendant.

What is most remarkable about these paintings technically is the brilliance of the brush drawing. Never before had anything like this been done, the bare, unpolished brushstroke left before us, mistakes and all, yet brilliantly creating forms in space. The subtle nuances of pressure and slight turnings of the lines create relatively powerful configurations of tangible forms and receding contours. Bridles wrap themselves around heads. Hands grip ropes. A robe spreads around striding boots. Terse ink lines define three-dimensional forms as surely as a sculptor models clay. Taught by centuries of connoisseurs and critics of Chinese painting—and conditioned by our own relatively recent appreciation of the qualities of sketches and drawings—we can recognize the graphic rawness and immediacy of Li's brush. But how did the people of his own time see so clearly what it has taken us so long to appreciate? How is it possible for so demanding an art to have risen so quickly to such high public esteem?

Ultimately, we can only guess. But in all probability the attention given to Li's art by so many so quickly owes primarily to the fact that he was befriended and admired by the small coterie of scholars, poets, and artists who were undoubtedly the most gifted and distinguished men of their time. Su Shih, Huang T'ing-chien, Wang Shen, Mi Fu, Ch'in Kuan, Tung Yu, Chang Lei, Ch'ao Pu-chih, and those scholars and officials, Buddhist priests, and Taoist monks who associated

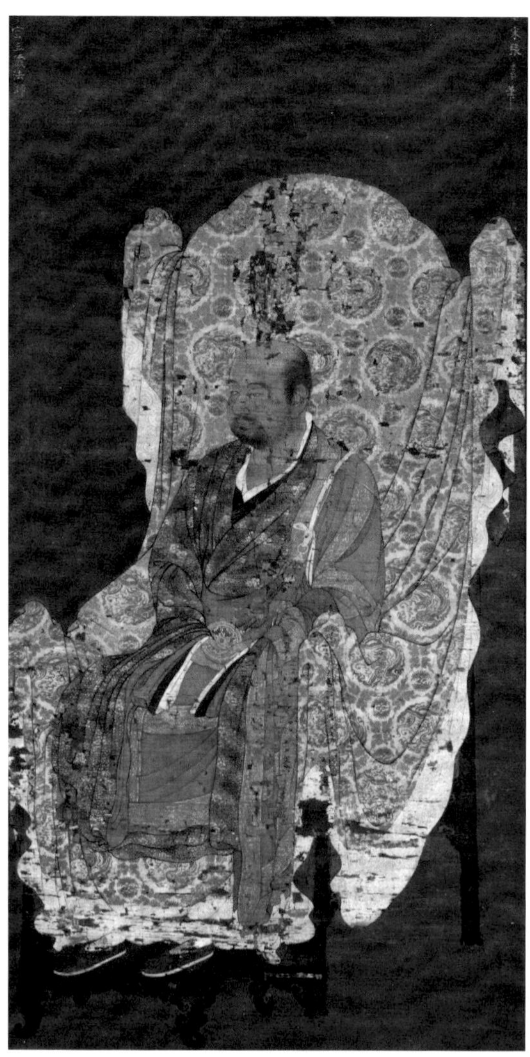

Figure 4. Unidentified 11th- or 12th-century artist, *Portrait of an Unknown Ch'an Master* (traditionally identified as Pu-kung). Hanging scroll, ink and color on silk, $46^{1}/_{2} \times 23^{3}/_{8}$ in. (118.1×59.4 cm). Kōzanji, Kyoto

with them were a concentration of talent, intelligence, and creative energy unequaled in Chinese history—and indeed rarely seen before or since.[23] Others of the group were also painters of great achievement, but for the coterie as a whole it was Li who represented the art of painting at its most learned and far-ranging. Bearing the public approval of this coterie, Li's art went forth in the world with credentials like those no other painter had ever before carried. And in return, the plain beauty and disturbing, provocative substance of his art gave rewards that surpassed all expectation.

Imperial Horses at Pasture (fig. 2) is at some level a copy of an earlier work. Li was a passionate student of the past, and he went to extraordinary lengths to be able to see and study great paintings by the classical masters.[24] To an interesting and suggestive degree, the masters he copied were those who have since been remembered as the patriarchs of the art: Ku K'ai-chih, Lu T'an-wei, Wu Tao-tzu, Han Kan, Li Ssu-hsün, and Wang Wei.[25] *Imperial Horses at Pasture* suggests the likelihood that Li's so-called copies were in fact relatively free re-creations, loosely based upon the model yet remade into a personal interpretation that expresses the artist's own thoughts and attitudes.

The historical model for Li's *Five Tribute Horses* is the earlier practice of such pictures rather than any specific example. Such compositions—in which a succession of tribute horses and grooms or attendants were arrayed horizontally, with colorful, decorative detail and a dramatic, entertaining flavor—had been painted by the great masters of horse painting, such as Han Kan and Tung-tan-wang. Li's *Five Tribute Horses* is a type of commentary on that tradition, taking the form of a series of portraits of actual horses and grooms presented as tribute to the Sung throne in the years 1086 to 1088, but presenting them in a new style that challenged the assumptions of the old style and the purposes of the earlier paintings. Li makes us reconsider the entire context of tribute bearing, and further suggests that we look empathetically at all men and at their relations with the world. External configurations, though an inexact reflection of internal realities, must be correct and true if we are to see beyond them—as Li makes it possible for us to do in both *Imperial Horses at Pasture* and *Five Tribute Horses*.

So far as we know today, no complete earlier version of the subject existed when Li Kung-lin painted his *Hsiao-ching hsiang*, or "visualizations of the *Classic of Filial Piety*," the third and last of his extant works.[26] This ancient text had been illustrated many centuries earlier, but by the eleventh century probably nothing more than fragmentary and debased bits of that precedent were still known, at best. Li therefore had to invent his so-called visualizations. Because it was his own invention, the *Classic of Filial Piety* belongs to the small group of pictorial narratives that represents Li's most profound and original creations. This group includes, in addition to the *Classic of Filial Piety*, the *Homecoming Ode* (*Kuei-ch'ü-lai-hsi*) of Ta'o Ch'ien, the *Nine Songs* of Ch'ü Yüan, the Hua-yen Sutra, the *Gathering at the Orchid Pavilion*, and a type of representation of arhats or lohans, the ascetic disciples of Sakyamuni Buddha, that profoundly influenced later Buddhist imagery.[27] Each of these pictorial inventions became a classical model that in turn influenced many generations of later artists.

The *Classic of Filial Piety*—or at least one version of the subject—was requested of Li Kung-lin by a certain Mr. Yang in 1085. Li's own account of the matter is of interest:

> Lord Yang of the Phoenix Pavilion said that the *Classic of Filial Piety* is the lock and key to the Six Arts and the root and foundation of all human conduct. He said to me, Lung-mien Shan-jen Li Kung-lin, "If you could depict these matters in order to show them to people, it would be of benefit." Therefore, in the sixth month of the eighth year of Yuan-feng, I chose one or two things from each chapter and depicted them.[28]

The present scroll has the look of a first draft, a series of sketches, and must be directly related to the initial painting of the subject in 1085. Three sections of the original eighteen are now lost, but their general character can be seen in early copies of the entire composition, which is the basis for all known later versions of the theme. Beside each painting is Li Kung-lin's own writing of the relevant chapter.

Although the entire work is discussed in detail later in this volume (pp. 73–155), here we would like to call attention to a few features that are of particular importance to an understanding of Li Kung-lin's art in the broadest sense. Like *Five Tribute Horses*, the *Classic of Filial Piety* is painted in the plain-ink *pai-miao* technique. A few traces of vermilion can still be found here and there, indicating that the work was very much like the *Five Tribute Horses* in style, except that the latter was done on paper, the former on silk. Because of the relative informality of the images in the *Classic of Filial Piety*, we might suspect that Mr. Yang and Li had a special relationship. Perhaps Mr. Yang sent Li the bolt of silk on which he subsequently painted the succession of eighteen images spontaneously and informally, as if discussing the content and meaning of the *Classic* with Mr. Yang through his pictures. At any rate, the clear implication of Li's note is that the pictures were done for Mr. Yang, so that a kind of dialogue is involved. Unfortunately, we do not know Mr. Yang's response.

The *Classic of Filial Piety* itself was a long-hallowed mainstay of the Confucian political and social tradition, although it was not designated as one of the official classics until the Sung dynasty. By Li's time, every schoolboy was probably required to memorize the eighteen sections or chapters.

It would not exaggerate the significance of the *Classic of Filial Piety* to observe that its contents—the governing of relationships among men—are the keystone of Chinese society, the "root and foundation of all human conduct," according to Mr. Yang. With these carefully regulated rules of conduct in place, society would be secure. We still see in China today the unchanging belief in the absolute necessity for the maintenance of such order. Harshly and inhumanely imposed, however, the patriarchal and hieratic structure of behavior described in the *Classic of Filial Piety* can become inhibiting, fear-inducing, and finally destructive.

It is one of the beauties of Li's depictions of the subject of carefully ordered human relationships that we can read both the virtues and the potential faults of the kind of prescribed relationships set forth in the text. Li's pictures convey commentary and criticism as they systematically present a pictorial account of both ideal and actual human society. In this ideal world, children sustain and support their parents; friends love friends; officials govern with honesty and courage; rulers rule with strength, fairness, and wisdom: human society is harmonious, ordered, and intelligent, governed by a carefully maintained order of relationships as clear and perfect as the musical notes of an ancient set of stone chimes.

But in fact, as Li shows us, the world often falls far short of this ideal. The wretched and the poor are regarded as dangerous. Honest men take their lives in their own hands and risk everything to speak honestly. Those who transgress the rules of society suffer harshly, while complacent emperors grow fat and remote. Alongside such behavior there continues to exist the other, so often unattained and perfect, world that we have the capacity to realize but mostly do not.

What Li presents again and again is the individual human being, each within his or her systematically governed web of relationships, both sustained by and trapped in them. The various ways in which he does this constitute the substance of his artistic originality and reveal the nature of his didactic intentions. Li Kung-lin set out, as he tells us, to do something that "would be of benefit"; we can examine his purposes by examining the structure of his art. To emphasize the individual human life within the idealized realm of a universal filial piety that controls the operations of human society, Li typically isolates one person within a pictorial structure composed of people in a communal or mass state. What is being measured in such works is the individual human action, responsibility, and obligation. Emperor, prince, minister, father, son, each finds himself alone in the fulfillment of necessary filial duties.

When these actions take place within the home, as in the several scenes of children serving their parents, we sense the loving intimacy and harmonious ideal that can exist. When they take place in public arenas, however, like the court or the streets, we often glimpse the artist's commentary on power. His prince, for example, in the illustration to chapter 3 of the text (see pl. 1), appears as a concerned and humane man riding in his carriage through the city streets. A company of armed guards protects him, flanking the carriage on both sides, preceding it, and presumably following it as well. They look threateningly and with suspicion at the common people along the way, one of whom appears to be shaking his fist in anger despite the watchful and glaring eyes of the head guard. Li isolates the poor and the crippled in the lower corner, separating them dramatically from the richly appointed and impressively bannered armed company of imperial aristocrats who fill the upper part of the composition, forming a powerful and overwhelming force in the pictorial structure. Elsewhere, Li brings the same structure of oppression, threat, and control to bear on an isolated honest official who dares to submit a criticism of the imperial court, and again on the helpless orphans, widows, and widowers who are ceremoniously and ritually greeted by their ruler in the illustration to chapter 8. In Li's visualization of this important symbolic act of filial piety, we see the abandoned and harmless surrounded by the visible threat of violence and isolated from the powerful forces that control their lives.

Li Kung-lin's contemporaries believed that his paintings could benefit human society, and that they often subtly incorporated admonitions or didactic messages in unexpected ways within their forms. In fact, his paintings reveal that for Li his art was a tool or a weapon, a moral vehicle that allowed him to set out his views of the men, institutions, ideals, and conflicts of his time. When he depicted the emperor of China, he commented upon that figure; a portrait of a high minister was a statement about actual ministers and about the lives of men, like his father, who served in official positions. Men are seen to be in conflict and forced into dangerous situations. Common people are shown to be a constant threat to those in power, except when their lives are neutralized through the operation of mutual respect and filiality. Occasionally, as in chapter 12, where the Essential Way is discussed, Li allows us to see a fluid, harmonious, and unstructured society without conflict or compulsion. This is the ideal that always beckons, but it is shown to exist only when there is no coercion or physical necessity. As he revealed so beautifully in his *Imperial Horses at Pasture*, when people are tightly controlled they behave like sheep, head down and submissive. They behave like people only when they are left alone, like the free and unencumbered horses at the end of that scroll, released from compulsion.

Before Li, painting did not have the capacity of poetry or prose to convey significant human meaning, to criticize or praise, to blame or admonish, or to reveal the artist's inner thoughts and emotions. In a way not seen earlier, Li let his art grow directly from the activities of his life. He painted his friends when they were drunk or happy, created spontaneous images of water buffalo and herdboys or rocks and bamboo to make visual poems corresponding to those his distinguished friends wrote with words, drew from ancient masterpieces material with which to reflect on the present, and fashioned his studies into political, social, and philosophical observations. It was only when painting acquired this capacity that it joined poetry and calligraphy as a *necessary* art in China.

1. *Hsüan-ho hua-p'u* (original preface 1120), translated into modern Chinese and annotated by Yü Chien-hua (Beijing, 1964), pp. 132–33.
2. For the late Northern Sung gentry and their views of painting, see Osvald Siren, *Chinese Painting: Leading Masters and Principles*, 7 vols. (New York, 1956–58), vol. 2, pp. 1–52; and Susan Bush, *The Chinese Literati on Painting: Su Shih (1037–1101) to Tung Ch'i-ch'ang (1555–1636)*, Harvard-Yenching Institute Studies 27 (Cambridge, Mass., 1971), pp. 29–82. The patrons of Li's extant paintings will be discussed below.
3. Published in *Chung-kuo li-tai hui-hua: Ku-kung po-wu-yüan ts'ang-hua chi*, vol. 2 (Beijing, 1981), pp. 24–43, and notes pp. 6–7.
4. *Hsüan-ho hua-p'u*, pp. 130–33, 182–83.
5. Ibid., p. 225.
6. Jan Fontein and Wu Tung, *Han and T'ang Murals* (Boston, 1976), pp. 90–103.
7. Agnes E. Meyer, *Chinese Painting as Reflected in the Thought and Art of Li Lung-mien, 1070–1106* (New York, 1923), pp. 247, 252–53, 256, 262.
8. Ibid., pp. 56–57.
9. Ibid., p. 54.
10. Ibid., p. 247.
11. Reproduced in *Chung-kuo li-tai hui-hua*, vol. 2, pp. 60–83, and notes pp. 8–12.
12. Chang An-chih, *Li Kung-lin* (Beijing, 1979), p. 17.
13. Translated, with modifications, from William Hung, *Tu Fu: China's Greatest Poet* (Cambridge, Mass., 1952), p. 84.

14. Richard M. Barnhart, "Landscape Painting Around 1085," in the Festschrift volume in honor of Frederick Mote, *The Power of Culture*, ed. Willard Peterson (Hong Kong: Chinese University Press), forthcoming.

15. *Hsüan-ho hua-p'u*, p. 131.

16. Meyer, *Chinese Painting*, pp. 287–88.

17. *Hsüan-ho hua-p'u*, p. 130.

18. See Meyer, *Chinese Painting*, pp. 288, 293, 316, 325–26, 327, for records of Li's portraits. The likelihood that the scroll was painted for the writer Chang Hsun was suggested to me by Deborah DelGais Muller, who is preparing an article on the painting. This assumption is strongly suggested by the earliest seal on the scroll, which simply reads "Hsun." Huang T'ing-chien's colophon would then have been written also for Chang Hsun, not Chang Lei, as has been assumed.

19. Richard M. Barnhart, "Li Kung-lin's *Hsiao Ching T'u*: Illustrations of the 'Classic of Filial Piety'" (Ph.D. diss., Princeton University, 1967), pp. 159–64.

20. *Sodai no kaiga: Tokubetsuten/Song Paintings from Japanese Collection*[s] (Nara, 1989), cat. 59, p. 94, is a recent publication of this famous old painting. Traditionally ascribed to the Buddhist painter Chang Ssu-kung, and identified as a portrait of the T'ang priest Pu-k'ung (705–774) because of a late inscription at the top of the painting, the portrait is in fact a work of the eleventh or twelfth century by an unidentified Buddhist priest of the Sung period.

21. A painting of tribute horses attributed to the T'ang master Han Kan, and its earlier and later associations, is discussed in Thomas Lawton, *Chinese Figure Painting* (Washington, D.C., 1973), cat. 47, pp. 186–90.

22. Siren, *Chinese Painting*, vol. 2, p. 43.

23. Bush, *Chinese Literati on Painting*, pp. 29–43.

24. Meyer, *Chinese Painting*, p. 102.

25. Richard M. Barnhart, "Li Kung-lin's Use of Past Styles," in Christian F. Murck, ed., *Artists and Traditions* (Princeton, 1976), pp. 51–71.

26. Barnhart, "Li Kung-lin's *Hsiao Ching T'u*," pp. 66–70, discusses earlier versions of the subject, none of which seems still to have existed in the eleventh century.

27. Meyer, *Chinese Painting*, pp. 271–75, 341–42. See also Lawton, *Chinese Figure Painting*, cat. 4, pp. 38–41.

28. Author's translation from Chou Mi, *Yun-yen kuo-yen lu* (*Mei-shu ts'ung-shu* ed.), reprinted in *I-shu ts'ung-pien* (Taipei, 1962), p. 37.

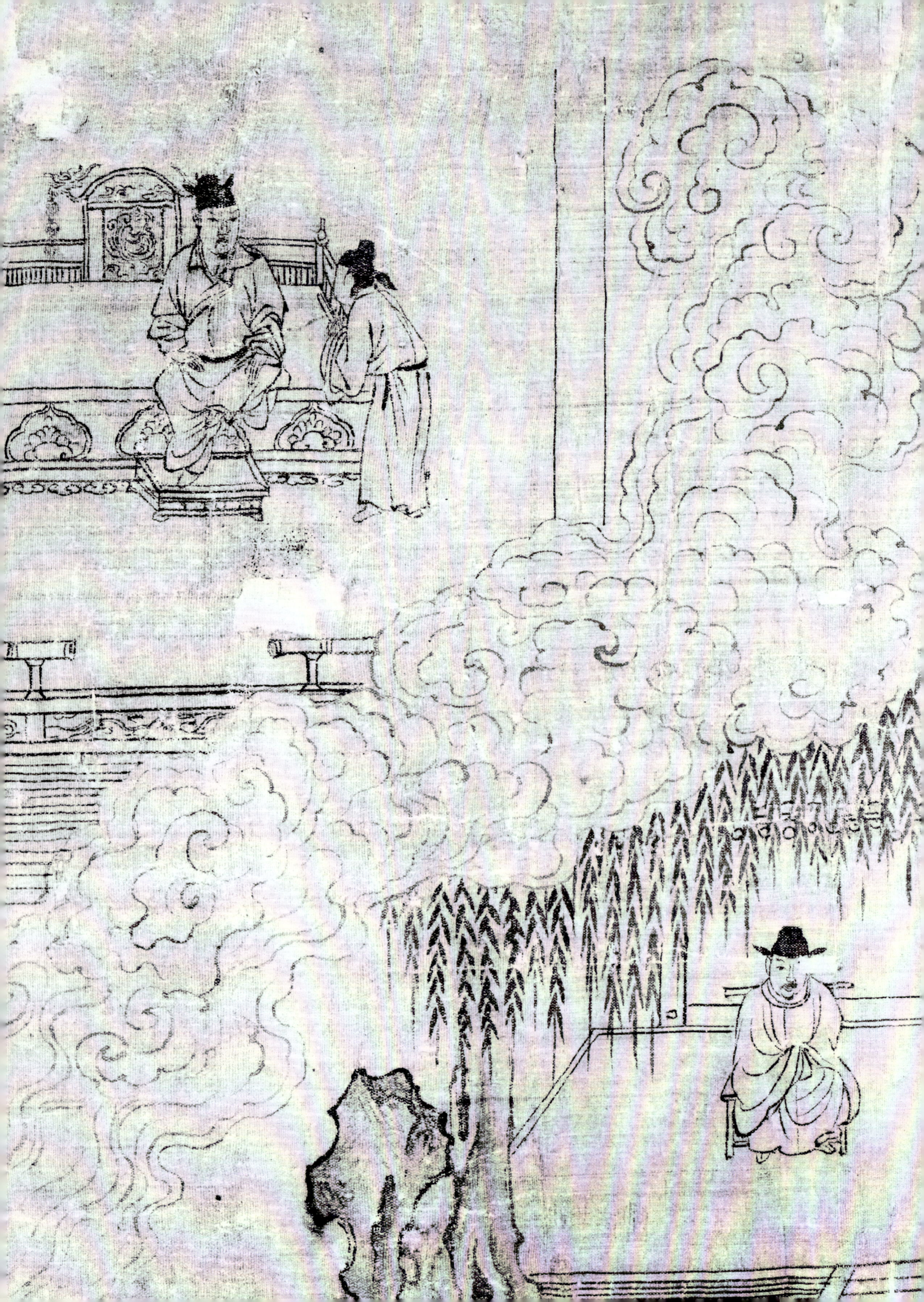

THE HERMIT OF LUNG-MIEN
A Biography of Li Kung-lin

Robert E. Harrist, Jr.

For his illustration of chapter 17 of the *Classic of Filial Piety*, Li Kung-lin combined two complementary scenes (fig. 5; see also pl. 14). In the upper left, a scholar-official at the imperial court addresses an imposing, seated figure, who must be the emperor himself. In the lower right, separated from the scene above by a diagonal band of cloud, the same scholar-official appears again, lost in thought as he sits at home in a garden pavilion. Although the obscure posts Li Kung-lin held in the Northern Sung (960–1127) government never demanded that he speak his mind in the imperial presence, as does the figure in the painting, the illustration is a fitting visual introduction to his biography. Like the scholar-official in his painting, Li struggled to reconcile the often conflicting ideals of active involvement in government service and contemplative retreat from its potentially corrupting demands—a conflict summed up in the *Classic of Filial Piety* by the words *chin*, "to advance," and *t'ui*, "to retire." In real life, however, Li Kung-lin never achieved the assured balance between these two ideals that he achieved pictorially in the illustration. While his public career in government carried him fitfully from one minor post to another, Li achieved fame for his private career as a painter and as an antiquarian.

The Scholar in Retreat

In the eyes of Northern Sung society, dominated by the precepts of Confucianism, the first significant event in Li Kung-lin's life surely was earning the *chin-shih* degree in 1070. Although historians currently are engaged in lively debate

Figure 5. Li Kung-lin, detail from chapter 17 of the *Classic of Filial Piety* (plate 14)

over the relationship between degree-holding and elite status, there can be no doubt that for men of talent and ambition living during the Northern Sung, this degree was the surest passport to becoming a scholar-official in the civil service bureaucracy, the most desirable career in imperial China.[1] The term *chin-shih* means literally "presented scholar," a reference to the fact that men who achieved this degree were presented formally to the emperor. In English, the term is often translated as "doctor of letters," which nicely underscores the fact that although men inducted into the civil service through the *chin-shih* examinations performed all manner of administrative duties, from drafting state documents to supervising water-conservancy projects, the examinations themselves tested a candidate's literary skills and his knowledge of the classical texts that formed the Confucian canon.

The son and grandson of scholar-officials from Shu-ch'eng in modern Anhwei Province, Li Kung-lin was fortunate in being born into a family that nurtured precisely that scholarly environment which could best prepare a *chin-shih* aspirant for the intellectual ordeal he would face. In fact, by the end of the Northern Sung dynasty, Li's family had produced nearly half the fourteen *chin-shih* degree holders known to have come from the prefecture of Lu-chou, the administrative unit that included Shu-ch'eng.[2] The year Li Kung-lin earned his degree, he shared honors with his younger brother Kung-yin, their cousin Li Chieh, and a man named Li Ch'ung-yüan, sometimes identified as another cousin but most likely a fellow native of Shu-ch'eng, with whom Li Kung-lin shared a common surname. All four men successfully completed the exhausting sequence of examinations that began at the prefectural level in Hefei, the seat of Lu-chou prefecture, and culminated with the Palace Examination, supervised by Emperor Shen-tsung (r. 1067–85) himself in K'ai-feng (then known as Pien-ching), capital of the Northern Sung.

John Fairbank has compared earning the *chin-shih* degree in imperial China with being awarded tenure at a university and simultaneously being elected to Congress in the United States today.[3] For men whose years of arduous scholarly preparation had at last brought them one of the highest marks of distinction their society could confer, the completion of the *chin-shih* examinations in K'ai-feng was an occasion for great rejoicing. In the fall of 1087, while he was grading examinations and perhaps remembering the celebrations that attended the conferral of his own *chin-shih* degree, Li Kung-lin wrote a poem describing the joy felt by families of the successful candidates. The closing lines read: "Joyous events, the celebrations will go on for days / They must rely on wine to carry it all off!"[4] The formal celebrations in K'ai-feng climaxed in a banquet hosted by the emperor at which the successful candidates were presented with flowers, ceremonial clothing, and other imperial gifts. The men also organized their own, less decorous, revel called the Feast of Hearing Happy News. In a poem describing this event, a euphoric graduate wrote:

We sang like crazy, and shouted loudly at each other;
We danced, and fell on the door-steps.
There was not much thinking at the time;
All we did was to enjoy the moment.[5]

Graduates often capped their festivities with visits to K'ai-feng's thriving brothel districts—a final fling before returning home in triumph and preparing to launch their careers in earnest.

Although newly minted *chin-shih* recipients sometimes had a brief wait before they were appointed to office, the normal course was to move directly from degree candidate to scholar-official. But Li Kung-lin, at just this point in his life, made a highly unorthodox decision: he turned his back on an official career, returned to his home district, and settled in a scenic area called the Lung-mien Mountains. Choosing "to retire" (*t'ui*) rather than "to advance" (*chin*), Li did not seek office for nearly ten years.

Why did Li Kung-lin decide to avoid official life for so long? Richard Barnhart has suggested that although Li seems to have held no strong political views himself, he may have hoped to avoid the factional struggles within the bureaucracy that attended the implementation of the famous reform policies of Wang An-shih (1021–1086) in the early 1070s.[6] During these years, with the support of the energetic Emperor Shen-tsung, Wang launched new administrative policies touching on everything from currency to horse breeding. These policies sparked intense political disputes between the reformers, who supported Wang, and the conservatives, led by Ssu-ma Kuang (1019–1086), who opposed both the specific measures Wang advocated and the utilitarian philosophy by which they were justified. While Li Kung-lin may well have been reluctant to become embroiled in these feuds, he may have had other, more private reasons for avoiding public life. According to his nephew Chang Ch'eng, Li Kung-lin's father had come to grief when his outspokenness, in "six essays that exceeded the norm," led to his dismissal from office.[7] His father's misadventures may have lessened the attractions of office-holding so much that Li Kung-lin decided to delay his own debut as a bureaucrat for as long as possible. Although their reasons for dropping out of public life are not clear, Li Chieh and Li Ch'ung-yüan also spent time with Li Kung-lin in the Lung-mien Mountains during the 1070s. Contemporaries dubbed the trio the Three Li of Lung-mien.

When he decided to retreat to the mountains and began calling himself the Hermit of Lung-mien,[8] Li Kung-lin joined the venerable line of hermits and recluses whose biographies enliven Chinese history and literature. Like countless hermits of earlier centuries, Li spent his retirement from public life in magnificent natural surroundings. His retreat lay in the Lung-mien Mountains, southwest of the city of Shu-ch'eng, deep in the Ta-pieh mountain range. The name Lung-mien, or "Sleeping Dragon," was inspired by the mountains' to-

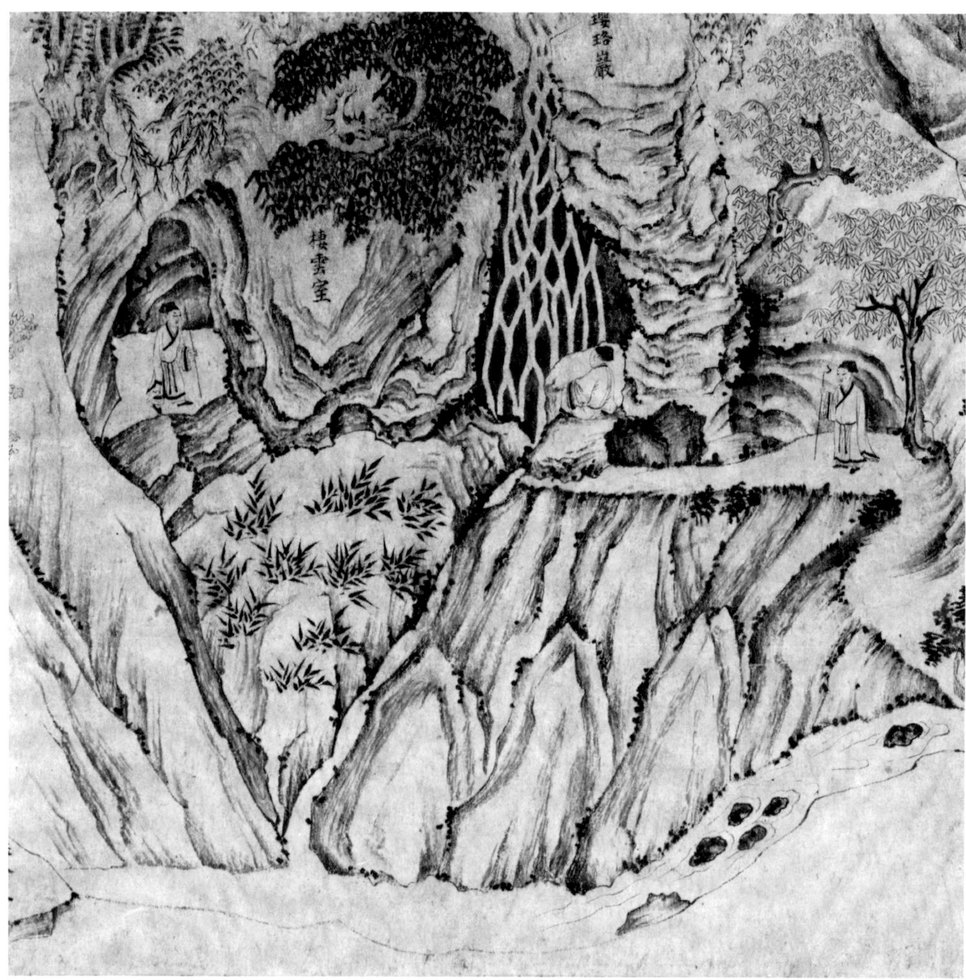

Figure 6. After Li Kung-lin, "Necklace Cliff" and "Chamber of Perching Clouds," from the *Lung-mien Mountain Villa*. Handscroll, ink on silk, 11¼ × 201½ in. (28.7 × 512 cm). Palace Museum, Beijing

pography: "wriggling, rising, falling," as they are described in a local gazetteer, the mountains were thought to resemble the form of a recumbent dragon.

Several years after Li had left the mountains to take up a government position in K'ai-feng, he painted a pictorial tour of his property titled the *Lung-mien Mountain Villa*, or, as it is usually abbreviated, *Mountain Villa*.[9] The poet, calligrapher, and statesman Su Shih (1037–1101) composed a well-known colophon for the painting, and his younger brother, Su Ch'e (1039–1112), wrote a preface and twenty poems—one for each of the major sites Li depicted—in imitation of the twenty "Wang-ch'uan" quatrains by the T'ang recluse-poet Wang Wei (701–761).[10] Both the draft and the final versions of *Mountain Villa* were lost long ago, but in extant copies we are offered glimpses of Li Kung-lin's life in the mountains.

Unlike the writings of his friends Su Shih, Su Ch'e, and Huang T'ing-chien (1045–1105), which have been preserved in *wen-chi*, or literary collections (and which can be read as intellectual and spiritual autobiographies of the writers), Li Kung-lin's literary works, aside from a few poems and scattered notes on

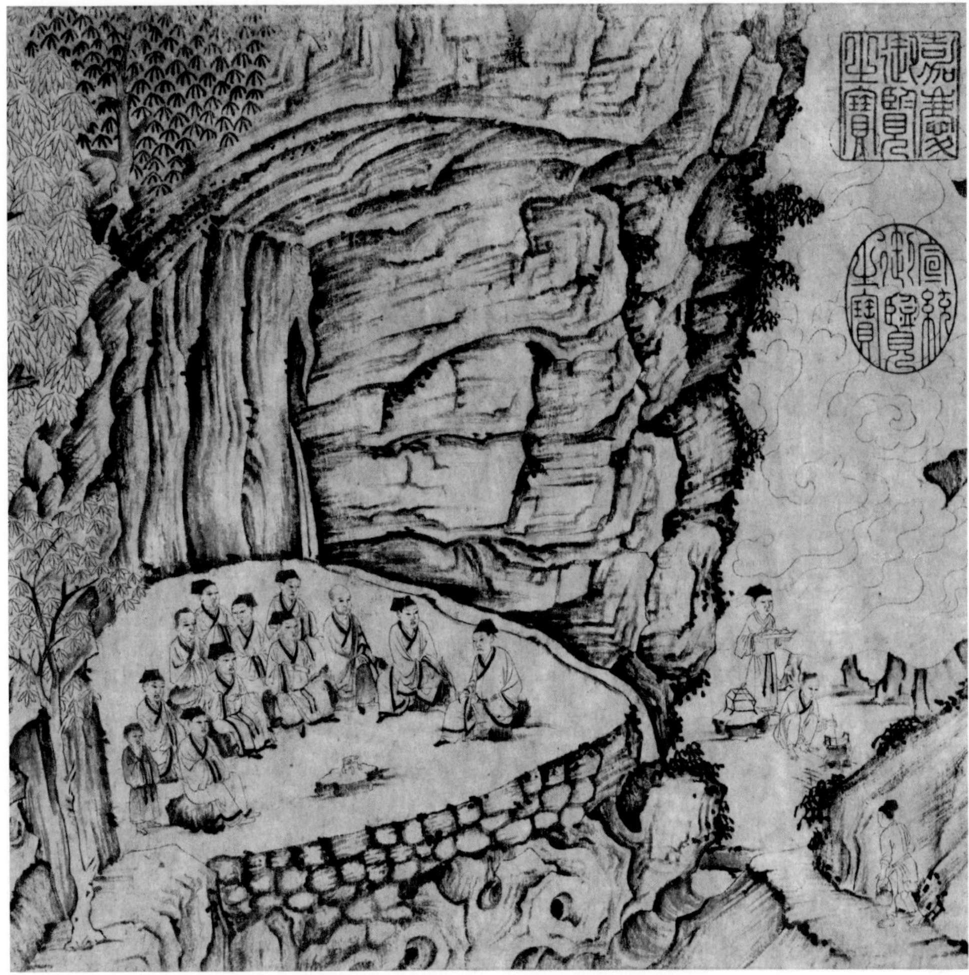

Figure 7. After Li Kung-lin, "Surpassing Gold Cliff," from the *Lung-mien Mountain Villa*

painting, have not survived. What we can know of how Li interpreted his own life must come from his paintings. None of his works was more autobiographical than *Mountain Villa*. While the *Classic of Filial Piety* comments on the obligations of official life and depicts the social and political hierarchy within which men of Li's class lived, *Mountain Villa* illustrates a world of private, intensely personal experiences.

The painting presents an inviting landscape of luxuriant trees, precipitous cliffs, strange rock formations, caves, streams, and waterfalls (fig. 6). But *Mountain Villa* is not merely a topographical survey of Li's property; it is also a record of his presence in the landscape and, in a sense, of his ownership of the land. In a sequence of self-portraits, Li depicts himself with two companions, probably Li Chieh and Li Ch'ung-yüan, as they linger by waterfalls, cool their feet in mountain streams, pause to drink wine in a cave, pick herbs, and sail downstream in a catamaran. At some sites they are accompanied by a Buddhist monk, and at the Surpassing Gold Cliff—a natural amphitheater sheltered by an overhanging bluff—they join an audience of eleven men listening to an outdoor lecture (fig. 7).

The autobiographical content of *Mountain Villa* becomes even clearer when we consider the special nature of the painting's subject matter, for the landscape it depicts is not simply anonymous mountain terrain but a rambling, unwalled garden designed by the artist himself. Here Li Kung-lin installed discreetly placed paths, bridges, man-made ponds, platforms, and huts that transformed his property into a subtly controlled environment for pleasure and contemplation. Although Chinese scholars had created, written about, and painted pictures of gardens for many centuries, the Northern Sung witnessed an unprecedented flourishing of garden art, nurtured not only by the dynasty's economic and political stability but also by the emergence of scholar-officials such as Li Kung-lin as the new elite of Chinese society. Poems and essays of the period amply document that, in addition to painting, calligraphy, and poetry, garden building flourished as a characteristic product of Northern Sung elite culture both in cities and in rural retreats.

Literature about gardens from this period shows that for Northern Sung scholars, garden building inevitably was an expression of the garden owner's mind.[11] One of the most compelling ways through which a proprietor asserted his taste and character in his garden was by giving poetic names to its structures and scenic spots. At Lung-mien, site names chosen by Li Kung-lin, like the man-made improvements he installed, helped to transform an anonymous landscape into a true garden. Lodge of Establishing Virtue, the name Li chose for his homestead and the principal structure at Lung-mien, alludes to a story by Chuang-tzu. In a place called Chien-te, or Establishing Virtue, people are "simple and naive, few in thoughts of self, scant in desires."[12] Li Kung-lin's choice of this name announces that the life he leads in the mountains is simple, unworldly, and rustic. Other names Li chose articulated his imaginative responses to the topography of the land and allow us to see it through his eyes. He chose the name Necklace Cliff, for example, for a site where a waterfall rushing down a cliff recalled the shapes of necklaces worn by Buddhist deities. At the Ling-ling Valley, streams coursing into a pool suggested to Li the words *ling-ling*, an onomatopoeic compound for the sound of splashing water.

Six of the twenty site names Li Kung-lin chose come from the vocabulary of Buddhism and reflect his lifelong interest in this religion, both as a source of subjects for his painting and as a personal belief. Although often said to have declined in China after the fall of the T'ang dynasty (618–906), Buddhism, especially the Ch'an sect (known in the West by its Japanese name, Zen), attracted many of the best minds of the Northern Sung and thoroughly penetrated scholarly life.[13] Li Kung-lin painted many Buddhist subjects, including illustrations of sutras, iconic representations of deities, the gathering of arhats, and imaginary portraits of famous monks and laymen. Unlike the Buddhist paintings of Wu Tao-tzu (8th century) of the T'ang, brushed with great boldness on temple walls and intended to inspire awe, Li's small-scale works, usually in his charac-

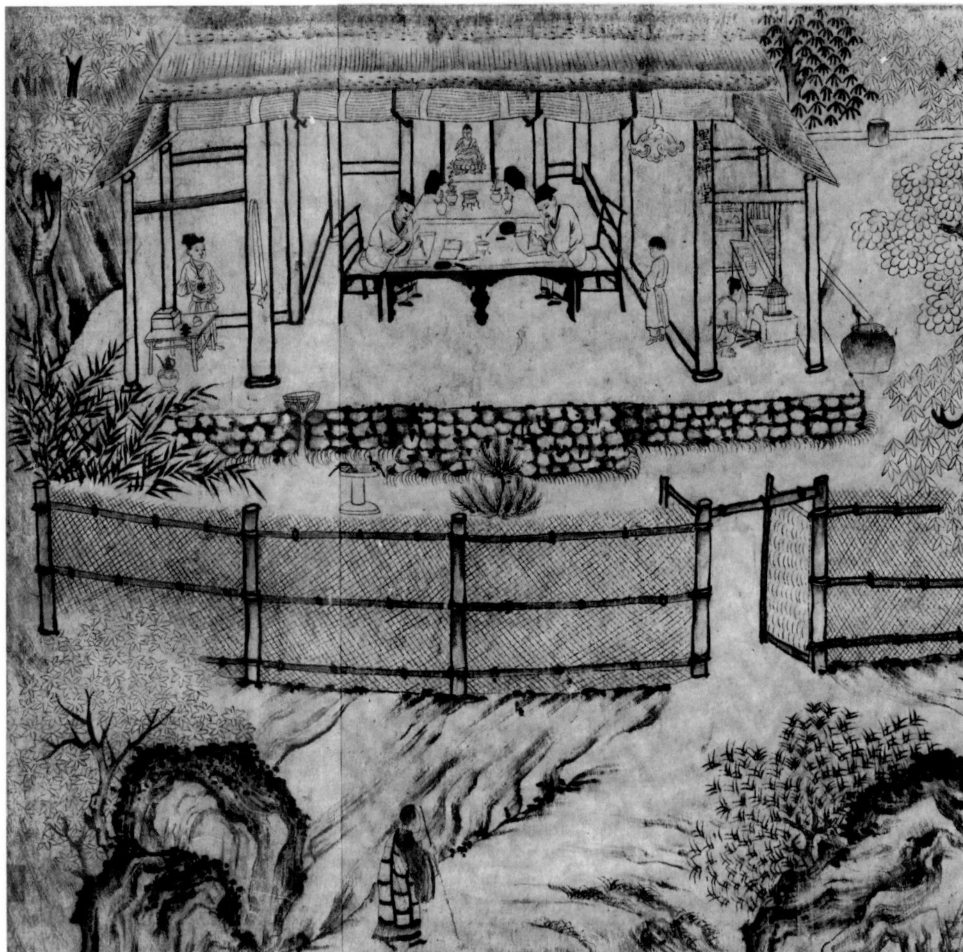

Figure 8. After Li Kung-lin, "The Hall of Ink Meditation," from the *Lung-mien Mountain Villa*

teristic *pai-miao* (ink outline) style on paper, were done for the private enjoyment of his literary friends. His paintings also could function, however, as fully efficacious icons. When Su Shih's second wife died in 1093, he asked Li to paint the images of Sakyamuni Buddha and his Ten Great Disciples, which Su dedicated as a votive offering to the memory of the dead woman.[14]

Of all the sites in *Mountain Villa*, it is a rustic building serving as a combination Buddhist retreat and artist's studio that Li Kung-lin depicts in the greatest detail. This site, the Hall of Ink Meditation, includes what may be the only self-portrait of an artist at work in all of Sung-dynasty painting (fig. 8). Inside a thatched hut, while their servants busy themselves in the antechambers, two men work at a large table. Li Kung-lin can be identified as the man who sits at the right, writing, or perhaps painting, a scroll; the man seated across from him copying a text that lies open on the table is probably Li Ch'ung-yüan, who collaborated with Li Kung-lin to produce a set of illustrated scrolls of the Hua-yen Sutra.[15] Ink stones, extra brushes, and a ewer rest on the table between the two men. Hanging on a partition at the back of the room is a scroll, probably the work of Li

Kung-lin himself, depicting the Amida Buddha seated on a lotus throne. On a small table in front of this icon are two wooden boxes, two vases of flowers, an incense burner, and two *ching-p'ing*, or "pure bottles," which contain water used for ablutions in Buddhist ceremonies. The blinds that form the front wall of the room are raised, and a Buddhist chime hangs from the rafters at the right.

This extraordinary image illustrates the idea suggested by the name of the hut, the Hall of Ink Meditation. "Ink meditation" (*mo-ch'an*) recalls the term "ink guest" (*mo-k'e*), a poetic euphemism for scholars or poets. In the context of site names at Li Kung-lin's retreat, the words "ink meditation" allude to the highly literary form of Buddhism, called *wen-tzu ch'an*, or "lettered Ch'an," practiced by his scholarly friends, such as Su Shih.[16] Li's painting seems to illustrate that no less than meditation or other Buddhist practices, painting and calligraphy—ink meditation—can be means of achieving insight and, quite possibly, enlightenment itself. Su Ch'e acknowledges this truth in his poem for this scene:

> *This mind has never been attached,*
> *merged in meditation* [ch'an] *with all things.*
> *How is it that a single ball of ink*
> *can unfold into all these hills and streams!*[17]

Like the landscape theorist and Buddhist layman Tsung Ping (375–443), Su Ch'e expresses wonder at the painter's ability to produce images whose power to move the viewer is comparable to that of real landscape.[18] Li's painted image and Su Ch'e's response to it also suggest that in the minds of Northern Sung scholars there was no conflict between painting or other cultural pursuits and the path to Buddhist salvation.

Politics, Painting, and Friendship

Aside from what Li Kung-lin shows us in *Mountain Villa*, we know little of his years of retreat in the 1070s. He surely had married by this time, and his two children, a boy and a girl, probably were born during this decade. One highlight of these years was the visit Li paid to Wang An-shih in Nanking sometime after 1076, when Wang retired there after leaving government service. This visit is documented in poems Wang wrote for Li and in a portrait of the retired statesman that Li Kung-lin painted on the wall of Wang's studio on the grounds of a Buddhist temple.[19] In light of his later friendships with Wang's political opponents, the brothers Su Shih and Su Ch'e, it may seem surprising that Li should have been on such good terms with Wang An-shih. Some have seen in his apparent sympathy for Wang's faction a tendency toward political fence-straddling. But in fact, the animosity felt by Su Shih and members of his circle toward Wang An-shih may have been exaggerated by later partisans of the warring reform and conservative camps. Li's amiable relationship with both Wang An-shih and the Su brothers is more understandable when we recall that Su Shih himself seems not to have held a grudge against the older man: Su called on Wang An-shih in Nanking in 1084, chatting with his old political foe and even toying with the idea of becoming his neighbor.[20]

Whether owing to financial necessity or a favorable response to changes in the political scene, Li ended his self-imposed exile and left the Lung-mien Mountains in 1079. In the spring of that year, he was in K'ai-feng as a member of the staff administering the first *chin-shih* examinations of the Yüan-feng (1078–86) reign.[21] There is no indication, however, that Li had yet accepted a full-time government post. How he came to be appointed to the examination staff is not known, but it was the initial step in the beginning of a long-deferred official career.

While Li was in the capital he widened his circle of literary friends, meeting the men who would become his intellectual soul mates and for whom he produced most of his paintings. It was probably during this period that he first met the poet and calligrapher Huang T'ing-chien. Huang, who had been serving in the capital since 1072 as an instructor at the National Academy, initiated the friendship by asking Li, whom he had not yet met, for a portrait of the T'ang poet Wang Wei.[22] Although Huang was somewhat disappointed by the portrait, in which Wang Wei sported a full beard, he and Li became close friends. Of all Li's literary associates, none wrote more extensively about his paintings than Huang T'ing-chien, who acknowledged that his conversations with Li about painting and poetry, especially the concept of *yün*, or "resonance," greatly deepened his own understanding of these arts.[23] When Huang T'ing-chien left the capital in 1080 to become prefect of T'ai-ho district (Kiangsi), Li Kung-lin, who soon would become District Defender in Nan-k'ang (Kiangsi), either traveled with him from K'ai-feng or met Huang as the latter passed through Lu-chou and visited the Lung-mien Mountains. Huang commemorated this visit to Li's beloved mountains in a witty quatrain playing on the words *lung mien* (literally, "dragon sleeps"):

> *Among the several mountains, where does the dragon sleep?*
> *In former days the dragon slept, today he is awake.*
> *Hearing the Way, he has followed a cloudy aura and departed,*
> *For it was not fitting that he rain only on a single plot of fields.*[24]

Huang T'ing-chien's poem for Li pokes gentle fun at his new friend, who, like a long-slumbering dragon rousing himself to action, had at last begun his career in earnest.

Li Kung-lin's post in Nan-k'ang was his first full-time job, assumed when he was nearly forty years old. About 1083, he was transferred to Ch'ang-yüan (Honan), a district in the metropolitan prefecture, not far from K'ai-feng. This move to the area of the capital was not accompanied by an elevation in rank: his new position was the same as that he had held in Nan-k'ang, District Defender, an appointment frequently given to new *chin-shih* holders but not a particularly distin-

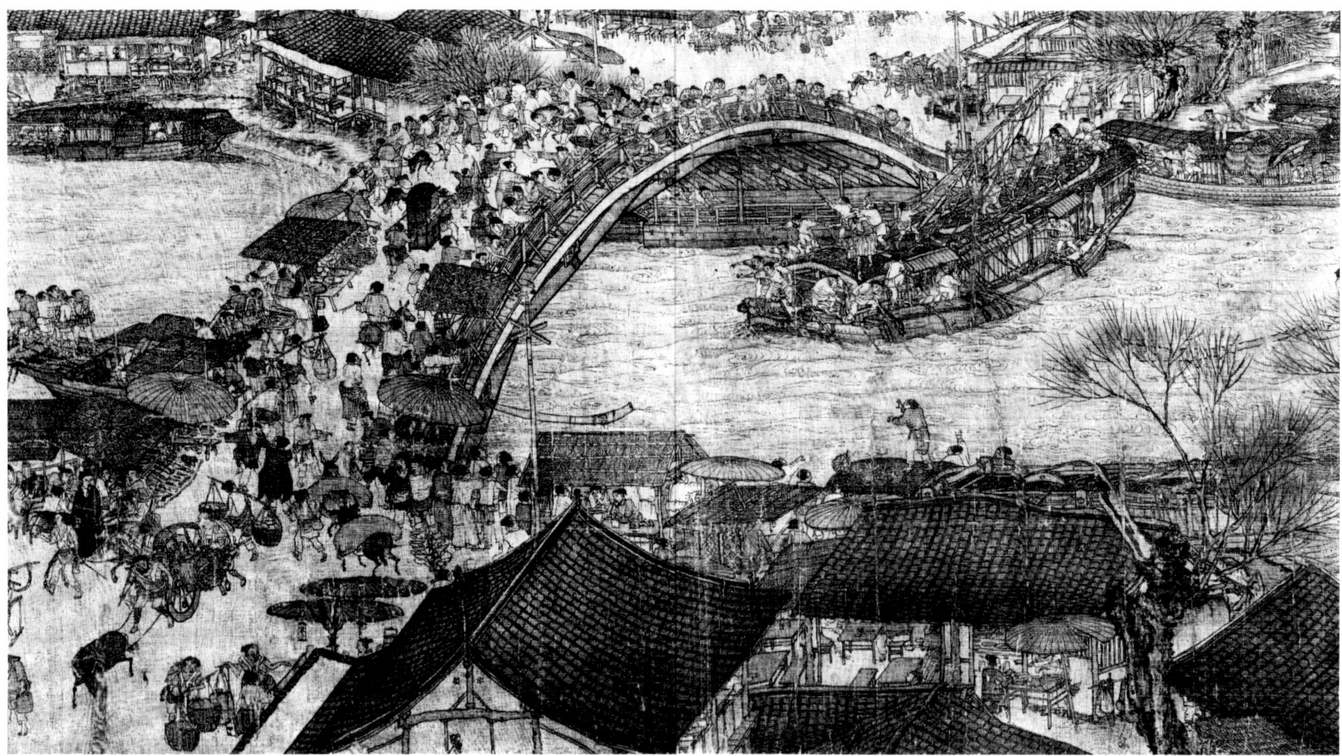

Figure 9. Chang Tse-tuan (early 12th century), detail from *Spring Festival on the River*. Handscroll, ink and light color on silk, $9^3/_4 \times 208^1/_4$ in. (24.8 × 528.7 cm). Palace Museum, Beijing

guished achievement for a mature scholar like Li Kung-lin. It was just before the end of his tenure in Ch'ang-yüan that Li painted at least one version of the *Classic of Filial Piety*. In an inscription he wrote on the painting, Li explained that at the suggestion of a certain Secretary Yang, he "chose one or two ideas" from the text and completed the scroll in the second month of 1085.[25]

A month later, after nineteen years on the throne, Emperor Shen-tsung died suddenly. Because his heir, Emperor Che-tsung (r. 1085–1101), was only ten years old, Shen-tsung's mother, the empress dowager Hsüan-jen (d. 1093), became regent, and in 1086 a new reign title, Yüan-yu (1086–94), was proclaimed. Under the regency of the empress dowager, Wang An-shih's reform policies were dismantled and the conservative party, led by Ssu-ma Kuang, returned to power. Within a short time the capital was filled with a group of brilliantly talented writers, calligraphers, and amateur painters, many of them recalled from remote postings to staff the central government administration under the new emperor. The years Li Kung-lin spent working among these men, from about 1086 to 1094, constituted the golden age of Northern Sung scholarly culture and were for Li himself the most productive period of his career as an artist.

Li Kung-lin was summoned to the capital early in the Yüan-yu reign, thanks to the recommendation of his friend and fellow 1070 *chin-shih* graduate Lu Tien. Li had arrived in K'ai-feng by early 1086 and established a residence in the eastern suburbs of the city, not far from the Rainbow Bridge, in the very area depicted in the opening sections of Chang Tse-tuan's (early 12th century?) great panorama of urban life *Spring Festival on the River* (fig. 9). Although Li's new position in the central government, Reviser in the Rear Section of the Secretariat Chancellery, has an impressive ring, it was in fact a low-ranking court post in which Li was required to edit official documents concerning the domestic administration of the imperial palace.

During his years in K'ai-feng, Li's closest associates were Su Shih, Su Ch'e, and Huang T'ing-chien, all recalled to the capital at the beginning of the Yüan-yu reign. After five years of banishment, travel, and a brief provincial assignment, Su Shih returned to the capital to join the staff of the Ministry of Rites late in 1085. His younger brother, Su Ch'e, arrived shortly after him and took up a new post in the Palace Library, where Huang T'ing-chien was a newly appointed editor, charged with compiling the *Veritable Records* of Emperor Shen-tsung's reign. Other close friends of Li Kung-lin who were summoned to the capital were the poets Ch'in Kuan (1049–1100), Chang Lei (1054–1114), and Ch'ao Pu-chih (1053–1110)—all followers of Su Shih—and the imperial son-in-law and painter Wang Shen (1036–after 1100).

Li Kung-lin's friendships with these men directly inspired most of the paintings he produced during his years in the capital. Unlike professional artists, Li did not paint on commission nor did he intend his paintings to be appreciated by a wide audience. When "persons of wealth and position" who wished to obtain his paintings approached him with requests, he stubbornly refused to respond; when asked for paintings by noted scholars, however, Li painted even for those he did not know.[26] As Wai-kam Ho has pointed out, it is impossible to understand the art of such Northern Sung scholar-officials as Li Kung-lin without recognizing the intimate relationship between art and friendship in their lives.[27] Among these men, as never before in China, painting began to function as a currency of friendship, serving much the same role that poetry had traditionally served as a private language accessible only to a highly literate elite.[28]

Su Shih requested or inspired more paintings than any of Li's other associates in K'ai-feng. After writing out the *Classic of the Yellow Court* in his matchless calligraphy, he had Li Kung-lin paint a frontispiece for the text. Li also added a portrait of himself and Su Shih at the end of the scroll.[29] In another portrait of Su Shih, Li depicted his friend sitting on a large rock. Huang T'ing-chien thought that this resembled Su Shih in a state of drunkenness, and he decided to ask Li for a similar portrait to display at gatherings of Su's friends.[30] In 1087 or 1088, Su Shih asked Li Kung-lin to paint a work titled *Three Horses*. This scroll depicted horses presented to the Northern Sung court by various barbarian tribes and included a portrait of a tribal chieftain who had been captured by the Chinese and presented to the emperor in 1087. Su Shih was greatly impressed by this rare example of the dynasty's military success in dealing with its menacing non-Chinese neighbors. The painting must have been one of Su's favorites, for he took it with him into exile to Hui-chou (Kwangtung) and inscribed it in 1097.[31] Su's final request for a painting from Li, made shortly before the two men parted for good, apparently was for the Buddhist images mentioned earlier that Su Shih had dedicated to his wife's memory in 1093. Although *Mountain Villa* was not painted at Su Shih's request, he and Su Ch'e were the first friends with whom Li Kung-lin shared his record of life in the Lung-mien Mountains.

In addition to requesting or inspiring paintings by Li Kung-lin, Su Shih also collaborated with Li in producing them. Shortly after the two men arrived in the capital, they collaborated on a painting of a pine tree and rocks, which they presented to one of Su's relatives, Liu Chung-yüan.[32] Later, Liu asked Li Kung-lin to add beneath the trees the figure of a foreign Buddhist monk. Li did so, transforming the painting into an illustration of lines from a poem by Tu Fu (712–770) that described such a scene.[33] Su Ch'e wrote a poem praising the painting, which bore the title *Easy Rest*, and Huang T'ing-chien composed two more.[34] Su and Li are said to have painted other collaborative works showing Su's favorite poet, T'ao Ch'ien (365–427), washing his feet, and another painting of a monk watching fish.[35]

Li Kung-lin's friendship with Su Shih also led to the production of paintings in the unlikely setting of the examination hall. In the spring of 1088, Su Shih served as Chief Examination Administrator for the departmental *chin-shih* examinations. He appointed as his assistants Huang T'ing-chien, Li Kung-lin, Ch'ao Pu-chih, and several other scholars from his circle of friends. During the weeks that the men were sequestered in the Imperial University, where the examinations were administered and graded, they found time to produce flurries of poetry.[36] Li Kung-lin also made several paintings. One evening Su Shih visited Li's quarters and found his friend suffering from stomach trouble and unable to eat. According to Su Shih, Li expressed his discomfort by painting a picture of a horse rolling in the dirt. Su, Huang T'ing-chien, Ch'ao Pu-chih, and several other examiners all wrote quatrains for this humorous sketch, which Li said he had done quite impetuously, taking up a piece of paper when he felt the horse "stomping to enter his brush."[37] This amusing vignette illustrates how thoroughly painting had become a part of everyday life for Li Kung-lin and his friends. Like occasional poems, which could be inspired by almost any event, Li's painting could transform even the most mundane experience into art.

Although most of Li Kung-lin's paintings during his years in K'ai-feng were produced for his famous literary friends—men celebrated during their own lifetimes for their poetry, prose, and calligraphy—Li also painted for less illustrious figures whose names are now almost forgotten. He offered several of his paintings as parting gifts to men who were leaving the capital. The most admired of these works, painted in 1086 for a man named An Fen-sou, was the *Yang Pass*, an illustration of Wang Wei's poem "Farewell to Yüan the Second on His Mission to An-hsi."[38] Like the man to whom Wang Wei addressed his poem in the eighth century, An Fen-sou was setting out for the remote northwestern corner of the Chinese empire, to a posting in Ho-hsi (modern Kansu). Li Kung-lin presented An with both the painting and a quatrain. Although poems had been written as parting gifts for centuries, Li Kung-lin may have been the first to combine a painting with a poem as a farewell offering.[39] Claiming that he was unable to express his feelings in words, Li made another painting of farewell, titled *Presenting Credentials*, for Liu Ching-wen, who was setting out to take office in Ta-ming (Hopei).[40] A painting of a similar theme by Li titled *Ch'in and Crane* depicted an official named Chao Pien (1008–1084), who carried with him to a posting in Szechwan only a pet crane and his *ch'in*.[41]

Informal visits with friends also could lead to painting. While calling on Chang Lei in 1086, Li dashed off a picture of two horses.[42] In the summer of 1089, during a visit to Lu Tien, Li Kung-lin was suddenly inspired to paint a portrait of Wang An-shih, whom he had visited in Nanking in the 1070s and with whom Lu Tien had studied as a young man.[43] And when Huang Shu-ta and Ch'en Lü-ch'ang stopped by Li's home in K'ai-feng one evening on their way back from the Fa-yün Monastery, where they had visited the Ch'an abbot Fa-hsiu (1027–1090), Li commemorated the occasion with a portrait of the two men. This painting showed Huang, dressed in a white robe, riding a donkey and singing while Ch'en walked behind, supporting himself with a staff—a sight so odd that residents of the capital were said to have mistaken the two men for a pair of immortals.[44]

Although Li Kung-lin fulfilled many requests from his friends, at least once he failed to produce a promised painting. His friend Ts'ai Chao (*chin-shih* 1079), who eventually composed Li's epitaph, once began a painting of some old trees and asked Li to finish it by adding river scenery, geese, and a boat—images Ts'ai conjured up in a poem he had written to complement the hoped-for painting. Li agreed to paint these images, but his laziness got the best of him, Ts'ai Chao complained, and the painting had to be finished by another artist.[45]

Another friend who played an important role in Li's life as a painter in K'ai-feng was Ts'ao Fu (*chin-shih* 1063). This man, who had once served on an examination staff with Li Kung-lin, was Chief Minister of the Imperial Stud during the early years of the Yüan-yu reign. Through his friendship with Ts'ao Fu, Li Kung-lin gained ready access to the imperial stables. There, he spent long hours studying the horses, so absorbed in his equine studies that he ignored other guests. It was apparently Li's fascination with the horses, many of which had been presented by foreign states, that inspired one of his most famous horse paintings, *Five Tribute Horses*. Now rumored to be in a private collection in Japan, this scroll was painted in K'ai-feng sometime between 1088, when the last of the horses Li depicted arrived at the court, and 1090, when Huang T'ing-chien wrote his colophon for the scroll.[46] During this period of Li's frequent visits to the imperial stables, which probably ended in 1088 when Ts'ao Fu left the capital, the Ch'an abbot Fa-hsiu issued his famous warning to the painter: if Li persisted in painting the animals, he would risk being reincarnated as a horse.[47] Fa-hsiu's stern words were said to have shocked Li into giving up horse painting in favor of Buddhist subjects; but, in fact, Li had been interested in Buddhism for many years before this, and there is no proof that he ever cured himself of his love of horses. Fa-hsiu's warning did, however, become an inside joke among Li's friends. When the monk cautioned Huang T'ing-chien about his excessive use of sensual language in his poetry, Huang asked if he, too, could expect to be punished by "ending up in the belly of a horse."[48]

The Artist as Antiquarian

Li Kung-lin's great fame as a painter has obscured his activities in a field that was equally important or, perhaps, even more important to him than his painting—collecting and studying the art of the distant past. His interest in collecting was fostered by his father, Li Hsü-i, who had assembled a distinguished collection of early calligraphy and painting. While he was still very young, Li Kung-lin began to study and copy works by the T'ang masters Wang Wei and Han Kan (715–after 781) that were owned by his father. This early introduction to works by great painters of the past enabled Li to "grasp the brushwork conception of the ancients"[49] and permanently fixed his taste for classical traditions of art. Li Kung-lin himself owned paintings by Chan Tzu-ch'ien (active ca. 581–609), Wu Tao-tzu, Han Kan, and Chou Fang (ca. 730–780). Although this list of works is impressive, Li did not collect paintings as voraciously as his friends Mi Fu (1052–1107) or Wang Shen, and he never wrote systematically about the scrolls he owned.

As a collector of bronzes and jades, however, Li amassed a collection that probably rivaled any outside the imperial palace or the households of imperial relatives. All the early biographies of Li speak of his wide knowledge of bronze vessels and jades and of his unparalleled expertise in deciphering archaic scripts. Li gained his erudition in these matters not merely by studying early texts but also by examining and purchasing ancient objects. According to Teng Ch'un's *Hua-chi,* "[Li] searched widely for ancient vessels, such as bells and caldrons, as well as for precious [jade] objects such as *kuei* tablets and *pi* discs."[50] Teng Ch'un also goes so far as to say that the energy Li Kung-lin channeled into his painting was only that left over from his antiquarian pursuits. When Li heard of an outstanding piece, he would think nothing of spending a large sum to acquire it, and a visitor to his home in K'ai-feng would have found rooms crowded with imposing objects from the Shang, Chou, and Han dynasties.

Much of Li Kung-lin's collection can be reconstructed by consulting the *K'ao-ku t'u,* a catalogue of ancient bronzes and jades compiled by the Neo-Confucian philosopher Lü Ta-lin (1044–1093). In addition to wood-block illustrations, this text contains facsimiles of rubbings and transcriptions of characters cast or carved on the objects, records of their sizes and weights, provenance, and owners, in addition to notes on miscellaneous historical and epigraphical points written by Lü Ta-lin himself or copied from other sources.[51] Of the total of 225 items catalogued, 55 are bronzes from the collection of Li Kung-lin. These include *ting, tun, yi, yu, hu, ku, chüeh,* and eight other types of ritual vessels from the Shang and Chou, as well as a bronze crossbow trigger, a halberd, and a bronze knife. Lü Ta-lin also recorded several Han-dynasty bronze lamps, an oven, belt hooks, and incense burners, all owned by Li Kung-lin. Because Li's collection included such a variety of bronze types from several dynasties, it is evident that his goal as a collector was to assemble a comprehensive survey of the bronze caster's art.

Chapter 8 of Lü Ta-lin's *K'ao-ku t'u* is devoted entirely to sixteen jades owned by Li Kung-lin. Li mentions nine of these in his preface to an essay by Su Shih titled "Record of the Washing Jade Basin."[52] According to Li's preface, in 1093 he obtained a Ma-t'ai stone and set it up in his studio. When Su Shih saw it, he urged Li to hollow out the stone to create a basin, in which, Su Shih said, Li could bathe his jades from time to time to bring out their luster. Su's "Record of the Washing Jade Basin" was inscribed on the basin's rim, and, at Su's suggestion, Li Kung-lin carved the shapes of his jades on its exterior. After Li's death, his son presented the basin to Emperor Hui-tsung (r. 1100–1126), taking care first to eradicate the text by Su Shih, whose writings were then proscribed. Hui-tsung eventually acquired all of Li Kung-lin's jades, with the exception of the *lu-lu* ring, which was buried with Li in his grave near Shu-ch'eng.[53]

The objects in Li Kung-lin's collection were the foundation of his study of archaeology. His major contribution to this field was a now-lost text in five chapters completed sometime before 1091 and titled *K'ao-ku t'u,* the same title Lü Ta-lin would give the catalogue he compiled a year or two later.[54] Although Li Kung-lin was one of many Northern Sung scholars who conducted epigraphical, archaeological, and antiquarian research and published treatises and catalogues on these subjects, he treated ancient bronzes and other artifacts not merely as sources of historical information but also as art objects, classifying them by categories of nomenclature that are still used today and recording important information about their origins, sizes, and functions. Li's text probably was the earliest catalogue to include extensive illustrations, another sign that his interest in the objects encompassed their purely aesthetic qualities. According to an early-twelfth-century source that describes Li Kung-lin's *K'ao-ku t'u*:

> For each object in each chapter he made an illustration and wrote a text. He explained the shapes of the objects and the engravings on them, the meanings of inscriptions, and the ways the objects were used. He summarized [his findings] in a preface and a postface. This was widely circulated, and scholars know that paying attention to the study of *ting* and *yi* of the Three Dynasties really began with [Li] Po-shih.[55]

From this description it is clear that the format of Li Kung-lin's *K'ao-ku t'u* was the model for Lü Ta-lin's catalogue, which contains nearly thirty entries copied from Li Kung-lin's lost text.[56] The most important of all Northern Sung archaeological catalogues, *Hsüan-ho po-ku t'u lu*, compiled at the command of Emperor Hui-tsung in the early twelfth century, also was based on the format of Li's *K'ao-ku t'u* and followed the system of nomenclature he used.[57]

It was through his private endeavors as a collector and an antiquarian that Li Kung-lin left his only mark on Sung political history, bringing about the change of a reign title and, indirectly, helping to advance the career of the infamous Ts'ai Ching (1046–1126), the corrupt prime minister of Emperor Hui-tsung's reign. This curious sequence of events began in 1096, when a certain Tuan I of Hsien-yang district (Shensi), site of the Ch'in-dynasty (249–207 B.C.) capital, excavated a luminous blue-green jade seal. The next year, after Tuan I presented this object to the court, Che-tsung commanded the Ministry of Rites, the Censorate, and other lower-ranking bureaus to investigate the seal's origins. In the third month of 1098, Ts'ai Ching, who was then a Recipient of Edicts in the Hanlin Academy, and thirteen other officials who had discussed the seal reported their findings in a memorial.[58] After consulting jade craftsmen and studying catalogues of seals and standard histories, they concluded that the seal was from the Ch'in dynasty and that it had been carved by the prime minister Li Ssu (d. 208 B.C.). The text of the seal, written in an archaic form of characters called "worm script," read: "Receive the mandate of heaven, in long life enjoy lasting prosperity."

Coming to light during Che-tsung's reign, Ts'ai Ching argued, the seal was a potent sign of Heaven's favor; though carved during the reign of the despised First Emperor of Ch'in (r. 221–210 B.C.), the seal had been captured by Kao-tsu (247–195 B.C.), founder of the illustrious Han dynasty (206 B.C.–A.D. 220), and became a symbol of dynastic legitimacy. To commemorate the appearance of this auspicious omen, which the memorial refers to as a *ling-fu*, or numinous tally, Ts'ai Ching urged the emperor to change the title of his reign. Che-tsung accepted this advice and, in the sixth month of 1098, after a ceremony enshrining the seal as a state treasure, changed the title of his reign from Shao-sheng, or "Continued Sageness," to Yüan-fu, or "Primal Tally."

What Ts'ai Ching's memorial omits is Li Kung-lin's role in the affair. Nearly one third of Li's biography in the *Sung-shih*, the official history of the Sung dynasty, is devoted to an account of his identification of the seal. When discussions among various scholars at court yielded no consensus on the seal's significance, Li Kung-lin was asked to settle the matter. The jade itself, Li argued, came from Lan-t'ien, in Hsien-yang district, and was the kind used during the Ch'in for the manufacture of imperial seals. The inscription and the method of carving, which, Li explained, was accomplished with a *k'un-wu* knife after the jade had been softened with toad grease, established that the seal had been made by

Li Ssu himself.[59] Although he was not credited in the memorial presented by Ts'ai Ching, it was probably in recognition of this impressive display of knowledge that Li was awarded the title Gentleman for Court Service. To his contemporaries in the capital, this was undoubtedly the high point of Li's otherwise humdrum official career.

Return to Lung-mien

According to the biography of Li Kung-lin in the *Hsüan-ho hua-p'u*, Li never forgot his beloved mountains and streams at Lung-mien during all his years in office. On holidays in the capital, he indulged his love of landscape by visiting gardens and scenic spots around the city in the company of one or two friends, avoiding "persons of wealth and authority."[60] His longing for a reclusive life and his lack of ambition puzzled some of his associates at court, who found it regrettable that Li had achieved fame only as a painter and had never risen to high office. Huang T'ing-chien once felt moved to defend his friend by explaining that Li was ". . . a man of the hills and the valleys. As to the passing glory of a famous name or the trappings of high rank, these are things with which he never concerned himself."[61] Li's yearning to escape the confines of life in officialdom was expressed in his *Mountain Villa*, as well as in other paintings, such as his several depictions of T'ao Ch'ien, the hermit admired most by Sung literati.

Before his departure from the capital, Li Kung-lin filled one final position in the central government, that of Legal Researcher in the Imperial Censorate. Li owed his transfer to the Censorate to Tung Tun-i (d. ca. 1110), an official who had won an excellent reputation for local administration and who was made Investigating Censor in 1091. The relationship between Tung and Li sheds light on an incident that has long puzzled the artist's biographers. According to Ch'ao Yüeh-chih (1059–1129), after Su Shih was banished to Kwangtung in 1094, Li happened to meet two of Su's followers on the street in K'ai-feng. Rather than greeting these men closely associated with his old friend, Li hid his face behind his fan and pretended not to see them.[62] Interpreting this as a sign of disloyalty to Su Shih, Ch'ao Yüeh-chih developed an intense dislike of Li and disposed of all Li's paintings in his collection. In spite of Ch'ao Yüeh-chih's indignant interpretation of Li Kung-lin's actions, there is no evidence that Su Shih and Li had parted as anything but the best of friends. Why, then, should Li have snubbed his old friend's followers on the streets of K'ai-feng? An answer emerges when this event is interpreted in the context of late-eleventh-century political life. After the death of the empress dowager Hsüan-jen in 1093, her grandson, the young emperor Che-tsung, assumed personal control of the government. Intent on reviving the reform policies favored by his father, Shen-tsung, and eager to distance himself from men closely associated with his domineering grandmother, Che-tsung sanctioned the banishment of Su Shih, Su Ch'e, Huang

T'ing-chien, and many others to remote provincial posts. With this sudden shift in the political fortunes of his closest friends, Li Kung-lin had good reason to believe that his own official career, lackluster though it was, would soon be ruined. His unwillingness to acknowledge publicly his association with the then-disgraced Su Shih by greeting Su's followers on the street can be seen as an understandable faltering of courage.

But there was a more subtle, and perhaps more painful, reason for Li Kung-lin to avoid Su Shih's followers. Tung Tun-i, who had recommended Li for the Censorate, was a determined enemy of Su Shih. Appointed to the Censorate in 1091, Tung immediately accused Su of having offended the memory of the late emperor Shen-tsung in an improperly worded memorial. Fortunately, thanks to the support of the empress dowager, Su Shih was cleared of this charge, and Tung was temporarily dismissed from the Censorate. But in 1094, after Su Shih had left the capital and Che-tsung had come to power, Tung Tun-i was restored to his former post and began launching fresh attacks on Su. Suddenly encountering Su Shih's disciples and abruptly reminded that the man responsible for his own rise also was responsible for the persecution of his close friend, Li Kung-lin had good cause to take refuge behind a discreetly held fan. This small moral compromise would seem to suggest that even Li Kung-lin, the unworldly hermit, could no longer remain untainted by the bitter factionalism that had disrupted the lives of his most intimate associates.

About 1097, after his closest friends had been banished from the capital, Li Kung-lin left the city for the last time to take up the post of Administrative Supervisor in Ssu-chou (Anhwei). In 1100, owing to illness, he asked to be relieved of his official duties, and he returned home to the Lung-mien Mountains. The illness that is said to have precipitated Li's final retirement was a form of paralysis that disabled his right hand. Although this disability may indeed have become acute by the time Li finally retired from all involvement in government, he had suffered from trouble in his arm for over a decade. In 1088, writing about one of Li's horse paintings, Huang T'ing-chien sadly commented that Li's affliction made it impossible for him to work. By the next year, however, Li had recovered sufficiently to paint for Lu Tien the portrait of Wang An-shih mentioned earlier. But even during those periods when Li was confined to bed, his thoughts were focused on his art. On one occasion, while he was lying sick in bed and moaning with pain, Li began to move his hand across his blanket as if he were painting. When his family admonished him, he laughed and said it was an old habit he could not break.[63]

Little is known of the final years of Li Kung-lin's life. Sequestered at his retreat, separated from his famous friends, Li once again became a sleeping dragon among the cliffs and ravines of Lung-mien. There, Li died at home in 1106.

1. For a survey of recent studies of the relationship between degree-holding and elite status, see Patricia Ebrey, "The Dynamics of Elite Domination in Sung China," *Harvard Journal of Asiatic Studies* 48, no. 2 (1988), pp. 493–519.

2. See John Chaffee, *The Thorny Gates of Learning: A Social History of Examinations* (Cambridge, 1985), table 26, p. 198. Although some sources state that Li Kung-lin was a descendant of the Southern T'ang imperial family, there is evidence that this claim may have been untrue. See Robert E. Harrist, Jr., "Li Kung-lin: A Note on the Origins of His Family," *National Palace Museum Bulletin* 25, no. 4 (1990).

3. John King Fairbank, *The Great Chinese Revolution, 1800–1985* (New York, 1986), p. 129.

4. In Chang Lei, *K'o-shan chi*, in *Ssu-k'u ch'üan-shu chen-pen ssu chi*, vol. 249 (Taipei, 1973), *chüan* 29, p. 14b.

5. Su Shun-ch'in, "Chi ti hou yü t'ung-nien yen Li ch'eng-hsiang chai," in *Su Shun-ch'in chi* (Shanghai, 1961), *chüan* 1, p. 4; translated by Thomas H. C. Lee, in *Government Education and Examinations in Sung China* (Hong Kong, 1985), p. 164.

6. Richard M. Barnhart, "Li Kung-lin's *Hsiao Ching T'u*: Illustrations of the 'Classic of Filial Piety'" (Ph.D. diss., Princeton University, 1967), p. 9.

7. Chang Ch'eng, *Hua-lu kuang-i*, in *Mei-shu ts'ung-shu*, vol. 16 (Shanghai, 1947), *shang*, p. 65.

8. The Hermit of Lung-mien (Lung-mien chü-shih) is a style name that Li Kung-lin chose for himself. Po-shih, his courtesy name, was the form in which he was commonly addressed by his friends.

9. For a study of this painting, see Robert E. Harrist, Jr., "A Scholar's Landscape: *Shan-chuang t'u* by Li Kung-lin" (Ph.D. diss., Princeton University, 1989).

10. Su Shih, "Shu Li Po-shih shan-chuang t'u hou," in *Tung-p'o t'i-pa*, in *I-shu ts'ung-pien*, vol. 22 (Taipei, 1962), *chüan* 5, pp. 95–96; and Su Ch'e, "T'i Li Kung-lin shan-chuang t'u erh-shih shou ping hsü," in *Luan-ch'eng chi* (Shanghai, 1987), vol. 1, *chüan* 16, pp. 386–91. For a partial English translation of Su Shih's colophon, see Hsiao-yen Shih and Susan Bush, eds., *Early Chinese Texts on Painting* (Cambridge, Mass., 1985), pp. 206–7.

11. For a survey of Northern Sung gardens, see Harrist, "A Scholar's Landscape," chap. 3.

12. Translation, with author's modifications, from Burton Watson, trans., *The Complete Works of Chuang-tzu* (New York, 1968), p. 211.

13. See Robert M. Gimello, "Marga and Culture: Learning, Letters, and Liberation in Northern Sung Ch'an," in Robert E. Buswell, Jr., and Robert M. Gimello, eds., *Paths to Liberation: The Marga and Its Transformation in Buddhist Thought*, Kurokawa Institute Studies in East Asian Buddhism 7 (Honolulu, 1992), pp. 371–437.

14. For the story of Su's request for these paintings, see Li I-ping, *Su Tung-p'o hsin-chuan* (Taipei, 1983), vol. 2, p. 780.

15. Yeh Meng-te, *Pi-shu lu-hua*, in *Ts'ung-shu chi-ch'eng chien-pien*, vol. 2787 (Shanghai, 1935), *shang*, p. 66.

16. Gimello, "Marga and Culture," p. 381.

17. Translated by Jonathan Chaves, in Laurance P. Roberts, *The Bernard Berenson Collection of Oriental Art at Villa I Tatti* (New York, 1991), p. 40.

18. See Tsung Ping, *Lun shan-shui hsü*, in Yü Chien-hua, ed., *Chung-kuo hua-lun lei-pien* (Beijing, 1957), vol. 1, pp. 583–84.

19. See Harrist, "A Scholar's Landscape," pp. 20–23.

20. George Hatch, biography of Su Shih, in Herbert Franke, ed., *Sung Biographies*, Münchener Ostasiatische Studien 16 (Wiesbaden, 1976), vol. 3, p. 954.

21. Li Kung-lin describes his activities in the capital in a note appended to a painting done several years later. See Wu Shih-tao, *Wu Li-pu shih-hua*, in *Chih-pu-tsu chai ts'ung-shu*, vol. 208 (Taipei, 1966), pp. 34b–35b.

22. Huang T'ing-chien, "Hsieh-chen tzu-tsan liu shou," in *Yü-chang Huang hsien-sheng wen-chi*, in *Ssu-pu ts'ung-k'an ch'u-pien so-pen*, vol. 54 (Taipei, 1967), *chüan* 14, p. 127.

23. See the discussion of Huang T'ing-chien's theories of art in Susan Bush, *The Chinese Literati on Painting: Su Shih (1037–1101) to Tung Ch'i-ch'ang (1555–1636)*, Harvard-Yenching Institute Studies 27 (Cambridge, Mass., 1971), pp. 43–51.

24. Recorded by Wang Hsiang-chih, *Yü-ti chi-sheng* (ca. 1221), in *Sung-tai ti-li shu ssu-chung* (Taipei, 1963), *chüan* 46, p. 13b.

25. Chou Mi, *Yun-yen kuo-yen lu*, in *Mei-shu ts'ung-shu*, vol. 6, p. 37.

26. *Hsüan-ho hua-p'u*, in *I-shu ts'ung-pien*, vol. 9, *chüan* 7, p. 201.

27. Wai-kam Ho, "Mi Fei," in *Encyclopedia of World Art* (New York, 1965), vol. 10, col. 85.

28. See Bush, *Chinese Literati on Painting*, pp. 7–9.

29. *Su Tung-p'o ch'üan-chi* (Beijing, 1986), vol. 1, *chüan* 20, p. 278.

30. Huang T'ing-chien, "Pa Tung-p'o shu-t'ieh hou," in *Shan-ku t'i-pa*, in *I-shu ts'ung-pien*, vol. 22, *chüan* 5, p. 46.

31. Su Shih, "San-ma t'u tsan," in *Su Shih wen-chi* (Beijing, 1986), *chüan* 21, pp. 610–11. Unfortunately, none of the paintings Li Kung-lin made for Su Shih has survived.

32. Su Shih, "T'i ch'i-chi t'u shih," in *Tung-p'o t'i-pa*, *chüan* 3, pp. 53–54.

33. Tu Fu, "Hsi wei shuang-sung t'u ko," in P'eng Ting-ch'iu, ed., *Ch'üan T'ang shih* (Beijing, 1960), vol. 4, p. 2305.

34. Su Ch'e, "Tzu-an yü Li Kung-lin hsüan-te kung hua ts'ui-shih ku-mu lao seng wei chih ch'i-chi t'u t'i ch'i hou," in *Luan-ch'eng chi*, vol. 1, *chüan* 15, p. 352; Huang T'ing-chien, "Tz'u yün Tzu-an Tzu-yu t'i ch'i-chi t'u" and "T'i Li Po-shih ch'i-chi t'u," in *Yü-chang Huang hsien-sheng wen-chi*, *chüan* 5, p. 44.

35. The painting of T'ao Ch'ien is the subject of a poem by Liu Ts'ung-i (1181–1224), "T'i Su Li ho-hua Yüan-ming chiao-tsu t'u," in Ch'en Pang-yen, ed., *Yü-ting li-tai t'i-hua shih lei*, in *Ssu-k'u ch'uan-shu chen-pen liu-chi*, vol. 372 (Taipei, 1976), *chüan* 37, pp. 15b–16a. The painting of a monk watching fish is mentioned by Huang T'ing-chien in "T'i Li Po-shih hua kuan-yü seng," in *Yü-chang Huang hsien-sheng wen-chi*, *chüan* 5, p. 46.

36. For a study of some of these poems, see Ronald Egan, "Poems on Painting: Su Shih and Huang T'ing-chien," *Harvard Journal of Asiatic Studies* 43, no. 2 (1983), pp. 413–51.

37. Su Shih, "Shu shih-yüan chung shih," in *Tung-p'o t'i-pa*, in *I-shu ts'ung-pien*, vol. 22, *chüan* 3, pp. 54–55.

38. Wang Wei, *Wang Yu-ch'eng chi chien-chu*, vol. 2 (Taipei, 1977), *chüan* 14, p. 557.

39. Bush, *Chinese Literati on Painting*, pp. 8–9. For Li's poem, titled "Hsiao shih ping hua-chüan feng-sung Fen-sou t'ung-nien chi feng i fu Hsi-ho mu-fu," see Sun Shao-yüan, ed., *Sheng-hua chi*, in *Ssu-k'u ch'uan-shu chen-pen pa-chi*, vol. 213 (Taipei, 1978), *chüan* 1, pp. 22a–22b.

40. Chang Shih-nan, *Yu-huan chi-wen* (Beijing, 1980), *chüan* 9, p. 76.

41. Su Shih, "T'i Li Po-shih hua Chao Ching-jen ch'in-ho t'u erh shou," in *Su Tung-p'o ch'üan-chi*, vol. 1, *chüan* 17, p. 241.

42. Agnes E. Meyer, *Chinese Painting as Reflected in the Thought and Art of Li Lung-mien, 1070–1106* (New York, 1923), vol. 2, p. 249.

43. Lu Tien, "Shu Wang Ching-kung yu Chung-shan hou," in *T'ao-shan chi*, in *Ssu-k'u ch'uan-shu chen-pen pieh-chi*, vol. 284 (Taipei, 1975) *chüan* 11, pp. 7b–8a.

44. Hu Tzu, *T'iao-hsi yü-yin ts'ung-hua ch'ien-chi* (Taipei, 1966), *chüan* 52, p. 353.

45. Liu Tsai, *Man-t'ang wen-chi*, in *Ssu-k'u ch'uan-shu chen-pen chiu-chi*, vol. 250 (Taipei, 1979), *chüan* 24, pp. 17b–18b.

46. See Chou Mi, *Yün-yen kuo-yen lu*, pp. 40–41.

47. *Hsüan-ho hua-p'u*, *chüan* 7, p. 200.

48. Recorded in Li O, ed., *Sung-shih chi-shih*, in *Kuo-hsüeh chi-pen ts'ung-shu*, vol. 181 (Taipei, 1968), *chüan* 92, p. 2265.

49. *Hsüan-ho hua-p'u*, *chüan* 7, p. 197.

50. Teng Ch'un, *Hua-chi*, in Yü An-lan, ed., *Hua-shih ts'ung-shu*, vol. 1 (Shanghai, 1963), *chüan* 3, p. 12.

51. The earliest extant edition of Lü's *K'ao-ku t'u* is dated 1299; copies are in Beijing and the Harvard-Yenching Library, Cambridge, Mass. The *Wen-yüan-ke ssu-k'u ch'üan-shu* edition is based on a Northern Sung wood-block edition and includes several entries missing from the 1299 edition. For a survey of Sung archaeological catalogues, see R. C. Rudolph, "Preliminary Notes on Sung Archaeology," *Journal of Asian Studies* 22, no. 2 (February 1963), pp. 169–77, and Robert Poor, "Notes on the Sung Dynasty Archaeological Catalogs," *Archives of the Chinese Art Society of America* 19 (1965), pp. 33–44.

52. Recorded by Wu Tseng, *Neng-kai-chai man-lu* (Beijing, 1960), *chüan* 14, p. 402; Su Shih, "Hsi-yü-ch'ih ming," in *Ching-chin Tung-p'o wen-chi shih-lüeh*, vol. 2 (Hong Kong, 1979), *chüan* 59, pp. 975–76.

53. Wu Tseng, *Neng-kai-chai man-lu*, *chüan* 14, p. 402.

54. None of the early sources gives a date for Li Kung-lin's *K'ao-ku t'u*, though in his *Chou-shih*, Chai Ch'i-nien lists this title before another, shorter text on archaeology by Li titled *Chou-chien*, which was completed in 1091. This implies that *K'ao-ku t'u* was completed before 1091. See Chai Ch'i-nien, *Chou-shih*, in *Ts'ung-shu chi-ch'eng chien-pien*, vol. 1513 (Shanghai, 1935), p. 11.

55. Ibid.

56. This was first noted by the twentieth-century epigrapher Jung Keng in his "Sung-tai chi-chin shu-chi shu-p'ing," in *Ch'ing-chu Ts'ai Yüan-p'ei liu-shih-wu sui lun-wen chi* (Beijing, 1933–35), vol. 2, pp. 663–65.

57. Ts'ai T'ao, *T'ieh-wei shan ts'ung-t'an* (Beijing, 1983), *chüan* 4, pp. 79–80.

58. Li Tao, *Hsü tzu-chih t'ung-chien ch'ang-pien* (reprint, Taipei, 1964), *chüan* 496, pp. 2a–4a; and Ma Tuan-lin, *Wen-hsien t'ung-k'ao*, vol. 1 (Shanghai, 1936), *chüan* 115, p. 1041.

59. T'o T'o et al., *Sung-shih* (Beijing, 1977), *chüan* 444, pp. 13125–26.

60. *Hsüan-ho hua-p'u*, *chüan* 7, p. 201.

61. Colophon for *Wu-ma t'u*, recorded by Chou Mi in *Yün-yen kuo-yen lu*, p. 40.

62. This story is recorded by Shao Po, in *Shao-shih wen-chien hou-lu* (Beijing, 1980), *chüan* 9, p. 76.

63. *Hsüan-ho hua-p'u*, *chüan* 7, p. 202.

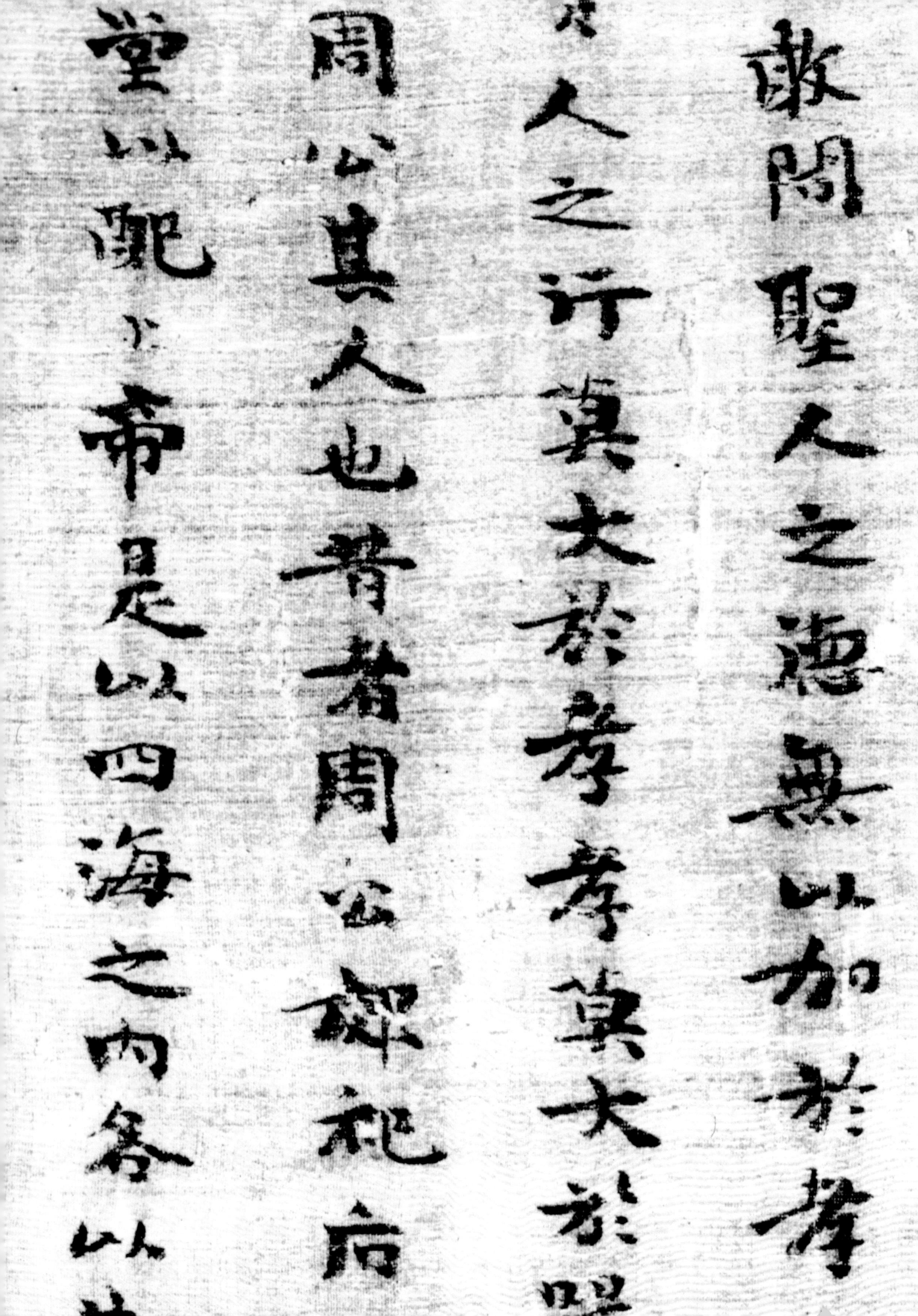

敢問聖人之德無以加於孝

人之行莫大於孝孝莫大於

周公其人也昔者周公郊祀后

堂以配上帝是以四海之內各以

THE CALLIGRAPHY OF LI KUNG-LIN IN THE *CLASSIC OF FILIAL PIETY*

Hui-liang J. Chu

In its present form, Li Kung-lin's calligraphic transcription of the *Classic of Filial Piety* is divided into sixteen sections; each section, except the first, is preceded by an illustration. The text consists of eighty-six lines, each of which contains eighteen to twenty-five characters. Most of the characters at the top and bottom of each column are missing or fragmentary as a result of damage sustained by the edges of the silk. When studied closely, this calligraphy, like Li's painted illustrations, reveals a brilliantly innovative synthesis of past styles and a bold departure from prevailing Northern Sung tastes (fig. 10).

The Calligraphy of Li Kung-lin

By the time Li Kung-lin transcribed the text of the *Classic of Filial Piety*, about 1086, Chinese calligraphy was already an ancient art and the subject of a vast body of critical and art-historical texts. All the basic script types still in use today had reached full maturity centuries before Li's time, and the practice of calligraphy was dominated by the styles of several towering figures of the past, especially Wang Hsi-chih (ca. 307–ca. 365) and Yen Chen-ch'ing (709–785). For the *Classic of Filial Piety*, Li Kung-lin employed small standard script (*hsiao-k'ai*), a miniaturized version of standard script (*k'ai-shu*) traditionally used for classical texts, government documents, Buddhist sutras, and other contexts for which a formal, highly regular form of calligraphy was appropriate. An early master of this script was Chung Yu (151–230), a chief minister of the short-lived Wei dynasty (220–65). During the Northern Sung, rubbings of works attributed to Chung Yu were available in the *Calligraphic Works in the Ch'un-hua Palace*, an imperial anthology of rubbings completed in 992.[1] Although they were copies of Chung Yu's writing made by later calligraphers, two examples of his style were

Figure 10. Li Kung-lin, detail from chapter 9 of the *Classic of Filial Piety* (plate 6)

especially important in the history of small standard script, *Memorial on an Announcement to Sun Ch'üan* (see fig. 21) and *Memorial Celebrating a Victory* (see fig. 22).[2] Wang Hsi-chih, revered for his mastery of running and cursive script, also produced works in small standard script that became important models during the T'ang and the Sung dynasties. *On General Yüeh I*, dated 348, is probably the most reliable example of Wang Hsi-chih's writing in this script type.[3] These small, squarish, regularly aligned characters written in carefully articulated brushwork profoundly influenced T'ang and Sung calligraphers.

By the end of the eighth century, both large and small standard-script calligraphy had been transformed by such masters as Ou-yang Hsün (557–641), Yü Shih-nan (558–638), Ch'u Sui-liang (596–658), and Yen Chen-ch'ing. Mature standard script of the T'ang is marked by perfectly proportioned characters of uniform size, arranged in a gridwork and written with complex strokes which require the calligrapher's brush to execute motions that have been given the names "lifting" (*t'i*), "pressing" (*an*), "turning" (*chuan*), "folding" (*che*), and "kicking" (*t'i*).

It was the style of the T'ang, transmitted with relatively little change through rubbings and samples of handwritten calligraphies, that dominated standard-script writing in the eleventh century, and it is against this background that Li's calligraphy in the *Classic of Filial Piety* must be seen. Compared with T'ang standard script, Li's calligraphy simplifies complex brush motions, introduces squat and imbalanced character structures, and breaks away from static, gridlike compositions in favor of a more dynamic arrangement of small and large characters. As we shall see, behind these innovations lay Li's extensive knowledge of Han-dynasty (206 B.C.–A.D. 220) and Northern Dynasties (386–581) stelae inscriptions, ink writings on paper from the Western Tsin (265–317) dynasty, and works attributed to Chung Yu available in the late Northern Sung dynasty.

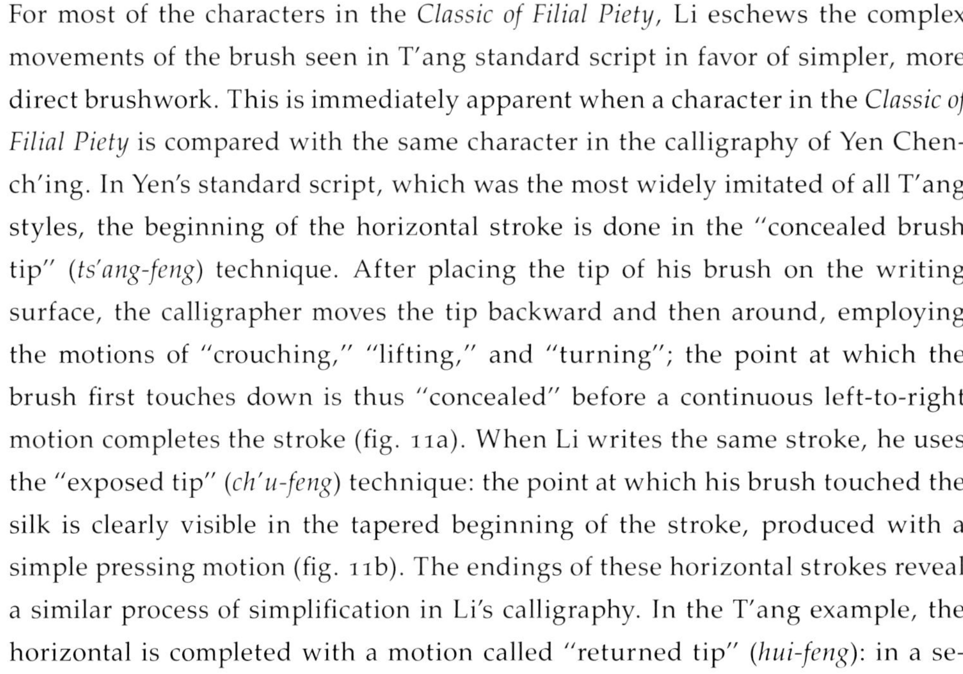

For most of the characters in the *Classic of Filial Piety*, Li eschews the complex movements of the brush seen in T'ang standard script in favor of simpler, more direct brushwork. This is immediately apparent when a character in the *Classic of Filial Piety* is compared with the same character in the calligraphy of Yen Chen-ch'ing. In Yen's standard script, which was the most widely imitated of all T'ang styles, the beginning of the horizontal stroke is done in the "concealed brush tip" (*ts'ang-feng*) technique. After placing the tip of his brush on the writing surface, the calligrapher moves the tip backward and then around, employing the motions of "crouching," "lifting," and "turning"; the point at which the brush first touches down is thus "concealed" before a continuous left-to-right motion completes the stroke (fig. 11a). When Li writes the same stroke, he uses the "exposed tip" (*ch'u-feng*) technique: the point at which his brush touched the silk is clearly visible in the tapered beginning of the stroke, produced with a simple pressing motion (fig. 11b). The endings of these horizontal strokes reveal a similar process of simplification in Li's calligraphy. In the T'ang example, the horizontal is completed with a motion called "returned tip" (*hui-feng*): in a se-

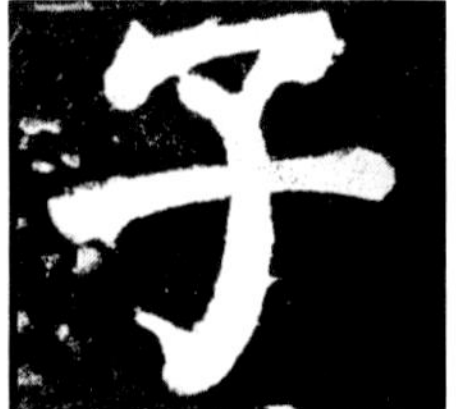

a

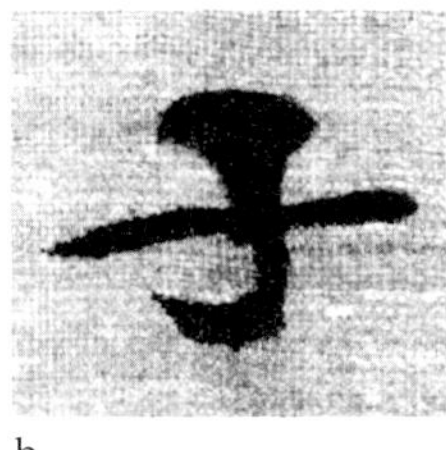

b

Figure 11. The character *tzu*

a. Yen Chen-ch'ing (709–785), detail from a rubbing of the *Stele for the Yen Family Shrine*, dated 770

b. Li Kung-lin, detail from the *Classic of Filial Piety*

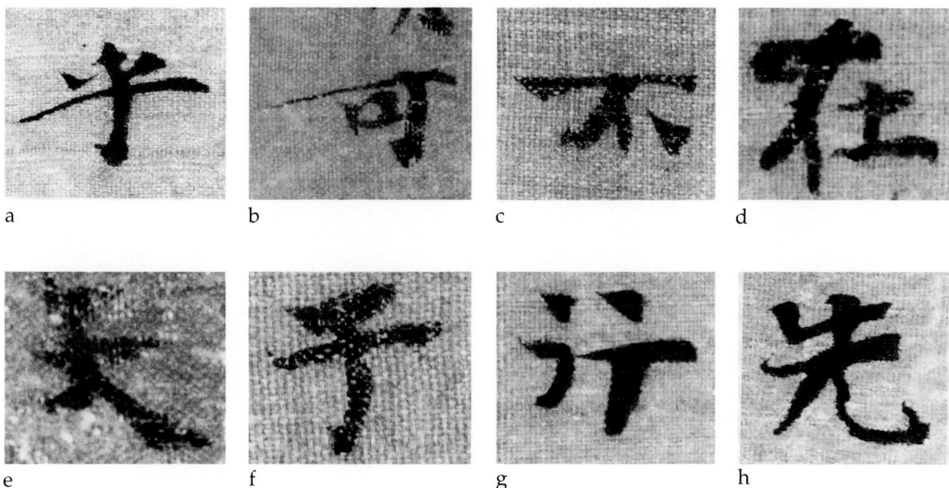

Figure 12a–h. Variations in beginnings and endings of horizontal brushwork, from Li Kung-lin, *Classic of Filial Piety*

quence of motions that reverses those of the "concealed tip" technique that began the stroke, Yen Chen-ch'ing moves his brush back to the left to form a well-defined knob. Li Kung-lin completes the same stroke by gradually lifting his brush as he completes the leftward motion. A similar process of simplification can be seen in the way the two calligraphers complete the hook strokes. The complex inner movements of the brush in Yen's calligraphy are replaced by a simple leftward "kick" in Li's writing.

In spite of this tendency to make his standard-script brushwork simpler than that of his T'ang predecessors, Li is never dull or repetitious. He wields the brush nimbly and with constant changes of speed, pressure, and direction to create fascinating graphic designs. This can be illustrated if we examine the horizontal strokes in the *Classic of Filial Piety*. These strokes, often exaggerated in length and greatly varied in shape, are the dominant visual motif in Li's calligraphy.

Li begins most of the horizontals with the "exposed tip" technique and then pulls the brush rightward in a simple movement, occasionally increasing pressure and thus widening the ending of the stroke (fig. 12a). When the pulling movement is done with the very tip of the brush, the stroke becomes thin as a thread (fig. 12b). Li frequently writes these thin horizontal strokes with a trembling motion that resembles the thin, trembling horizontal strokes in Chung Yu's *Memorial Celebrating a Victory*. This third-century work is echoed also in Li's horizontal strokes begun with a rapid pressing and lifting motion that forms a triangular shape (fig. 12c). Although Li begins some horizontals with a "concealed tip," this is not the complex T'ang technique that involves "crouching," "lifting," and "turning" movements but rather an abrupt application of pressure that produces a blunt shape totally unlike that found in T'ang standard script (fig. 12d).

The endings of most horizontal strokes in Li's calligraphy are executed in the "exposed tip" technique (fig. 12e). However, there is great variety in the way the brush leaves the silk. It may rise or fall or maintain the horizontal motion without any change. When the brush is pressed down slightly before being lifted, a flared, clerical-script form is produced (fig. 12f). Often the endings are written with an abrupt motion that can create either round or square shapes with no trace of the brush tip left on the silk (fig. 12g). In some characters, horizontal strokes end with an extremely quick motion that produces a stark, sharp-edged shape (fig. 12h), also reminiscent of Han-dynasty clerical script.

The type of analysis applied above to the horizontal strokes in Li's *Classic of Filial Piety* could be applied to many different types of strokes in the text and would reveal the artist's determination to avoid monotonous repetition of forms that might have resulted from his radical simplification of T'ang brushwork. Li's inventiveness is especially clear when we examine how he varies his brushwork in writing repeated characters. The most frequently used character in the *Classic of Filial Piety* is *chih,* a function word that appears over seventy times. This character consists of four strokes: a dot (*tien*), a rightward ascending diagonal (*t'iao*), a leftward descending diagonal (*p'ieh*), and a rightward descending diagonal (*na*) that ends in a flared, wedge-shaped silhouette. No two versions of this character are quite alike. Li's writing of the final downward diagonal is especially varied; subtle changes in the way the stroke is begun, the speed at which it is written, and the timing of the lifting and pressing motions make each stroke different in length, thickness, and shape. And although for the character to remain legible the basic positions of the strokes cannot be changed, Li varies the angles at which the strokes are written as well as the spaces between them so that the same character appears in many different guises. Other characters, such as *pu* ("not"), which appears fifty-four times, and *yeh* (a function word), which appears thirty-five times, also show Li avoiding repetition in his manner of writing horizontal strokes and hook strokes in identical characters. There are well-known precedents in the history of earlier calligraphy for Li's approach to writing repeated characters. The most famous is the *Preface to the Orchid Pavilion*, by Wang Hsi-chih. In this work, the most famous piece of calligraphy in history, there are twenty appearances of the character *chih*: no two are alike.[4] Li surely knew this revered work, which had been carefully studied for centuries.[5] But there is an important difference between Wang Hsi-chih's approach to repeated characters and Li's. Wang Hsi-chih wrote the *Preface to the Orchid Pavilion* in semicursive script, a script type that normally allows for considerable variation in the way repeated characters are written; Li's *Classic of Filial Piety* is written in small standard script, a script type that traditionally demanded strict regularity. By bringing to his calligraphy in small standard script the spirit of free expression and inventiveness normally restricted to more cursive styles, Li Kung-lin achieved a startlingly innovative form of writing.

Another source of visual interest in Li's calligraphy lies in his preference for sharp contrasts of thick and thin strokes. As standard script developed over the centuries from the time of Wang Hsi-chih to the T'ang, strokes became increasingly even in thickness. In the calligraphy of Yen Chen-ch'ing, especially works from late in his life, the thickness of the strokes is highly uniform. This tendency

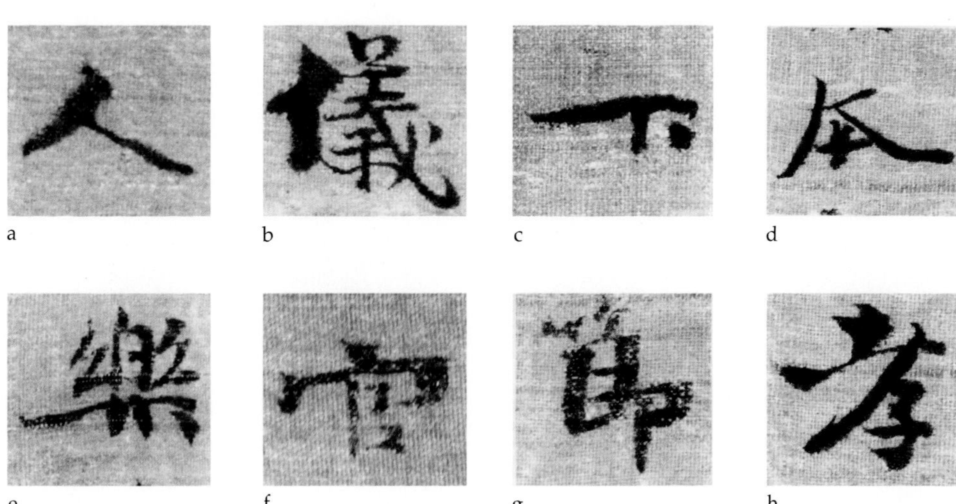

Figure 13a–h. Variations in character composition, from Li Kung-lin, *Classic of Filial Piety*

continued into the Northern Sung with little change. In the *Classic of Filial Piety*, however, sharp contrasts between thick and thin strokes are one of the most striking features. Common characters, such as *jen* ("man"; fig. 13a), *min* ("people"), and *pu* ("not"), all display this contrast between dark, heavy strokes written with considerable pressure on the brush tip and light, delicately brushed strokes in which the brush seems barely to graze the silk. In some characters Li stresses the radicals, making these signifiers of meaning heavier and more assertive than other elements in the characters (fig. 13b). He also uses sharp contrasts of thick and thin among groups of two or more characters. Whether it is within individual characters or between adjacent characters, the play of heavy and light, thick and thin creates a strong visual rhythm that enlivens Li's calligraphy throughout the scroll.

Just as Li's brushwork turns away from the complexity of T'ang models, often evoking styles of the remote past, so does the structure of his characters depart from the rectangular and balanced forms of T'ang standard script. In general, characters in the *Classic of Filial Piety* are squat and precariously balanced, recalling Eastern Han stelae inscriptions in clerical script and the small standard script of Chung Yu. By the T'ang period, this archaic squatness—the tendency of characters to expand horizontally rather than vertically—had given way to a taste for tall, rectangular, and perfectly balanced structures. Li Kung-lin evokes archaic structural principles in several ways. Often he elongates horizontal strokes and shortens vertical strokes to make characters low and compact (fig. 13c). In some characters he stretches the diagonals out of proportion (fig. 13d), and often he makes radicals that are oddly compressed (fig. 13e).

The imbalanced compositional structures Li favors, which differ so greatly from those in T'ang calligraphy, are created in several ways. In many characters radicals are enlarged (fig. 13f), and in characters composed of more than one radical either the left and right elements are misaligned (fig. 13g) or the upper and lower elements are not on the same vertical axis (fig. 13h). Unusually elongated or shortened strokes also create an effect of imbalance.

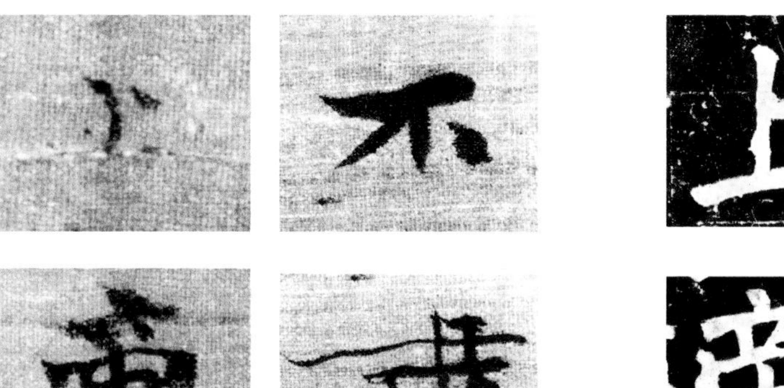
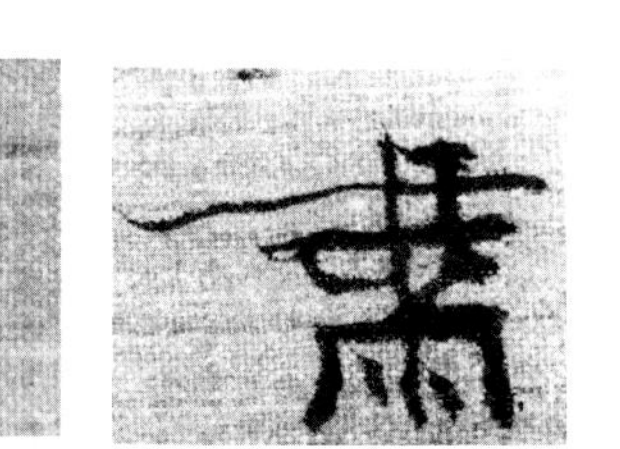
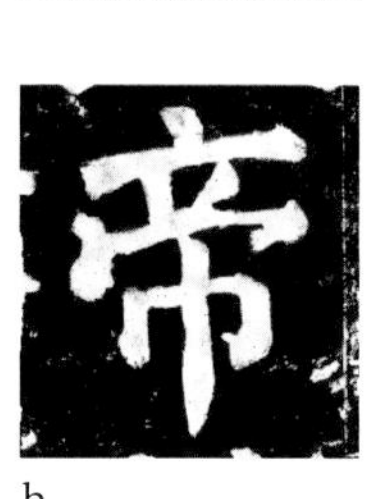
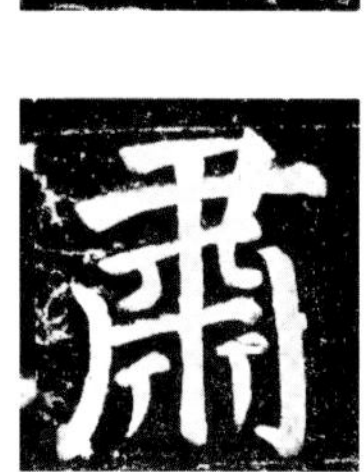

a b

Figure 14. The characters *shang, ti, pu,* and *su*

a. Li Kung-lin, *Classic of Filial Piety*

b. Yen Chen-ch'ing (709–785), rubbing of the *Stele for the Yen Family Shrine,* dated 770

Li Kung-lin's innovative departures from the norms of small-standard-script brushwork and character structure are complemented by his equally fresh approach to the size and spatial arrangement of the characters. In T'ang standard script, the sizes of characters are equal regardless of the number of strokes they contain, and each character fills an imaginary square. Rejecting this convention, Li frequently varies the sizes of his characters according to the number of strokes they contain. For example, *shang* ("above"), *ti* ("emperor"), *pu* ("not"), and *su* ("serious") differ greatly in size because of the different numbers of strokes they contain. Compare Li's writing of these characters (fig. 14a) with Yen Chen-ch'ing's, in which all the characters are the same size (fig. 14b). However, the number of strokes in a given character does not always account for the size in which Li Kung-lin chooses to write it. *T'ien* ("heaven") and *hsia* ("below"), in the thirty-fifth line, both contain only a few strokes, yet their sizes are very different. Here, Li Kung-lin's aesthetic judgment and spontaneity played a decisive role. Because the characters vary greatly in size, and because their imbalanced structures create an irregular pattern of rectangular, triangular, rhomboidal, and even trapezoidal forms, they cannot be arranged in a rigid gridwork like characters in T'ang standard script. This irregular spacing suggests that, as in his approach to repeated characters, Li has borrowed certain features from cursive and semicursive script, in which characters are more freely arranged, to transform his small standard script into a dynamic, expressive mode of writing.

Li Kung-lin's Study of the Past and the Sources of His Style

As the preceding analysis of Li Kung-lin's *Classic of Filial Piety* reveals, his style in small standard script turns away from the conventions of the T'ang dynasty, still dominant during the Northern Sung, in favor of simpler forms that evoke traditions of pre-T'ang calligraphy. Li's sources for this revival and his synthesis of past styles can be traced to stelae inscriptions of the Han and Northern Wei, writings on paper from the Western Tsin, and, most important, from the Chung Yu tradition.

The second half of the eleventh century witnessed a burst of interest in early calligraphy carved on stelae, or *pei*.[6] Scholars and calligraphers collected rubbings of these inscriptions and studied them for their artistic as well as for their historical and literary value, and rubbings of ancient stelae were popular gifts in literati circles. The renowned poet and calligrapher Su Shih (1037–1101) once gave fifteen such rubbings to his younger brother Su Ch'e (1039–1112).[7] Scholars also gathered the actual stelae in private collections. Sun Chüeh (1028–1090), an uncle of the famous calligrapher Huang T'ing-chien (1045–1105), collected many ancient stelae and displayed them in his studio, which he called the Pavilion of Marvelous Ink. Tseng Kung (1019–1083), Su Shih, Su Ch'e, and other cultural luminaries wrote essays and poems to commemorate Sun's collection.[8]

Records of stelae, including their inscriptions and locations, appear in the essays and poems of Northern Sung writers, in miscellaneous notes, and, most important, in books on epigraphy, such as the *Record of Ancient Calligraphy*, by Ou-yang Hsiu (1007–1072); *Records of Calligraphy on Bronze and Stone*, by Tseng Kung; and *Colophons to Calligraphy Collected by Kuang-ch'uan*, by Tung Yu (active early 12th century).[9] Among these works, Ou-yang Hsiu's was the most valuable record of ancient calligraphy available to Northern Sung scholars. Ou-yang lists seventy-eight stelae inscriptions from the Han and thirteen from the Northern Dynasties. Several of these stelae are still extant: *Mount Hua Temple Stele* (dated 165), *Stele for I-ying* (dated 153), *Ritual Vessels Stele* (dated 156), *Stele for Shih Ch'en* (dated 169)—all of the Eastern Han period—and the *Inscription at Stone Gate* (dated 509), from the Northern Wei. Although not recorded in texts on epigraphy, certain other stelae inscriptions also were well known in the Northern Sung. For example, an inscription dated 1096 on the back of the *Stele for Chia Ssu-po* (dated 519), from the Northern Wei, states that rubbings taken from this stele were circulated among scholars in the early eleventh century and that the stele itself was found hidden in a stable in the late eleventh century.[10]

These records show that calligraphers of the Northern Sung had ample opportunity to study rubbings of Han and Northern Wei stelae or, if they were diligent enough to seek them out, to see extant stelae. Li Kung-lin took full advantage of these materials, and his knowledge of stelae inscriptions is revealed in his calligraphy for the *Classic of Filial Piety*. This can be demonstrated by comparing characters from Li's work with those from several Han and Northern Dynasties stelae. The Han examples are *Ode to Shih-men* (dated 148), *Stele for I-ying, Mount Hua Temple Stele, Stele for Shih Ch'en, Ode to Hsi-hsia* (dated 171), *Stele for Ts'ao Ch'üan* (dated 185), and *Stele for Chang Ch'ien* (dated 186). These are excellent examples of Eastern Han clerical script, and four of them were recorded by Ou-yang Hsiu and Tseng Kung.[11] The Northern Dynasties stelae—examples of *tsao-*

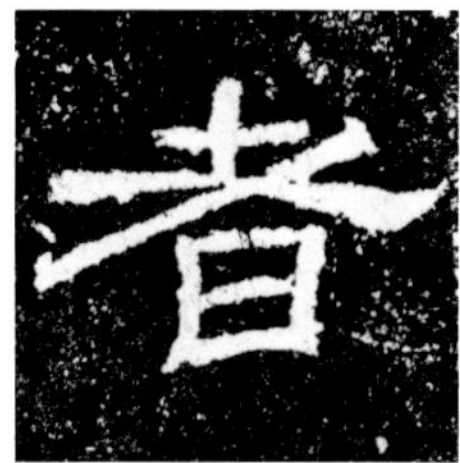
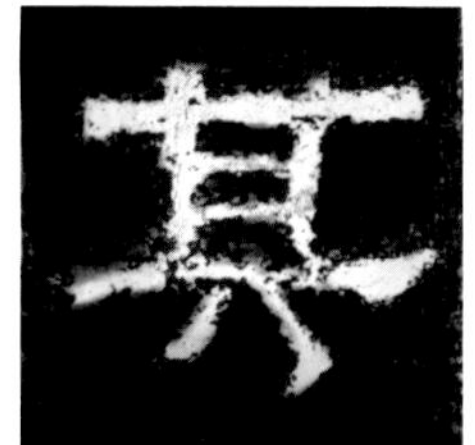
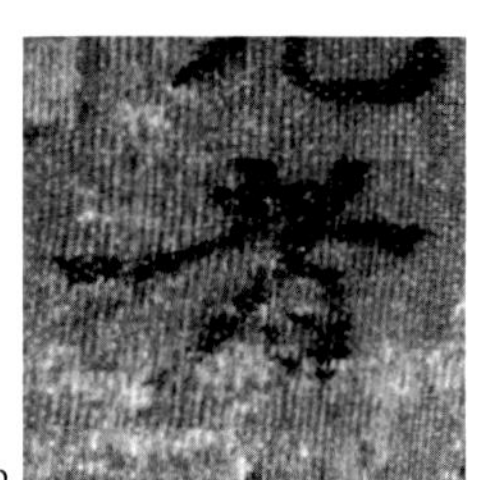
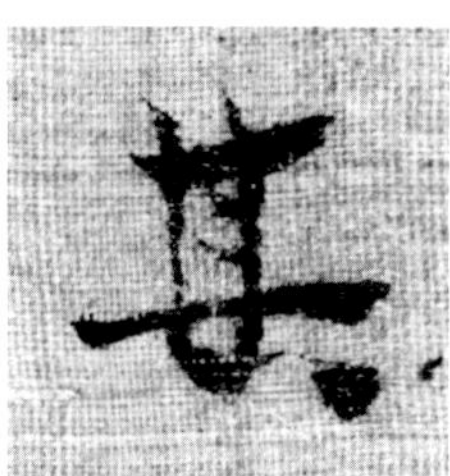

Figure 15. Horizontal brushstrokes with flared endings using "exposed tip" technique

a. Rubbing of the *Stele for I-ying*, dated 153

b. Li Kung-lin, *Classic of Filial Piety*

hsiang chi, or inscriptions on Buddhist statues—include: *Inscriptions on Buddhist Statues Dedicated by Niu Ch'üeh* (dated 495), *Inscriptions on Buddhist Statues Dedicated by Shih-p'ing Kung* (dated 498), *Inscriptions on Buddhist Statues Dedicated by Sun Ch'iu-sheng* (dated 502), and *Inscriptions on Buddhist Statues Dedicated by Wei Ling-ts'ang* (ca. 500–503).[12]

The flared endings of horizontal strokes are a prominent feature of mature Han clerical script. Completed with a pressing motion just before the brush is lifted, these endings are written in the "exposed tip" technique (fig. 15a). This kind of ending disappeared in standard script and was replaced by endings written with the more complicated "returned tip" discussed earlier. But it is precisely this type of complexity in T'ang brushwork that Li Kung-lin, inspired by Han and Northern Dynasties examples, rejects in his *Classic of Filial Piety* (fig. 15b). In adopting the flared horizontal endings from clerical script for a work in small standard script, Li evokes a style of calligraphy that was current nearly a thousand years before his time. But he was not content with merely imitating this motif from ancient calligraphy; indeed, he transforms it into a far more varied

Figure 16. Square brushwork (*fang pi*)

a. Rubbing of the stele *Ode on the Western Gorges*, dated 171

b. *Inscription of Buddhist Statues Dedicated by Niu Ch'üeh*, dated 495

c. Li Kung-lin, *Classic of Filial Piety*

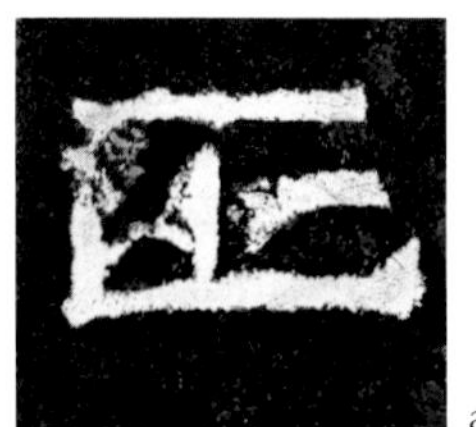
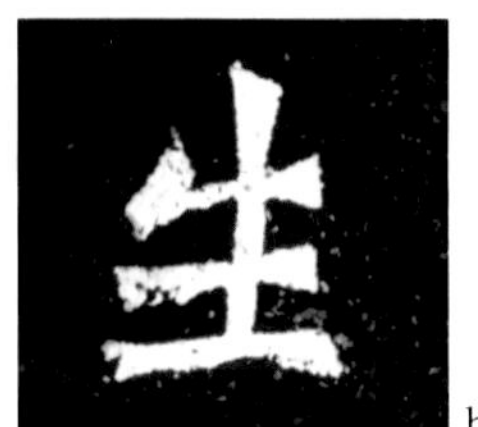
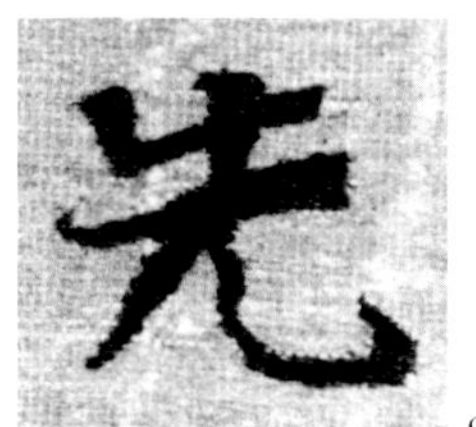

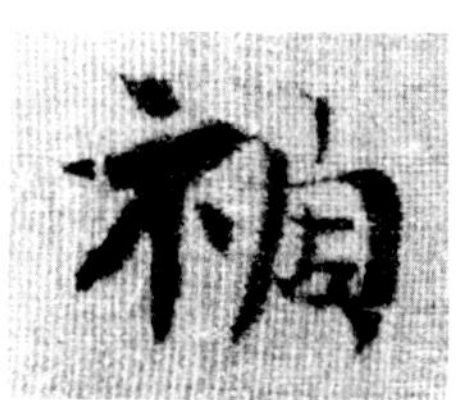
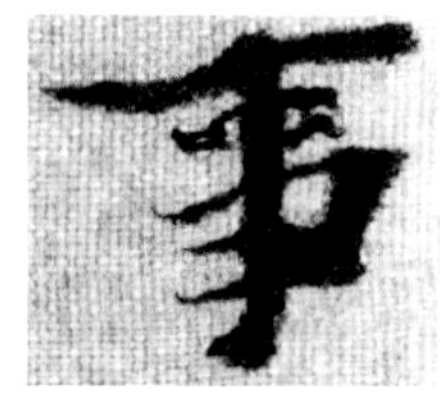
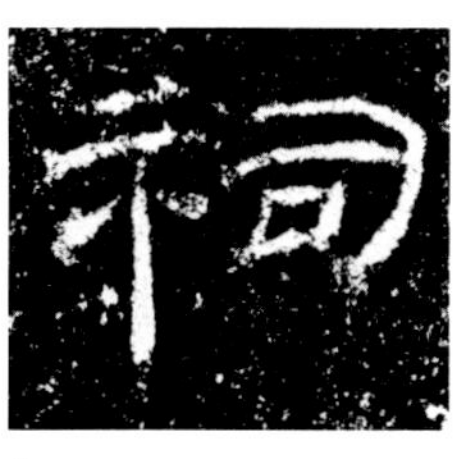
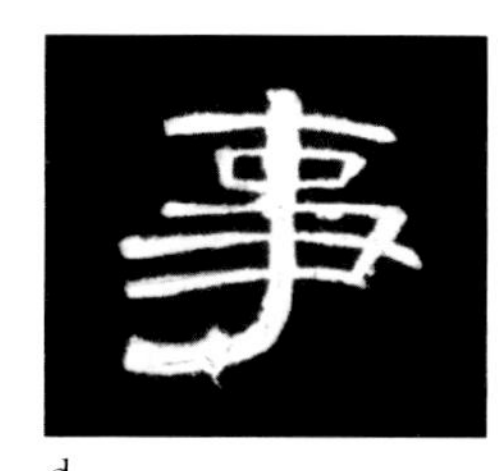

Figure 17. Corner strokes

a. Li Kung-lin, *Classic of Filial Piety*

b. Li Kung-lin, *Classic of Filial Piety*

c. *Stele for I-ying*, dated 153

d. *Stele for Ts'ao Ch'üan*, dated 185

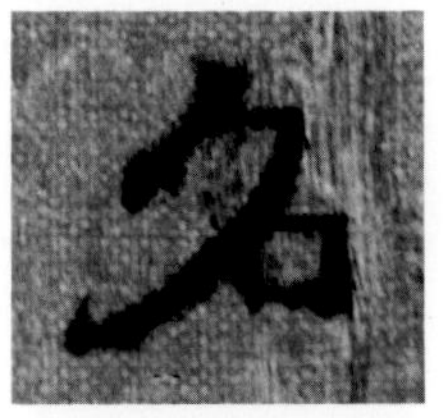
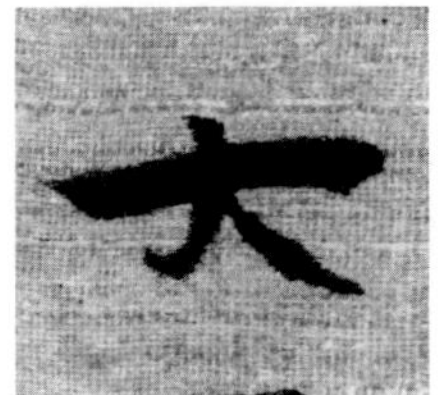
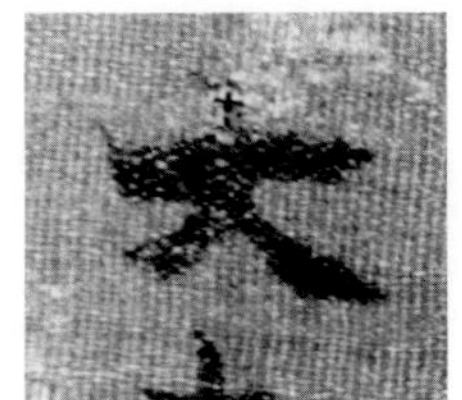
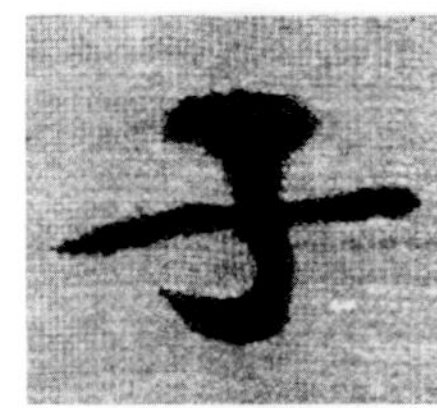
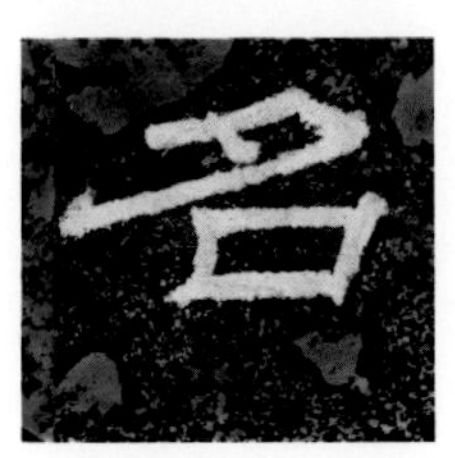
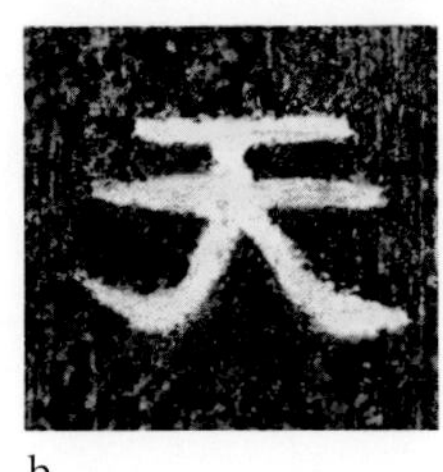
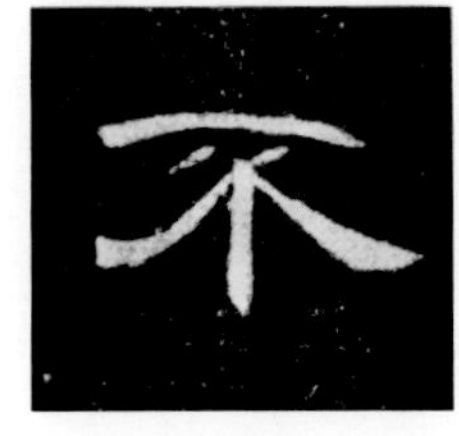
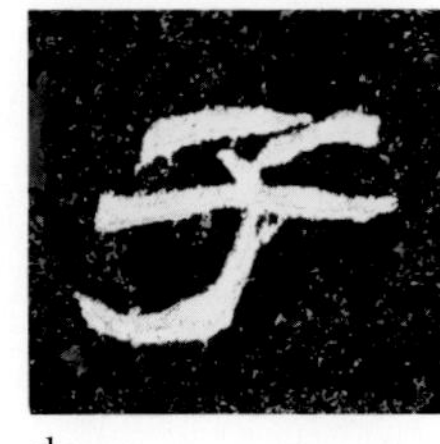

a b c d

Figure 18. Endings of leftward descending diagonal brushstrokes

a. Li Kung-lin, *Classic of Filial Piety; Stele for I-ying*, dated 153

b. Li Kung-lin, *Classic of Filial Piety; Stele for Chang Ch'ien*, dated 186

c. Li Kung-lin, *Classic of Filial Piety; Stele for Ts'ao Ch'üan*, dated 185

d. Li Kung-lin, *Classic of Filial Piety; Stele for I-ying*, dated 153

and dynamic range of forms than can be found in actual Han writings, thus creating a personal style unlike that of any other Northern Sung calligrapher.

The short horizontal strokes in Han stelae occasionally end in sharply defined squarish shapes (fig. 16a). These developed into the "square brushwork" (*fang pi*) that produces the characteristic chiseled effect in Northern Dynasties stelae inscriptions of the fifth and sixth centuries (fig. 16b). As a comparison of similar characters shows, Li integrated this square brushwork into his own style, stressing in his ink-written characters forms that were closely associated with calligraphy carved in stone (fig. 16c). The corner strokes in Li's *Classic of Filial Piety* also derive from stelae inscriptions. They are done either in smooth, rounded turns (fig. 17a) or in sharp, angular turns (fig. 17b). These strokes, far more simplified than those of T'ang standard script, can be associated with no other style of calligraphy except that found on Han stelae (figs. 17c, 17d).

Li's adaptations from Han stelae inscriptions can also be seen in his leftward descending diagonals. For example, the hooked endings (fig. 18a), arc-shaped endings (fig. 18b), and squared endings (fig. 18c) all resemble the Han forms with which they are paired in the illustrations. So do the squared endings and the arc-shaped endings (fig. 18d) of the hook strokes. Li does not, however, merely copy these archaic styles of writing. His brushwork is far more fluent and natural than that reflected in the carved stelae inscriptions, which tends to be slow and stylized.

Many of the dots in Li's calligraphy were written with the "square brush" technique, which creates sharply defined triangular shapes (fig. 19a). Such dots first appear in Chinese calligraphy in Han stelae (fig. 19b), though in these works the dots were not yet standardized and their shapes reveal traces of the soft, resilient brush hairs. In the calligraphy of the Northern Dynasties, the dots are sharper and more regular, and they are a distinctive feature of stelae inscriptions from this period (fig. 19c). Although the triangular dots in the *Classic of Filial Piety* are

Figure 19. Triangular dots

a. *Min*, from the *Classic of Filial Piety*

b. *T'ou*, from the *Stele for I-ying*, dated 153

c. *Hsien*, from *Inscriptions on Buddhist Statues Dedicated by Shih-p'ing Kung*, dated 498

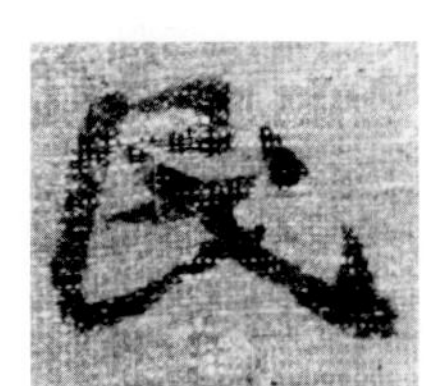

a

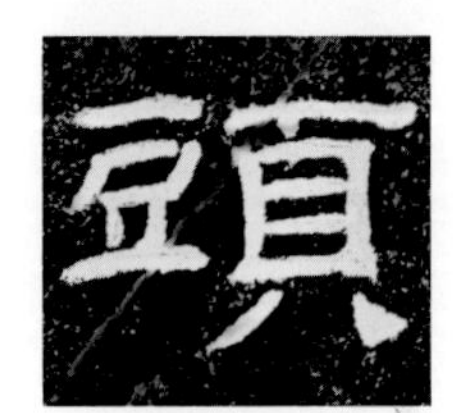

b

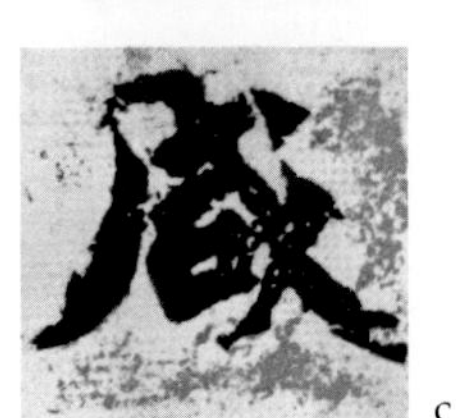

c

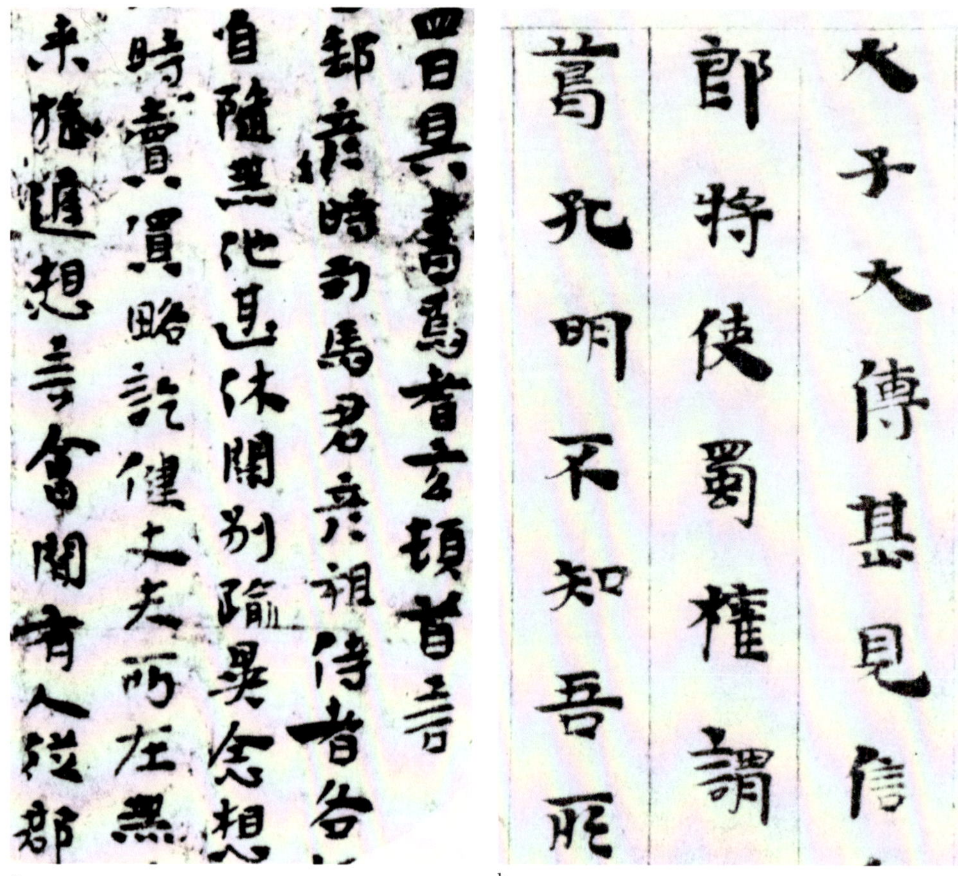

Figure 20. Third-century letters and sutras

a. Anonymous, fragment of a letter, ca. 3rd century. Ink on paper. Excavated at Loulan, Kansu Province. Private collection, Japan

b. Anonymous, *History of the Three Kingdoms*, ca. late 3rd century. Handscroll, ink on paper. Museum of Calligraphy, Tokyo

a b

much closer to these fifth- and sixth-century works, some of them still exhibit the soft, bulging edges seen in the Han-dynasty examples.

During the late Northern Sung, calligraphers studied not only ancient inscriptions carved on stone but also early inscriptions executed on paper. The striking contrasts between thick and thin strokes in the *Classic of Filial Piety* noted earlier can be related to the small-standard-script calligraphy seen in letters, sutras, and other texts written on paper from the third century that attracted the attention of Li's contemporaries. Huang T'ing-chien, for example, once commented that an ancient transcription of a Buddhist sutra was "pure and forceful, square and weighty," and far surpassed the calligraphy of Hsiao Tzu-yün (487–549), a calligrapher who practiced the Chung Yu style.[13] Huang's description of this calligraphy could apply also to third-century writings on paper that were discovered in the early twentieth century.[14] Huang's remarks comparing this sutra with writing by a follower of Chung Yu also reveal that as early as the eleventh century connoisseurs recognized a relationship between the Chung Yu tradition and the style of calligraphy used for sutras.

The most distinctive stylistic feature of third-century letters and sutras (figs. 20a, b) is the alternation of heavy and light with thick and thin strokes. The heaviest strokes are the rightward descending diagonals. These repeated forms and the contrasts between thick and thin strokes within individual characters

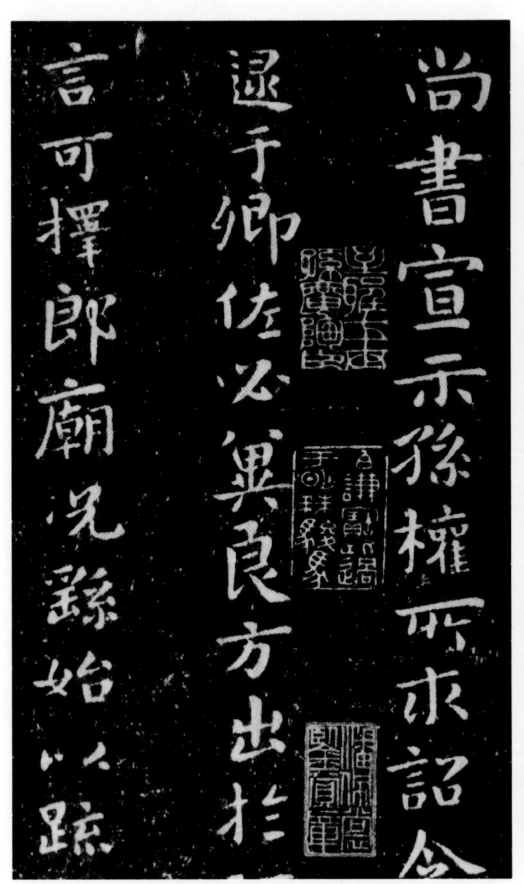

21

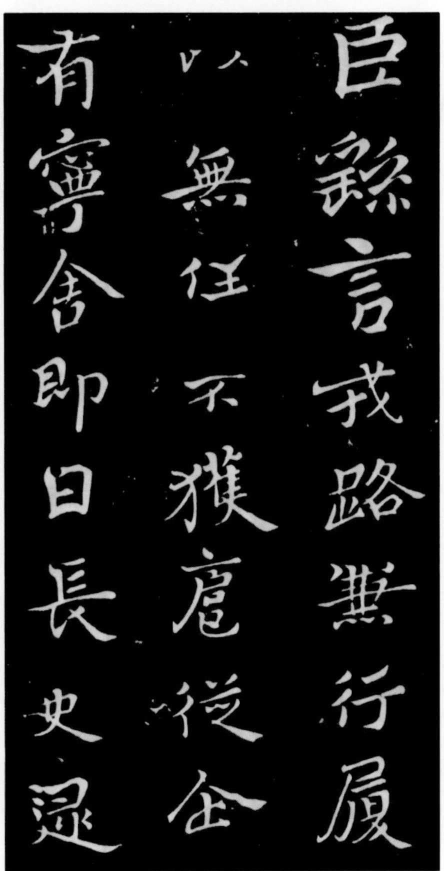

22

Figure 21. Chung Yu (151–230), rubbing of the *Memorial on an Announcement to Sun Ch'üan*, ca. 221

Figure 22. Chung Yu (151–230), rubbing of the *Memorial Celebrating a Victory*, ca. 219

give these writings a strongly accented visual rhythm. In the *Classic of Filial Piety*, Li achieves a very similar effect. But instead of repeatedly accenting a single type of stroke, he stresses different strokes at will, and strong contrasts of thickness appear not only between strokes but also between radicals, entire characters, and even groups of characters. Once again, we see Li drawing inspiration from an ancient style to achieve an innovative transformation of small standard script.

Of all the influences that can be identified in Li Kung-lin's calligraphy, the most important are the rubbings attributed to Chung Yu. The style of this third-century calligrapher was represented in the Northern Sung by rubbings collected in the *Calligraphic Works in the Ch'un-hua Palace*. Among the six works in the anthology,[15] the *Memorial on an Announcement to Sun Ch'üan* (fig. 21) was thought to have most successfully preserved the essence of Chung Yu's style, even though this work was recognized as a copy by Wang Hsi-chih. Although its authenticity was doubted by a few connoisseurs, *Memorial Celebrating a Victory* (fig. 22) also was generally accepted as a representative work.[16] These two examples, therefore, are our primary evidence for how Chung Yu's style was perceived in the Northern Sung. Returning to the *Classic of Filial Piety*, we find that most of the unusual brushwork and structural principles of Li's calligraphy are related to these two works.

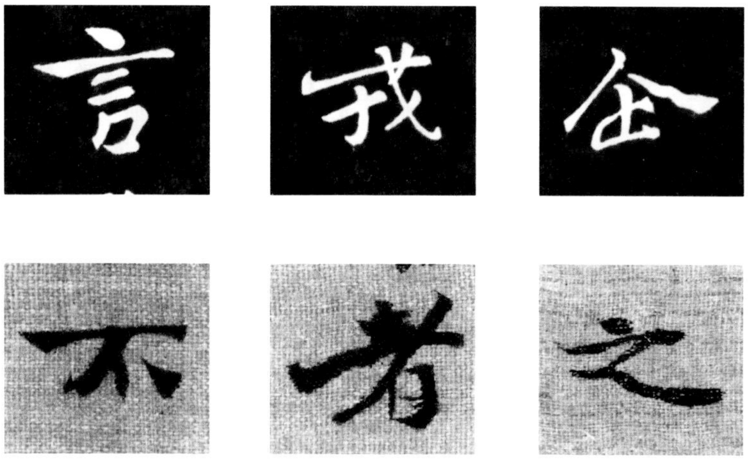

a b c

Figure 23. Comparison of brushwork in Chung Yu (151–230), *Memorial Celebrating a Victory*, ca. 219, and Li Kung-lin, *Classic of Filial Piety*

a. Triangular beginnings

b. Hooked beginnings and endings

c. Irregular silhouettes

Generally speaking, the *Memorial Celebrating a Victory* exerted more influence on Li Kung-lin's brushwork, and the *Memorial on an Announcement to Sun Ch'üan* more influence on the structure of his characters. Similarities between Li's brushwork and the unusual brushwork in the *Memorial Celebrating a Victory* are not difficult to see. These include the "exposed tip" technique that produces triangular beginnings of horizontal strokes (fig. 23a), the "turning" and "kicking" movements that form the hooked beginnings of horizontals and the hooked endings of diagonals (fig. 23b), and the uneven movements of the brush that produce irregular silhouettes in both horizontal and diagonal strokes

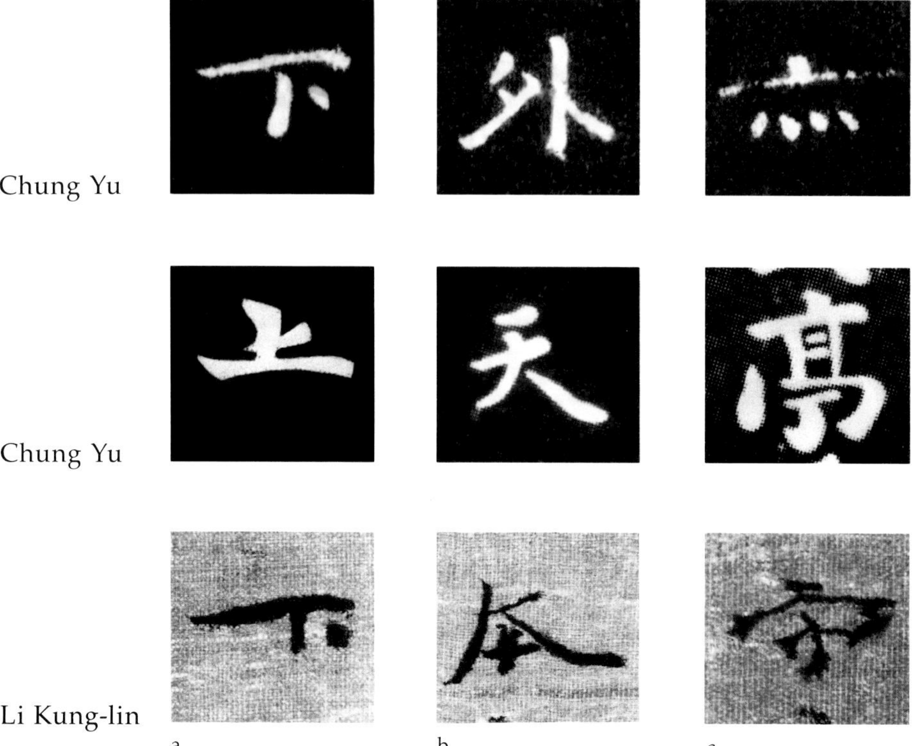

Figure 24. Comparison of brushwork in Chung Yu (151–230), *Memorial on an Announcement to Sun Ch'üan*, ca. 221; Chung Yu, *Memorial Celebrating a Victory*, ca. 219; and Li Kung-lin, *Classic of Filial Piety*

a. Elongated strokes and shortened strokes

b. Exaggerated diagonals

c. Compressed radicals

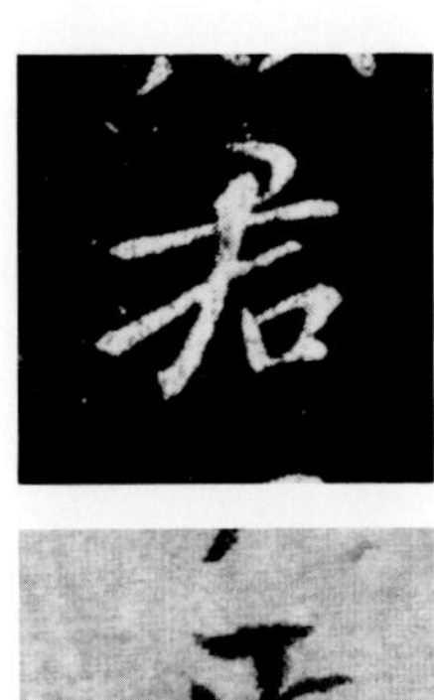
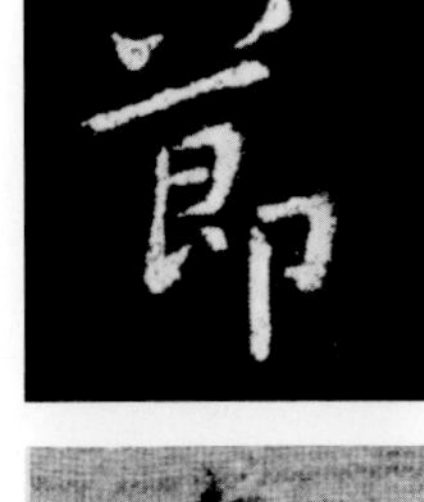
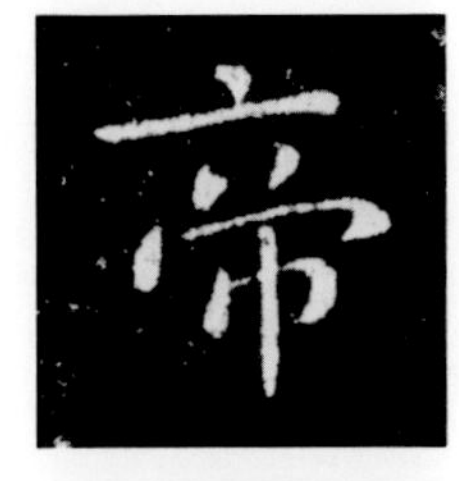
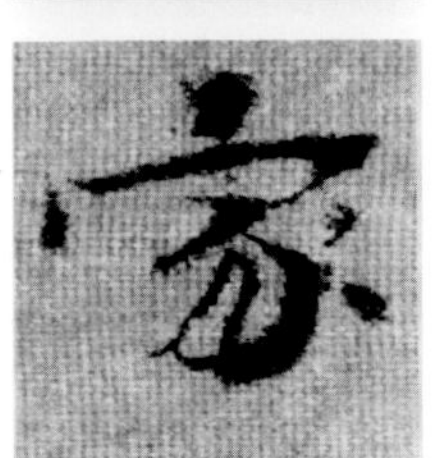

a b c

Figure 25. Comparison of brushwork in Chung Yu (151–230), *Memorial on an Announcement to Sun Ch'üan*, ca. 221, and in Li Kung-lin, *Classic of Filial Piety*

a. Exaggerated radicals

b. Misaligned radicals

c. Misaligned elements

(fig. 23c). Some features of the *Memorial Celebrating a Victory* are amplified or exaggerated in Li's writing, such as horizontal strokes that are long and tremulous.

The *Memorial on an Announcement to Sun Ch'üan* and the *Memorial Celebrating a Victory* also inspired the basic structure of Li's characters, and all three works display the squat, imbalanced structures that are the hallmark of the Chung Yu tradition. In both Li's and Chung Yu's writing, elongated horizontal strokes, shortened vertical strokes (fig. 24a), exaggerated diagonals (fig. 24b), and compressed radicals (fig. 24c) make characters seem squat and dumpy. A sense of imbalance is achieved by exaggerated radicals (fig. 25a), misaligned radicals (fig. 25b), and the placing of upper and lower elements of characters on different vertical axes (fig. 25c).

Synthesizing and transforming stylistic features of several different calligraphic traditions, Li Kung-lin invented a style of calligraphy unique in the history of small standard script. His simplified brushwork, based on a rejection of T'ang conventions, was a landmark in the history of the Chung Yu tradition.[17] No other calligrapher's work in this script type displays such an innovative approach to the past. The originality of Li's calligraphy equals the originality of his painting. Painting in the *pai-miao*, or plain-ink, drawing style which dispensed with colors and emphasized brushwork, Li opened a new chapter in the history of Chinese painting. To create this new style, Li returned to the past for inspiration. He studied the classical masters extensively and based his own style on a synthesis of their achievements. Richard Barnhart offers perhaps the most succinct evaluation of his art: "[Li Kung-lin] conveyed his forms in an artistic vocabulary drawn from the greatest masters of the past, quoting and paraphrasing their styles, techniques, and motifs so subtly that an extended composition by Li Kung-lin could be annotated as fully as the poetry of Huang T'ing-chien."[18] Like his paintings, the calligraphy of the *Classic of Filial Piety* displays a subtle integration of features drawn from various ancient styles and can be appreciated best with the aid of such annotations as those offered above.

Li Kung-lin and His Friends: Other Innovations in Northern Sung Small Standard Script

Most calligraphers of the eleventh century followed late-T'ang or early-Sung models of small standard script with little alteration. The calligraphy of Ts'ai Hsiang (1012–1067) is the finest representative of this conservative tradition, beautifully displayed in his *Memorial of Thanks for the Bestowal of the Emperor's Personal Calligraphy* (fig. 26). A few calligraphers, however, developed fresh, unconventional styles. In addition to Li Kung-lin himself, several of Li's close

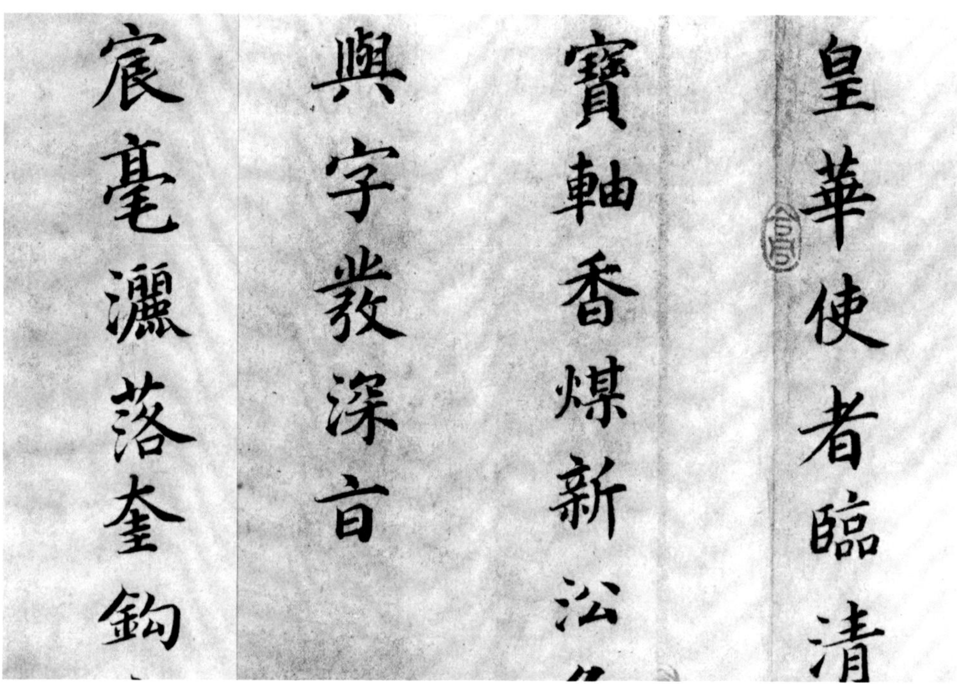

Figure 26. Ts'ai Hsiang (1012–1067), detail from the *Memorial of Thanks for the Bestowal of the Emperor's Personal Calligraphy*, dated 1052. Handscroll, ink on paper. Museum of Calligraphy, Tokyo

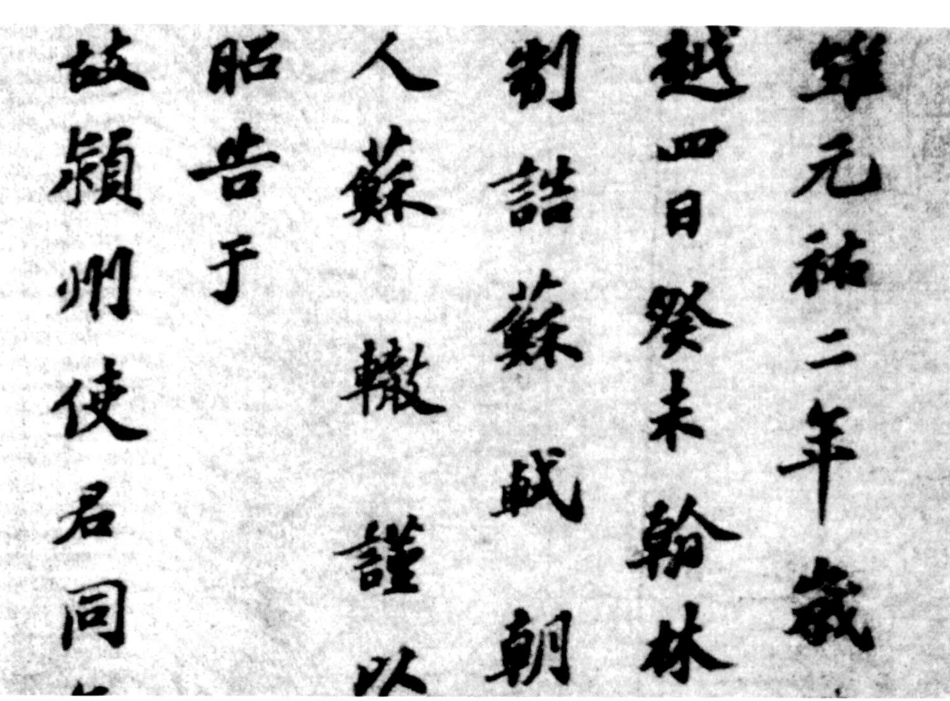

Figure 27. Su Shih (1037–1101), detail from the *Elegiac Address to Huang Chi-tao*, dated 1087. Handscroll, ink on paper. Shanghai Museum

friends were among the most inventive and original Northern Sung calligraphers: Su Shih, Huang T'ing-chien, and Mi Fu (1051–1107). Together with Ts'ai Hsiang, these men were hailed as the Four Northern Sung Masters. In this section, we shall compare works by Su, Huang, and Mi with Ts'ai Hsiang's and will examine the continuities between the calligraphy of Li Kung-lin and that of his three friends. The works by Li's friends are all from their later years and represent the culmination of their experience with the art of calligraphy: the *Elegiac Address to Huang Chi-tao* (fig. 27), by Su Shih; *Epitaph for Shih Fu* (fig. 28), by Huang T'ing-chien; and *Epitaph for the Honorable Ch'ung Kuo-kung* (fig. 29), by Mi Fu.[19]

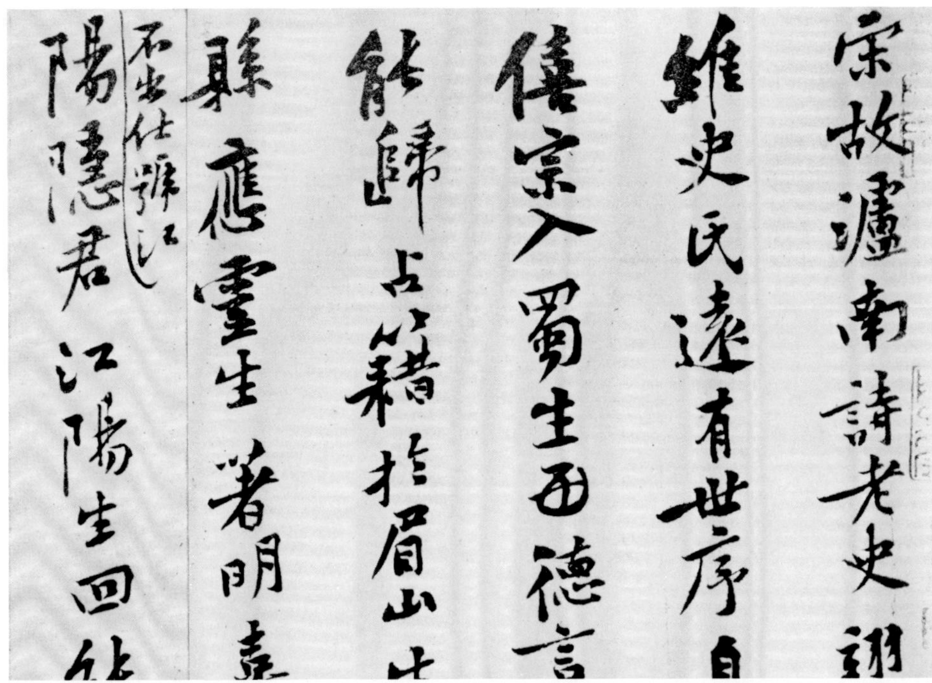

Figure 28. Huang T'ing-chien (1045–1105), detail from the *Epitaph for Shih Fu*, dated 1099. Handscroll, ink on paper. Tokyo National Museum

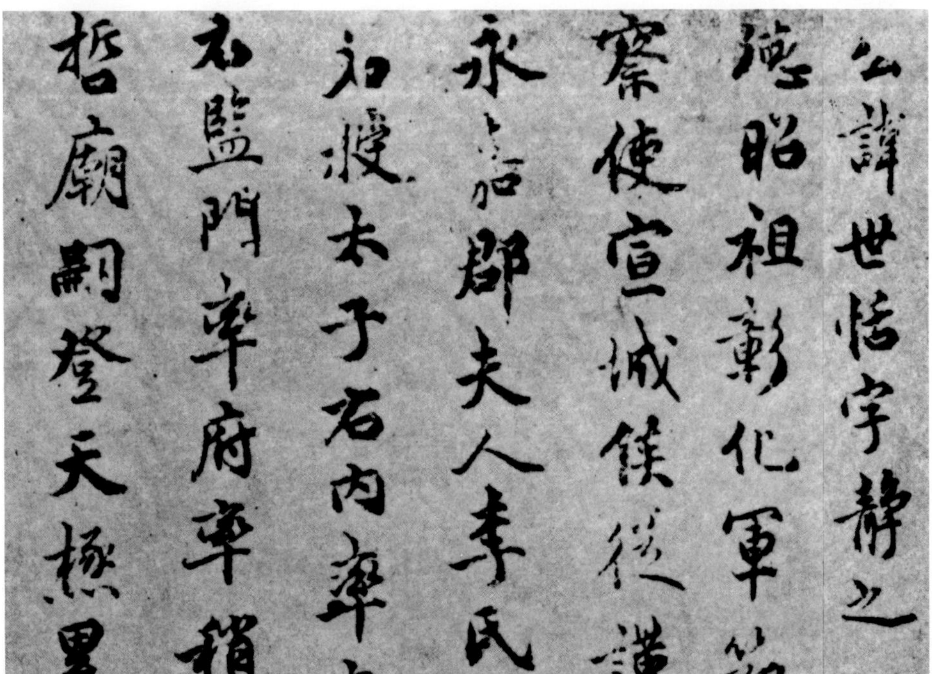

Figure 29. Mi Fu (1052–1107), detail from the *Epitaph for the Honorable Ch'ung Kuo-kung*, dated 1107. Handscroll, ink on paper. Palace Museum, Beijing

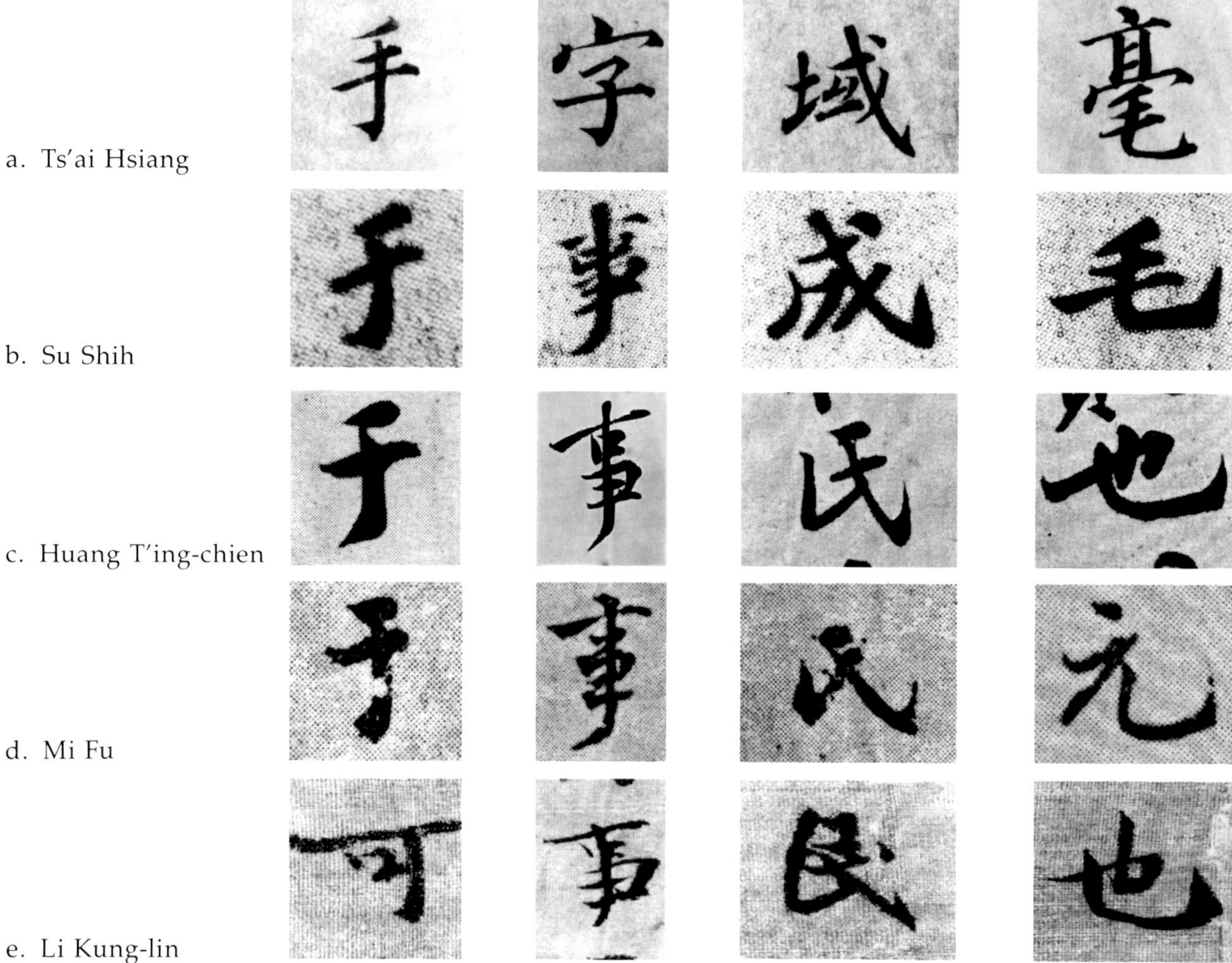

Figure 30. Comparison of brushwork in
- a. Ts'ai Hsiang, *Memorial of Thanks for the Bestowal of the Emperor's Personal Calligraphy*
- b. Su Shih, *Elegiac Address to Huang Chi-tao*
- c. Huang T'ing-chien, *Epitaph to Shih Fu*
- d. Mi Fu, *Epitaph for the Honorable Ch'ung Kuo-kung*
- e. Li Kung-lin, *Classic of Filial Piety*

When we compare the brushwork of Ts'ai Hsiang with that of Su, Huang, and Mi, the differences are easily recognized. Ts'ai's brushwork is far more complex. Taking hook strokes as an example, we see that in Ts'ai's writing vertical hooks (fig. 30a, cols. 1, 2), diagonal hooks, and horizontal hooks (fig. 30a, col. 3) all employ the motions of "pressing," "crouching," "returning," and "kicking" that are typical of late-T'ang and early-Sung standard script. In the calligraphy of Su, Huang, and Mi, the same types of strokes are written with much simpler movements of the brush. When completing a vertical hook, these calligraphers stop the motion of the brush quite suddenly, with a slight "kick" at the end (fig. 30, col. 1) or with a smooth leftward sweep that eliminates the motions Ts'ai Hsiang uses (fig. 30, col. 2). Comparable simplifications can be seen in the diagonal hooks (fig. 30, col. 3) and the horizontal hooks, which end with a short upward "kick" (fig. 30, col. 4). In the *Classic of Filial Piety*, we find an array of simplified hook strokes (fig. 30e) quite similar to those written by Li Kung-lin's three friends.

Other types of strokes by Su, Huang, and Mi, as well as those by Li Kung-lin, display the same tendency toward simplification. These include the "exposed

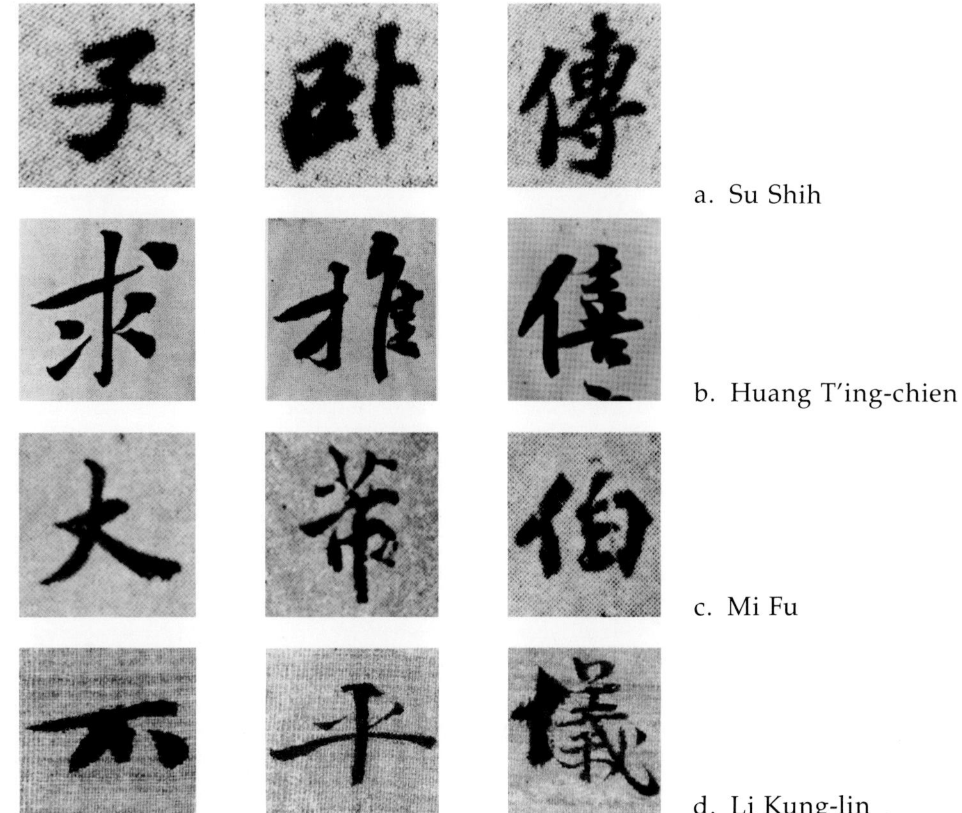

Figure 31. Comparison of simplified brushwork in
a. Su Shih
b. Huang T'ing-chien
c. Mi Fu
d. Li Kung-lin
(See fig. 30 for sources.)

tip" beginnings of horizontals (fig. 31, col. 1), the abrupt endings of verticals (fig. 31, col. 2), and the "square brush" beginnings of diagonal strokes (fig. 31, col. 3). All of these contrast to the more conservative calligraphy of Ts'ai Hsiang.

Like Li Kung-lin, his three friends display a strong preference for imbalanced character structure. Clearly, the well-formed equilibrium of T'ang standard script held little interest for these calligraphers, who created dynamic tensions in characters through the exaggeration of strokes and the unconventional arrangement of radicals. Although the basic shapes of their characters vary according to differences in their artistic temperaments and preferences—Su Shih's characters are squat; Huang T'ing-chien's and Mi Fu's are rectangular—the three writers employ similar structural principles. Frequently, they exaggerate a single stroke, such as the horizontal, diagonal, or hook, to make characters appear tilted (fig. 32, col. 1). Sometimes they exaggerate two diagonals in a character so that its structure becomes ill-proportioned (fig. 32, col. 2). They also misalign radicals horizontally or place them on different vertical axes (fig. 32, col. 3). As should now be clear, all these structural devices were used by Li Kung-lin in the *Classic of Filial Piety* to imbue his writing with a strong, dynamic momentum.

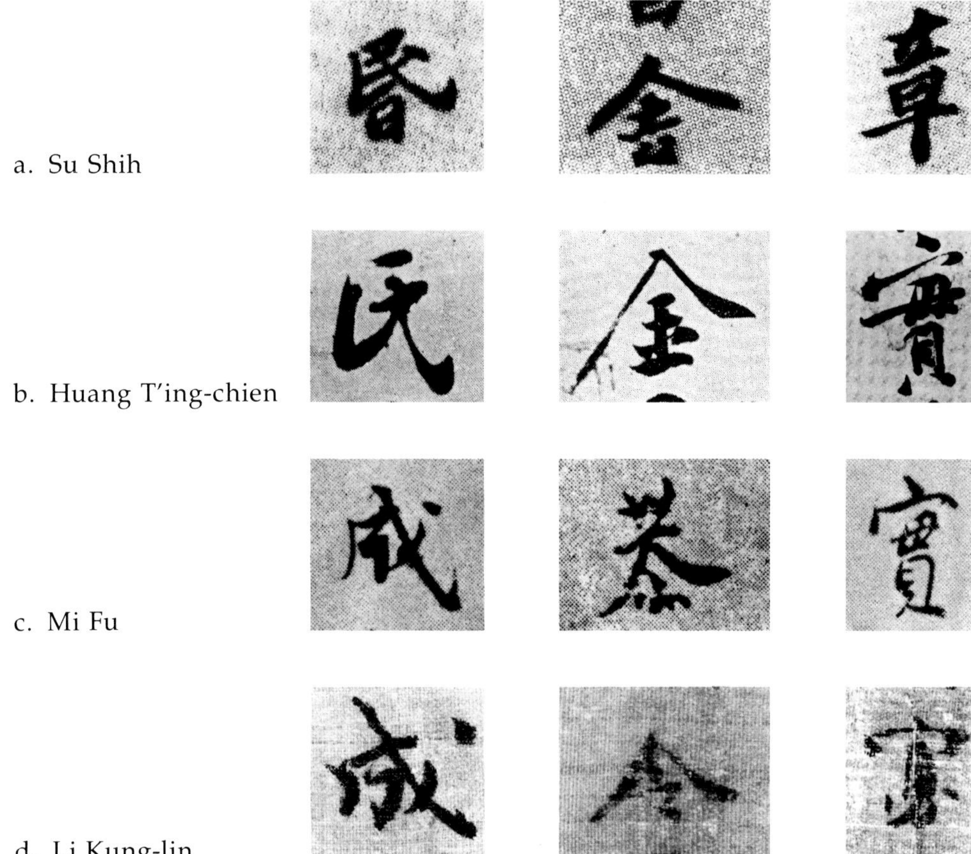

Figure 32. Comparison of imbalanced character structure in
a. Su Shih
b. Huang T'ing-chien
c. Mi Fu
d. Li Kung-lin
(See fig. 30 for sources.)

The simplified brushwork and imbalanced structures in the small-standard-script calligraphy of Su Shih, Huang T'ing-chien, Mi Fu, and Li Kung-lin mark a fundamental departure from T'ang and early-Sung models. The impression conveyed by the calligraphy of Su, Huang, and Mi, as well as by Li Kung-lin in the *Classic of Filial Piety*, is one of great naturalness. Abandoning the labored perfection of T'ang models, these late Northern Sung calligraphers allowed characters to flow from the mind to the hand and onto the writing surface with confidence and ease. Their major concern was to express the inner self at the moment of writing; brush techniques and character structures were simply vehicles of expression. As long as inner feeling was conveyed, there was no concern about what T'ang calligraphers might have regarded as technical imperfections.

1. *Ch'un-hua ko t'ieh* is a ten-volume anthology compiled by Wang Chu (d. 992), a renowned connoisseur. Although Wang was criticized for his mistakes in choosing the specimens, the anthology was widely popular in the Sung, as is clear from the fact that over thirty recarved editions were issued. There are many studies of this anthology. The earliest is Tseng Ch'un (active mid-13th century), *Shih-k'o p'u hsü* (1242; *Ts'ung-shu chi-ch'eng ch'u-pien*). The most extensive modern studies are Jung Keng, *Ts'ung-t'ieh mu* (Hong Kong, 1980); and Sesson Uno, *Hōjō* (Tokyo, 1970). Brief introductions to the anthology appear in Shen C. Y. Fu, "Huang T'ing-chien's Calligraphy and His *Scroll for Chang Ta-t'ung*: A Masterpiece Written in Exile" (Ph.D. diss., Princeton University, 1976), pp. 199–200; and Lothar Ledderose, *Mi Fu and the Classical Tradition of Chinese Calligraphy* (Princeton, 1979), pp. 10–12.

2. *Memorial on an Announcement to Sun Ch'üan* was presented by Chung Yu to Ts'ao P'i (187–226), Emperor Wei Wen-ti, to ensure loyalty to Sun Ch'üan (182–252), the King of Wu, who requested

that he be able to serve the Wei regime. *Memorial Celebrating a Victory* was presented by Chung Yu to Ts'ao Ts'ao (155–200), counselor-in-chief during Emperor Han Hsien-ti's reign (189–220), to congratulate him on a victory over his enemy Kuan Yü (d. 219). In the Northern Sung dynasty there were two versions of *Memorial Celebrating a Victory* known to connoisseurs.

3. *On General Yüeh I* was composed by Hsia-hou Hsüan (b. 209) to record the achievements of General Yüeh I (active late 3rd century B.C.). In A.D. 348 Wang Hsi-chih transcribed the text, which became the most representative example of Wang's small standard script.

4. This had been recognized by the early T'ang period. Ho Yen-chih (active early 8th century) recorded the history of the *Preface to the Orchid Pavilion* in his *Lan t'ing chi* of 714.

5. The *Lan t'ing chi* is mentioned by Sang Shih-ch'ang (active late 12th century) in *Lan t'ing k'ao* (preface by Kao Wen-hu, dated 1208), which includes a detailed account of Northern Sung scholarship on the *Preface to the Orchid Pavilion*.

6. The term "stelae" is used here in its broad sense to include calligraphy carved on stone in any format.

7. Su Ch'e, *Luan-ch'eng chi* (Shanghai, 1929), *chüan* 1, p. 18.

8. See Tseng Kung, *Yüan-feng lei-kao*, in *Ssu-pu ts'ung-k'an chu-pien*, *chüan* 7, p. 61; Su Shih, *Tung-p'o chi* (Taipei, 1967), *chüan* 3, p. 10; and Su Ch'e, *Luan-ch'eng chi*, *chüan* 4, p. 11.

9. Ou-yang Hsiu's *Chi-ku lu* has a preface dated 1063. This ten-volume work records ancient calligraphy seen by the author, Ou-yang Hsiu, including inscriptions on bronzes, stones, and recut copies of inscriptions. The dates of the items range from the Shang dynasty (ca. 1600–1028 B.C.) to the Northern Sung. This book is included in the *Ou-yang Wen-chung kung chüan-chi*, in *Ssu-pu ts'ung-k'an ch'u-pien*, vols. 46–50. *Chin-shih lu*, by Tseng Kung, contained five hundred *chüan* and was mentioned in the biography of the author; unfortunately, it is no longer extant, but the preface and fourteen items appear in Tseng Kung's collected works, *Yüan-feng lei-kao*, in *Ssu-pu ts'ung-k'an chu-pien*, *chüan* 50, pp. 319–22. Tung Yu's *Kuang-ch'uan hua pa* (Shanghai, 1949) is a ten-volume work that contains records of nineteen Eastern Han stelae.

10. *Shodō zenshū* (Tokyo, 1930–31), ser. 2, vol. 6, p. 169.

11. *Mount Hua Temple Stele*, *Stele for I-ying*, and *Stele for Shih Ch'en* were recorded by Ou-yang Hsiu in *Chi-ku lu*, *chüan* 1, p. 2. *Ode to Hsi-hsia* was recorded by Tseng Kung in *Yüan-feng lei-kao*, in *Ssu-pu ts'ung-k'an chu-pien*, *chüan* 50, p. 320.

12. See *Shodō zenshū*, ser. 2, vol. 6, for the illustrations of these examples.

13. Huang T'ing-chien, *Colophons by Huang T'ing-chien*, in *Sung nien ming-chia hui-pien*, *chüan* 4, p. 36.

14. At the beginning of the twentieth century, archaeologists conducted successive excavations in northwestern China. They discovered numerous wooden and bamboo slips of the Han, Wei, and Tsin dynasties, as well as many letters, drafts, and sutras of the Tsin. These discoveries greatly expanded our knowledge of second- and third-century calligraphy. See *Shodō zenshū*, ser. 2, vol. 2, p. 149; vol. 3, pp. 145–46, 150–51.

15. These are *Memorial on an Announcement to Sun Ch'üan*, *Huan shih t'ieh*, *Pai ch'i t'ieh*, *Ch'ang huan t'ieh*, *Hsüeh han t'ieh*, and *Ch'ang-feng t'ieh*.

16. Ou-yang Hsiu offered some controversial opinions about *Memorial Celebrating a Victory* in *Chi-ku lu*. However, at the end of the Northern Sung it had come to be regarded as the most representative work by Chung Yu.

17. Li Kung-lin's style in the *Classic of Filial Piety* was the source for the *Memorial Recommending Chi Chih*, a spurious work attributed to Chung Yu that first appeared in the early Southern Sung period and exerted great influence on the development of the Chung Yu tradition. For the relationship between the *Classic of Filial Piety* and the *Memorial Recommending Chi Chih*, see Hui-liang J. Chu, "The Chung Yu (A.D. 151–230) Tradition: A Pivotal Development in Sung Calligraphy" (Ph.D. diss., Princeton University, 1990), chap. 3.

18. Richard M. Barnhart, "Li Kung-lin's *Hsiao Ching T'u*: Illustrations of the 'Classic of Filial Piety'" (Ph.D. diss., Princeton University, 1967), p. 36.

19. *Elegiac Address to Huang Chi-tao* (Shanghai Museum) was written in 1087, when Su Shih was fifty-two. *Epitaph for Shih Fu* (Tokyo National Museum) was written after 1099, when Huang T'ing-chien was at least fifty-five. *Epitaph for the Honorable Ch'ung Kuo-kung* (Palace Museum, Beijing) was written in 1107, when Mi Fu was fifty-seven. *Memorial of Thanks for the Bestowal of the Emperor's Personal Calligraphy* (Museum of Calligraphy, Tokyo) was written in 1052, when Ts'ai Hsiang was forty-one.

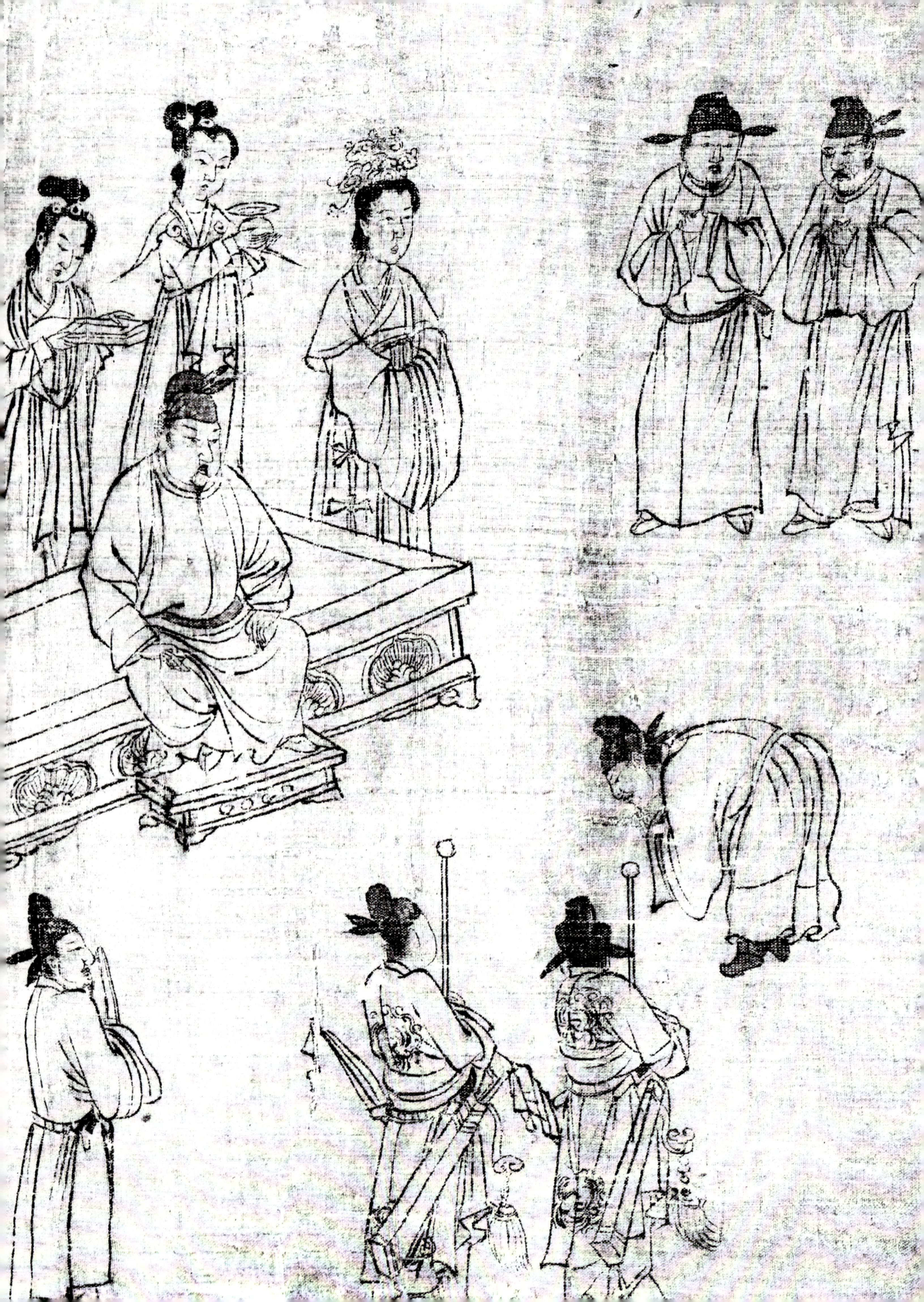

THE *CLASSIC OF FILIAL PIETY* IN CHINESE ART HISTORY

Richard M. Barnhart

The text transcribed and illustrated by Li Kung-lin, the *Hsiao-ching*, or *Classic of Filial Piety*, is one of the classics that constitute the orthodox canon of Confucianism (fig. 33).[1] A slight volume composed of eighteen brief chapters or sections, it takes the form of a dialogue between Confucius and his disciple Tseng-tzu on the meaning and application of filial piety in the affairs of the individual and of the state.

Modern scholars date the text to the period between 350 and 200 B.C., long after either Confucius or his immediate disciples lived. But by the eleventh century, only three views regarding the authorship had been advanced; it was held to have been written by Confucius himself, by Tseng-tzu, or by a disciple of Tseng-tzu who faithfully transmitted the conversation of the two philosophers. The major critical problem confronting scholars of the eleventh century was not, therefore, one of date or of authorship, since each of the three views advanced held the text to be an authentic record, but of priority between the two versions of the text then extant, the so-called modern text, which is now regarded as the older, and what was then known as the old text. The differences between them are slight, not amounting to much more than a few characters, but the old text includes one additional, very brief section and is divided into twenty-two instead of eighteen chapters. Nonetheless, a number of the greatest scholars of the eleventh century, including Ssu-ma Kuang (1019–1086), occupied themselves with the problem of priority. Many argued on behalf of the old text, as would Chu Hsi (1130–1200) a century later, when a new phase of critical examination was opened up.

The modern, or new, text had the advantage of imperial patronage. In 722, the T'ang emperor Hsüan-tsung authorized an imperial edition of the new text, for

Figure 33. Li Kung-lin, detail from chapter 15 of the *Classic of Filial Piety* (pl. 12)

which he himself wrote the commentary and a preface. A second imperial edition, with expanded commentary, was authorized by the Sung emperor Taitsung in 996 and completed in 1001 under the editorship of Hsing Ping (932–1010). It was this version of the text that was followed by Li Kung-lin.

Hsiao, or "filial piety," is a concept central to the Confucian ethic. It has been called "the root of all virtue, and that from which all moral teaching grows" (see below, chapter 1). Some authorities hold that Confucius himself never placed such emphasis on filial piety, and certainly the quality of human behavior most strongly advocated by Confucius in the *Analects* is *jen*, "goodness," or "human heartedness." In one passage, however, he clearly indicates that filial piety is the very root of *jen*: "The superior man devotes himself to what is fundamental, for when that has been established right courses naturally evolve; and are not filial devotion [*hsiao*] and respect for the elders in the family the very foundation of human heartedness [*jen*]?"[2] Filial piety is, with *jen*, one of the most pervasive themes of the *Analects*, but there is no extended development of the concept until the appearance of the *Classic of Filial Piety*. By the earlier Han dynasty (206 B.C.–A.D. 220), filial piety had emerged as a central concept of moral behavior in the structure of both the family and the state. The posthumous titles of all the Han emperors, for example, have as a prefix the word *hsiao*, testifying to the official regard in which the concept was held. Henceforward, the authorized histories of each dynasty would include honored examples of filial sons, brothers, and officials, and popular stories of particularly admirable filial behavior would grow steadily in number.

The ideal, even in much later periods, was not a hollow one. During the Sung dynasty, several of Li Kung-lin's friends were distinguished for their exemplary filial behavior. Huang T'ing-chien (1045–1105), the great poet and calligrapher, for example, became one of the twenty-four paragons through his selfless devotion to his mother. Another friend, Li Chih, or Li Fang-shu, was more extraordinary still. Despite a natural genius for writing, he postponed his own career until three generations of his ancestors—over thirty relatives in all—had been properly buried and mourned. Because he had been orphaned as a youth and was without financial resources of any kind, this decision meant years of hardship and personal sacrifice. When Li left to begin the travels that his self-appointed obligation made necessary, the distinguished poet Su Shih was moved to take off his own clothing and give it to him.

The ideal of filial piety has motivated men in every age and at every level of society. The text itself has been read and memorized by students since the Han dynasty, and its precepts have been deeply embedded in their minds. Another mark of the veneration in which it is held is the role it has played in art.

The fourteenth-century scholar Sung Lien (1310–1381) wrote that the *Classic of Filial Piety* was the most frequently illustrated of all the Confucian classics.[3] Surviving examples and literary records appear to support his observation. The earliest illustrations may have been done by the fourth-century artist Hsieh Chih. Another early set was completed during the Liang dynasty (502–556).[4] While some partial trace of these works may have endured into the T'ang dynasty, it does not seem that they survived into the Sung in any form at all. At any rate, no early version of the subject is mentioned in any Sung record. The earliest extant version of the *Hsiao-ching* is Li Kung-lin's, which is the first of the group of nine complete or partial sets of illustrations that are known today.

This group is of interest for a number of reasons. First, ranging in time from the eleventh to the eighteenth century, it offers a substantial survey of eight centuries of narrative illustration in China and represents a model of the evolution of classical illustration in later imperial China. Below are listed and briefly described each of the nine:

1. The present scroll by Li Kung-lin; ink on silk, originally with a few touches of color. Fifteen of the original chapter illustrations remain, and parts or all of each section of text except the first chapter. The Metropolitan Museum of Art, New York.[5]
2. An exact copy of the Metropolitan Museum scroll; ink on paper, made before the original suffered its present damage, that is, before the seventeenth century. All eighteen illustrations and texts are complete, and a copy of Li Kung-lin's original colophon is attached. Portions of this copy are illustrated below as figures 37, 40, and 44. National Palace Museum, Taipei.[6]
3. A partial copy (five paintings, six texts in seal script) based upon the Metropolitan Museum scroll; ink on silk. This fragmentary set appears to be of very high quality and may have been copied directly from the original. The painting is dated by Shanghai Museum authorities to the Yüan period (1279–1368). One section is reproduced here as figure 34. The Shanghai Museum.[7]
4. An album, containing fifteen paintings and accompanying texts, attributed to the twelfth-century painter Ma Ho-chih; ink and color on silk. Originally this was a handscroll, like the three versions above, but was later cut up and remounted as an album. The painter was not Ma Ho-chih, but presumably an unknown member of the imperial painting academy contemporary with Ma or slightly later. A complete copy of the original scroll, done in the eighteenth century by the court painter Chin T'ing-piao, preserves the three lost compositions (Chin T'ing-piao's copy is listed below as no. 9). A portion of the "Ma Ho-chih" version is reproduced below as figure 42. National Palace Museum, Taipei.[8]
5. An anonymous late Sung or Yüan (12th–14th century) handscroll; color on silk, with nine chapters of text and illustration. This is the version of the subject later attributed to the seventh-century master Yen Li-pen. Liaoning Provincial Museum, Shen-yang.[9]

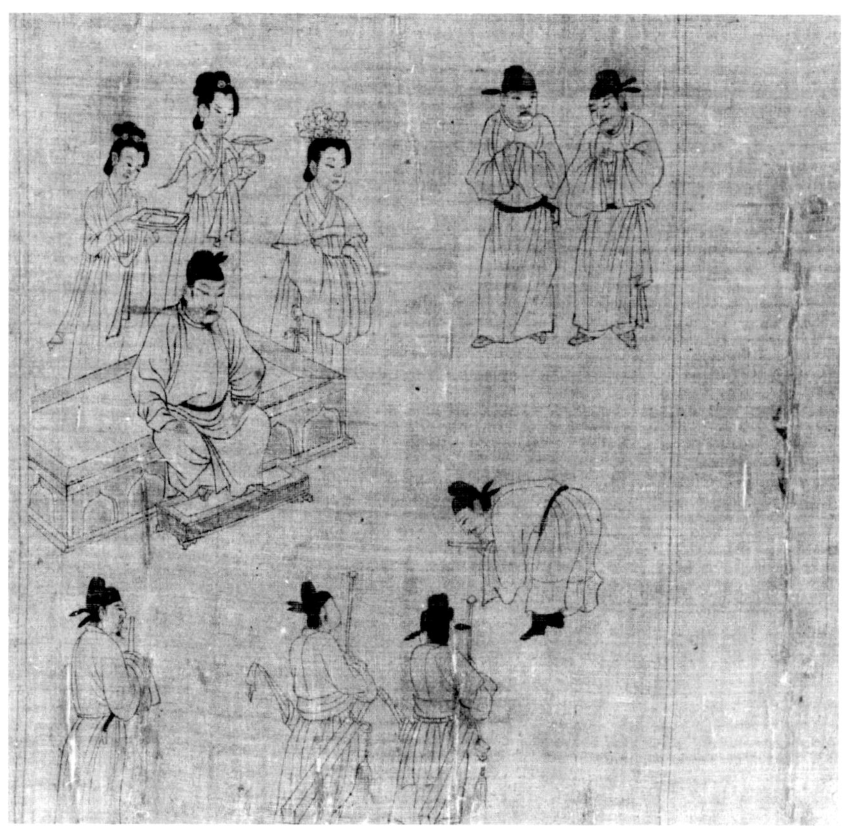

Figure 34. Unidentified artist (14th century), after Li Kung-lin, chapter 15 of the *Classic of Filial Piety*. Handscroll, ink on silk, 8½ × 62¼ in. (21.4 × 158 cm). Shanghai Museum

6. A handscroll in eighteen chapters, complete, with the signature of Chao Meng-fu (1254–1327); ink on silk. National Palace Museum, Taipei.[10]

7. A printed book with the text of eighteen chapters and colloquial translation, and fifteen wood-block print illustrations, published in 1308 as *Hsin-k'an ch'uan-hsiang Ch'eng-chai Hsiao-ching chih-chieh*. One section is reproduced here as figure 35.[11]

8. A handscroll in eighteen chapters, with paintings by Ch'iu Ying (ca. 1494–1552) and text written by Wen Cheng-ming (1470–1559); ink and color on silk. According to Wen's colophon, the painting was copied from a Sung version by Wang Tzu-cheng (active 11th century). It is related to nos. 4 and 5 above, but is not identical to either. National Palace Museum, Taipei.[12]

9. A complete copy, in handscroll form, by the court painter Chin T'ing-piao (mid-18th century) of the Ma Ho-chih version listed above as no. 4, done before the latter suffered the loss of three sections, and presumably before it was changed from a handscroll into an album; color on silk. National Palace Museum, Taipei.[13]

Among other recorded versions of the work that are no longer extant, so far as we know, was one by Li's student Ting Hsi-han.[14] In any case, the pictorial tradition of illustrations of the *Classic of Filial Piety* begins with Li Kung-lin, for all practical purposes.

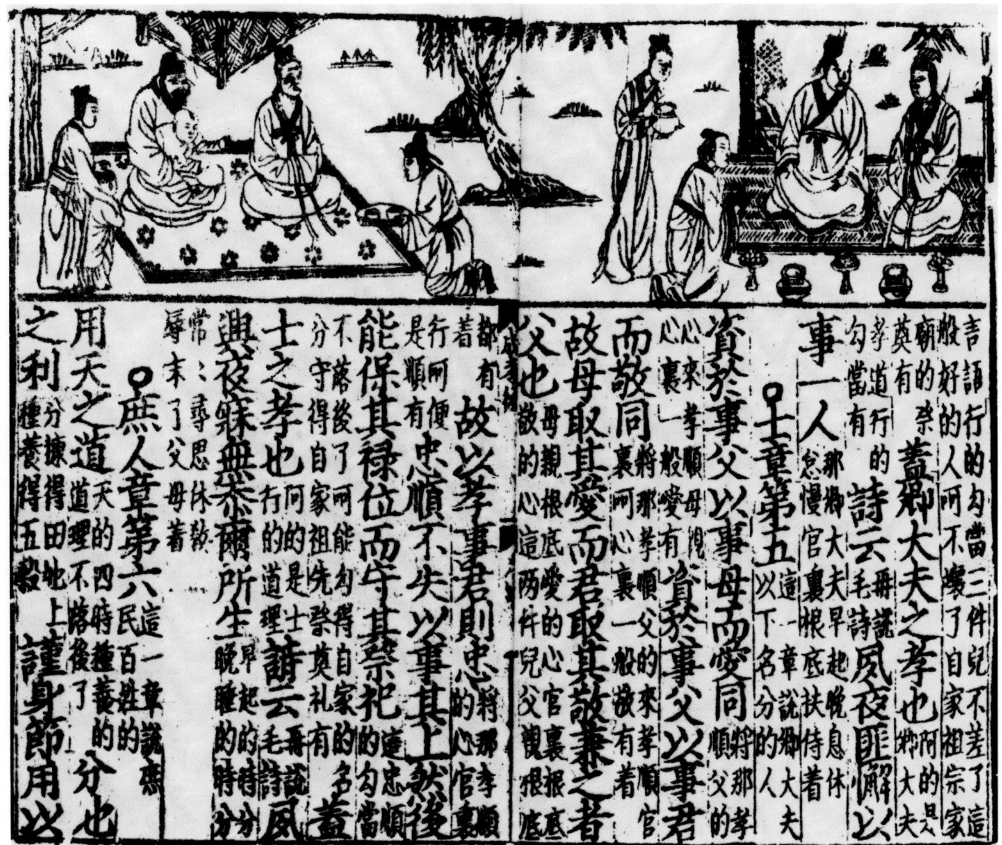

Figure 35. Chapters 5 and 6 of the *New Edition, Completely Illustrated, of Ch'eng-chai's "Classic of Filial Piety,"* 1308. Wood-block print edition of the *Classic of Filial Piety*

In the following analysis and description of Li's compositions, reference will be made to some of the other versions, especially to the complete copy in Taipei, which allows us at least a glimpse of the three missing segments of the original scroll. In general, however, the relationship between Li's original painting and the later versions is that of a classical model to its later perpetuation, in widely varying degrees of exaggeration. There is a vague correlation to the musical relationship of theme to variations. Li's painting appears to be the only one in the sequence of nine that creates its own compositions and thematic images, establishes its own formal and stylistic character, and serves as a pictorial reflection of the artist's thought. The later works, by contrast, share a general feeling of institutional anonymity and differ from one another primarily in superficial detail, not in substance. Li's work, uniquely, interprets a classical theme as if providing a learned commentary from the viewpoint of the activities, values, people, policies, and events of the artist's own time. It is, in other words, an original work of art of the highest order; all other versions are but reflections of it.

The present scroll, in its fragmentary and much-damaged form, measures 473 centimeters (about 15½ feet) in length and, though irregular because of the wear and tear of the silk at the top and bottom, averages about 21 to 22 centimeters (between 8¼ and 8½ inches) in height. Colophons add approximately 19 feet in overall length. The silk, darkened and worn after centuries of rolling and unrolling, is now a deep brown. There is an occasional faint tinge of green visible, curiously enhancing the scroll's venerable appearance, like the weathered patina on an ancient bronze vessel. The silk is damaged over its entire surface and was repaired several times, as well as substantially retouched and repainted in numerous sections.

Most recently, the entire scroll has been thoroughly cleaned and repaired, with all earlier retouching and repairing removed insofar as possible (that process is the subject of Appendix 2, in the present volume).

In its original form, the scroll was composed of eighteen illustrations separated by the eighteen corresponding chapters of the text. The text of each chapter follows the painting that illustrates it. Text and illustration are separated by double and sometimes by triple parallel brush lines drawn with a straightedge. The warped appearance of those framing lines is a good indication of the disfiguring damage the silk has sustained. Sometime before the seventeenth century, the opening section of the scroll—consisting of the first two illustrations, the first section of text and part of the second, and the illustration to section 6—was lost. In addition, the end of the scroll is irregularly torn, and throughout its length portions of the text and illustrations at top and bottom are lost. The originally continuous silk has, moreover, been torn apart at six places and hangs together by only a thread at another. At the end of the scroll, a tiny bit of silk bearing both the signature "Kung-lin" and a largely illegible seal directly below has been patched into place, having been completely separated when the end of the silk was torn away (fig. 36). Under a very strong light, the first character of the seal can still be deciphered; it reads: "Li."

It is clear that the centuries have left the scroll in a ravaged state, a few fragile pieces of battered, broken silk. Yet to unroll the painting today and come upon these tiny, ghostlike figures acting out the timeless rituals of an ancient civilization is strangely reassuring. That the work has survived at all is miraculous.

The paintings are done in a fine *pai-miao*, or ink-outline, technique. The barely visible color is achieved with occasional ink washes of silvery gray and possibly a few touches of vermilion and dark green. The vermilion and green, however, have nearly disappeared, surviving only as faint tints of now uncertain placement. Within the limitations of his technique the painter achieved a remarkable degree of tonal subtlety, contrasting strong black lines and pale washes in a variety of combinations. Each figure is portrayed with an acute sensitivity to nuances of characterization and social status; from emperor to beggar, each is readily identifiable. Architecture, furniture, and landscape accessories are limited; the human element is everywhere paramount.

The text is written in the small *k'ai*, or model, script. The character *ching*, "to respect," occurs twenty-three times; in each case the final stroke is missing. The characters *jang*, "to yield," and *k'uang*, "to correct," each occur once, and they, too, lack their final strokes. *K'uang* was part of the given name of the founder of the Sung dynasty, Emperor T'ai-tsu (r. 960–95); *ching* was the name of his grand-

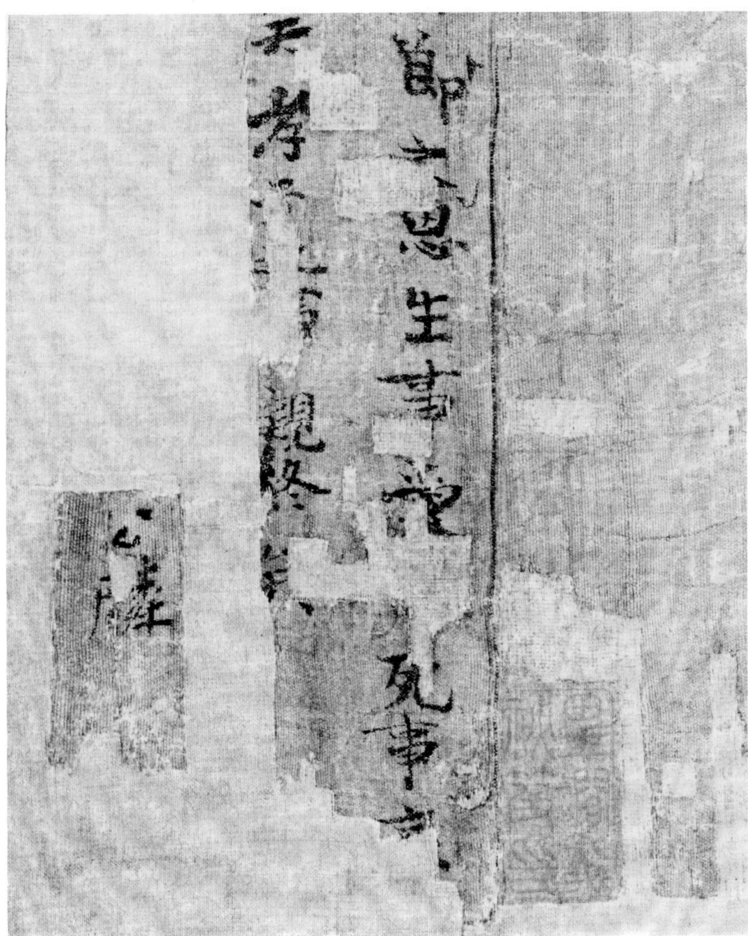

Figure 36. Li Kung-lin, detail from the *Classic of Filial Piety*, with signature and seal

father; and *jang* was the given name of the father of Emperor Ying-ts'ung (r. 1064–67). Normally, a Sung writer would have substituted other characters to avoid offending the imperial family, but in the case of a classical Confucian text they are simply written with a stroke missing. Copyists rarely observe such subtleties, however. Indeed, they generally quite unconsciously observe the imperial taboos of their own period and thus give themselves away. In the Taipei copy of the Princeton scroll, for example, none of the Sung taboos is consistently observed.

The style of the calligraphy is a profound evocation of the manner of the early Six Dynasties period (4th–5th century). Its restrained, classical spirit perfectly complements the paintings, which, if one were to cite a single tradition, share the simplicity and refinement of Ku K'ai-chih's *Admonitions* handscroll, dating originally to the fourth century. Li Kung-lin's contemporaries compared his calligraphy to that of the masters of the Chin (317–419) and Wei (386–534) dynasties, his painting to the tradition of Ku K'ai-chih (344–405) and Lu T'an-wei (late 5th century), and his personality to the great poets, painters, and eccentrics of the Chin dynasty.[15]

When it entered the collection of the eminent scholar of the arts Tung Ch'i-ch'ang (1555–1636) early in the seventeenth century, the Metropolitan Museum's scroll had an uncertain provenance. There was only one earlier colophon attached. Dated to a cyclical year corresponding in all probability to either 1230 or 1290, the colophon is signed "Han-man-weng," a name not otherwise identifiable. The text, very similar to a biography of Li Kung-lin published in 1167, is written in a fluid, elegant, and vibrant manner, close to that of the distinguished late-Sung master Chang Chi-chih (1186–1266). From the seventeenth century to the twentieth, however, a succession of owners and admirers have written colophons for the scroll. Tung Ch'i-ch'ang wrote four of them, the last dated 1609, and in 1603 had the text of chapter 9 reproduced for his collection of classical calligraphy. A later owner, the collector Pi Lung, wrote no fewer than six colophons during the last decade of the eighteenth century. Another eighteenth-century owner built a special hall to house the work, and in the nineteenth century a reproduction by stone engraving was made and ink rubbings of it circulated widely, attracting still more admirers. Appendix 1, in the present volume, summarizes the documentation and transmission of the scroll.

While we have no certain information about the provenance of the scroll between 1085, the year in which it was probably painted, and around 1600, when it was acquired by Tung Ch'i-ch'ang, we know that it was among the most admired and celebrated works by an artist whose reputation never declined. Beginning with Li Kung-lin's friend Su Shih, a succession of poets, painters, scholars, and collectors owned, saw, and wrote about the scroll and about other versions attributed to Li, as well as about the many copies of his works and paintings. To judge from this recorded history, Li Kung-lin's *Classic of Filial Piety* has been one of the preeminent monuments of Chinese cultural and art history for over a thousand years. The effect it has had upon those who have seen and studied it during the millennium may be suggested by a colophon written by the late-fifteenth-century scholar Lu Wan:

> In Li Kung-lin's illustrations of the *Classic of Filial Piety*, although he says that he selected only one or two concepts to accompany the chapters, in fact, from the emperor down to the common people, the details of decorous and dignified behavior, the pattern of the heavenly sacrifices, the customs of the countryside, the regulation of vessels and implements, the nature of the nourishment and raising of the family—all are quite complete. When Su Shih said that Li Kung-lin's spirit was joined to the myriad things and that his knowledge penetrated all human crafts, what he meant can be understood by those who study this scroll. Those who have praised his painting are of course numerous. As to his calligraphy, however, although the histories declare him wonderful beyond compare, his writing is seldom seen. Now, as I look at the force of his brush, I seem to see a great man hurrying respectfully to and fro in the newly arranged purity of the ancestral temple, jade pendants tinkling at his waist. Clear, simple, and dignified, it preserves the spirit and resonance of the ancient Chin and Sung periods.[16]

CHAPTER 1
The Scope and Meaning of the Treatise

Once when Confucius was unoccupied, and Tseng-tzu was sitting in attendance, the Master said: "Shen, the ancient kings had a perfect virtue and all-embracing rule of conduct, through which they were in accord with all under heaven. By the practice of it the people were brought to live in peace and harmony, and there was no ill will between superiors and inferiors. Do you know what it was?" Tseng-tzu arose from his mat and said, "How could I, Shen, who am so devoid of intelligence, know this?" The Master said, "It is filial piety that is the root of all virtue, and that from which all moral teaching grows. Sit down again and I will explain the subject to you. Our bodies, down to every strand of hair and bit of skin, are received from our parents, and we do not dare to injure or wound them. This is the beginning of filial piety. When we have established our character by the practice of the Way, so as to make our name known to future ages and thereby to glorify our parents, that is the end of filial piety. It commences with the service of our parents; it proceeds to the service of our ruler; it is completed by the establishment of our character. It is said in the Book of Songs:

> *Ever think of your ancestors,*
> *Cultivating your virtue."*[17]

Li Kung-lin's illustration for this first, introductory section of the text is lost, almost certainly destroyed by the damage inflicted on the opening section of the handscroll through its repeated opening, unrolling, and closing. That process has resulted in the loss of the first section of the scroll, consisting of one complete chapter of text and part of another and two paintings. The very close, though pedestrian, copy of the entire scroll in the National Palace Museum, Taipei, made before the original suffered its present damage, preserves the first composition (fig. 37). In it, Confucius sits on a low *k'ang*, or traditional Chinese couch, expounding on the nature of filial piety to his attentive disciples. Ten of them are arrayed like a frame to his back and sides, while the eleventh, Tseng-tzu, sits slightly apart and to the front. It is Tseng-tzu to whom Confucius had addressed his opening question. Now the Master, his right hand raised in explanation, begins to expound on the principles of filial piety.

Since all available evidence indicates that Li Kung-lin himself selected the individual compositions for each of the chapters, choosing the sections of text on which to focus for each illustration, we may look upon them as a form of intellectual commentary and as a personal reflection upon both filial piety and the nature of Sung society. When read in this way, they offer a rich survey not only of the people and activities of late-eleventh-century China but also of Li Kung-lin's own assessment of his tradition and the nature of its reality in his lifetime.

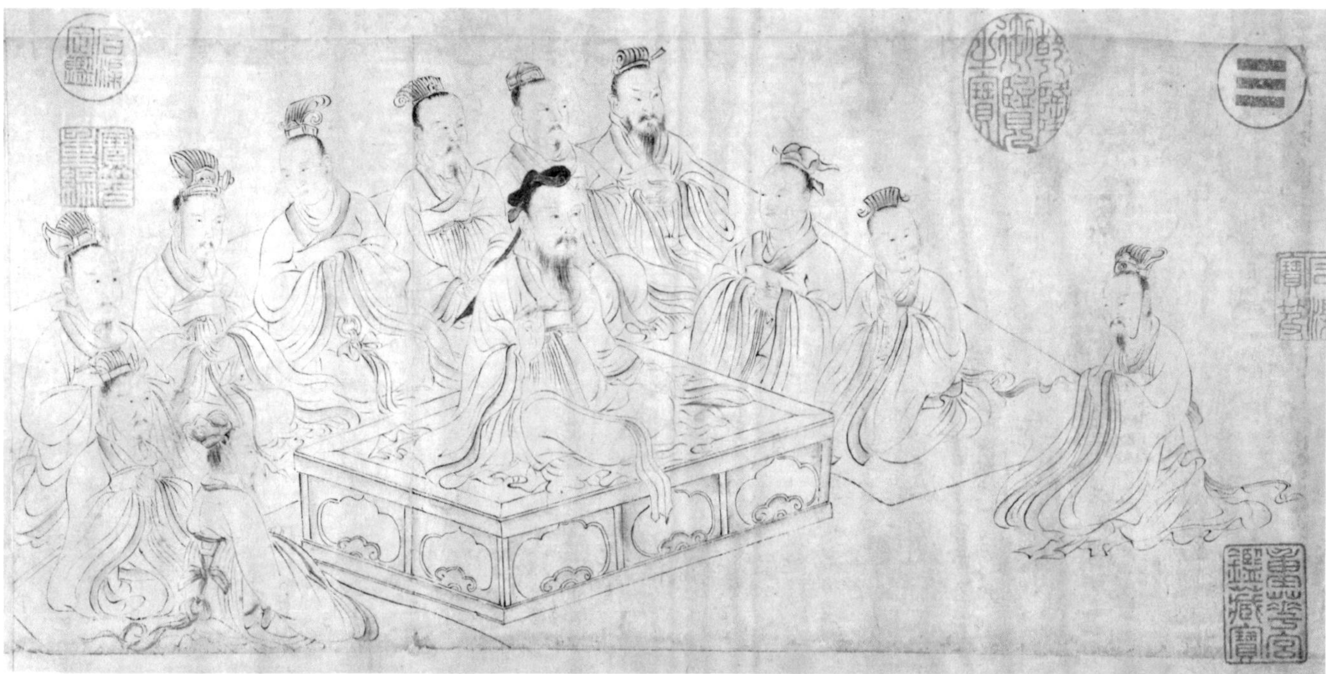

Figure 37. Unidentified artist (14th century?), after Li Kung-lin, detail from chapter 1 of the *Classic of Filial Piety*. Handscroll, ink on paper, 8 1/16 × 276 3/8 in. (20.5 × 702.1 cm). National Palace Museum, Taipei

In this opening painting, for example, Li introduces one of the consistent themes of his commentary, the separation of the individual from the larger group. Tseng-tzu, the favorite disciple of Confucius and affectionately addressed by him as Shen, is here called on to separate himself from the others and to respond to the Master. Of course, it would not be appropriate for a mere disciple to supply the answer to Confucius's profoundly important question, so he merely sits attentively, his eyes lowered in reverence, as the Master speaks. In this and later illustrations, Li seems to convey his awareness of the pressures placed on the individual in a society that values above all the hieratic patriarchal family and community. Li's own hereditary family was of the old aristocracy, now disenfranchised, and the class of society to which he belonged was the scholar-bureaucracy. His intermittent, lengthy, but unsuccessful career as a petty bureaucrat and minor officer in local administration was probably accompanied by a continuing inner debate over the personal choice between filial service to the state and private, individual explorations through a life devoted to art and scholarship.

There are other interesting comments made in this initial illustration. Confucius, China's greatest teacher, is distinguished from his disciples in several ways. Although he is elevated slightly above them by the height of the *k'ang* on which he sits, he is shown closely among them, as one of the group. He alone wears a black scholar's hat, however, and he is slightly larger than any of the disciples. By depicting Confucius as physically larger than mere mortals, Li adapts an old convention used traditionally in the depiction of kings and emperors. This was appropriate, since Confucius had long ago been elevated to the

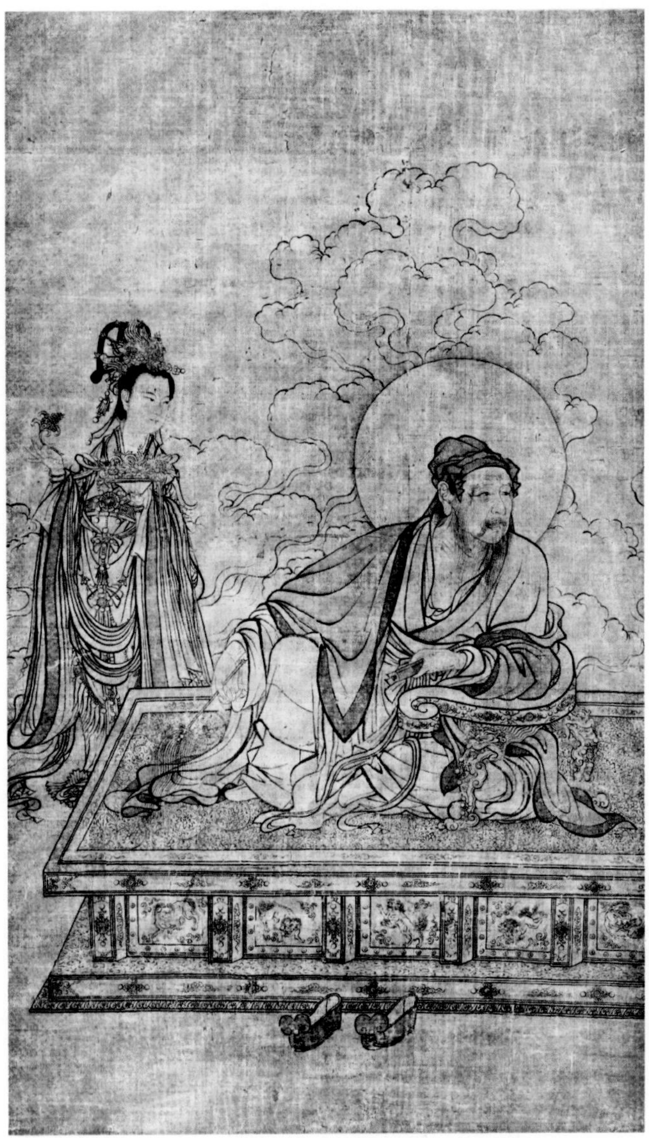

Figure 38. Attributed to Li Kung-lin, *Vimalakirti*. Hanging scroll, ink on silk, 35 × 20¼ in. (89 × 51.3 cm). Bureau of Cultural Affairs, Tokyo

position of teacher, even by the emperor of China. In symbolizing teaching and learning, he represents the Sung ideal of self-acquired knowledge gained through discipline and intelligence, an ideal by which society as a whole could hope to function effectively.

If there were earlier paintings of Confucius similar to this one, they do not seem to have survived. The earlier type of imaginary portrait of Confucius that has survived is a standing figure, which is also the traditional convention for the depiction of meritorious officials and scholars.[18] Instead of that rather formal, public tradition, Li may have had reference to two quite different traditions of ideal portraiture. Classic T'ang and Sung depictions of Vimalakirti, the Chinese lay saint of Buddhism, typically show him seated on a *k'ang* and dressed much like Confucius in Li's composition. The painting illustrated here (fig. 38) is in fact attributed to Li, though it is probably a distant copy of one of his lost original works.[19]

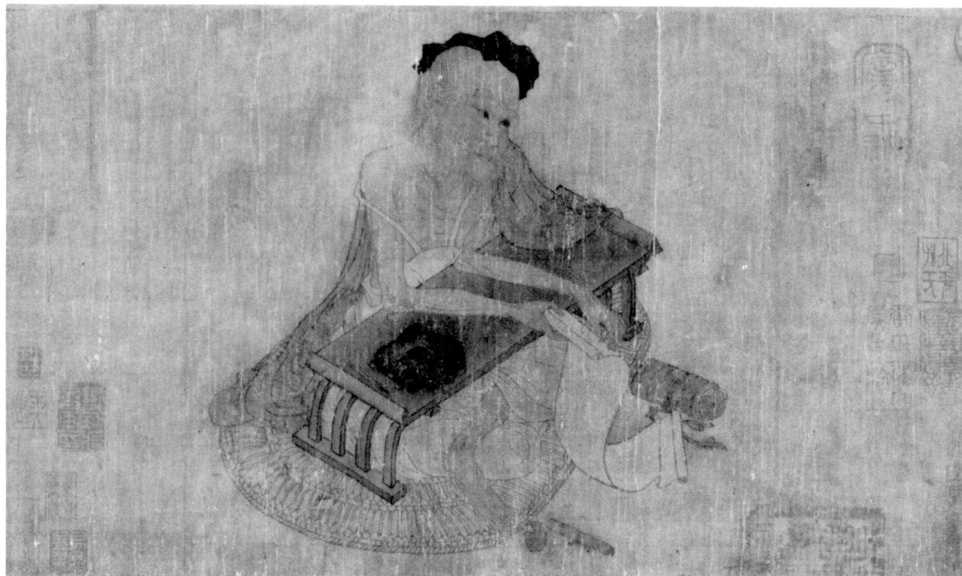

Figure 39. Attributed to Wang Wei (701–761), *Fu Sheng Expounding the Classics*. Handscroll, ink and color on silk, 10 × 17 5/8 in. (25.4 × 44.7 cm). Osaka Municipal Museum of Art

A second notable pictorial tradition that focused on the transmission and explication of classic Confucian texts depicted the great Han scholar Fu Sheng, who transmitted the classics from memory many years after they had all been destroyed at the order of the First Emperor, Ch'in Shih-huang-ti (259–210 B.C.). In the fragmentary image of Fu Sheng (3rd century B.C.) attributed to the T'ang master Wang Wei (701–761; fig. 39), the saintly old man leans his emaciated body forward to point out passages in the scroll that he holds out toward the official who, in the original painting, knelt before him, much as Tseng-tzu kneels before Confucius. That part of the Wang Wei scroll is now lost, though it appears in later versions.[20]

What Li Kung-lin does with these traditions is to intensify their inherent drama by grouping Confucius and his disciples tightly together, with Tseng-tzu somewhat apart, and by allowing only one point of entry into the composition, the space between the Master and Tseng-tzu, which continues out to the viewer. We are immediately engaged in the structure of the narrative by being asked to become the fourth point of a horizontal diamond, the other points of which are marked by Tseng-tzu, the uppermost disciple, and the disciple at the far left. We have become the audience in a small, intimate theater, almost sitting onstage, with the actors at touching distance.

It was undoubtedly one of Li Kung-lin's most significant achievements to have found the means by which to engage his audience so closely within the continuing story of his paintings. We begin with this frontispiece, as it were, which sets in motion the discourse that follows, as the Master continues to speak.

CHAPTER 2
Filial Piety in the Son of Heaven

He who loves his parents will not dare to hate any man. He who respects his parents will not dare to be contemptuous of any man. When love and respect are thus carried to the utmost in the service of his parents, the lessons of his virtue affect all the people and he becomes a model to all within the Four Seas. This is the filial piety of the Son of Heaven. As it is said in the Marquis of Fu on Punishment:

> *The One Man has goodness,*
> *And his people rely on him.*[21]

Each chapter in the *Classic of Filial Piety* pertains to a different expression of filial piety, and their arrangement in its hieratic order is like a model of traditional Chinese society. After the initial proclamation on the subject of filial piety, the text begins with the filiality of the emperor. In the Taipei copy of Li Kung-lin's lost illustration of this chapter (fig. 40), we see a fat emperor being ceremoniously helped to his trembling knees by two attendants. Carefully, they lower the huge mass of their sovereign to the floor as he prepares to prostrate himself in abject filiality before his mother. Twenty men and women of the imperial entourage look on impassively at this display. We must assume that an emperor of China was free to demonstrate his love and respect for his mother in less dramatic—even more sincere—ways than this. The depiction of this overstuffed, overdressed, and overly protected man being helped to his knees while dozens of observers look on impassively appears to be a pointed and ironic commentary on the relatively simple words of the text. At the very least, the painter seems to be implying that in the official court society in which he was compelled to spend so many years, only the most obvious gesture made any impression; only the most dramatic ceremony carried any meaning. By contrast, in the simple human scenes of family gatherings that Li presents elsewhere in the scroll, subtle gestures and unaffected interactions are sufficient; their meaning is understood.

Because the emperor served as a model for all to follow, the several roles he played often required visibility and public display. One such role was that of the son. Throughout the history of imperial China, the nature of the relationship between the reigning emperor and his mother was always carefully scrutinized, because so many other relationships emanated from it.

The emperor's mother lived in separate, palatial quarters, limited to women and eunuchs. She was served there by a vast entourage of women who were organized, like the male bureaucracy, into different ranks, duties, and salaries that were similarly subject to detailed regulatory structures. A visit by the emperor to his mother necessarily required advance negotiations and careful preparation. The public display of this preparation probably resulted in the kind of ritualistic

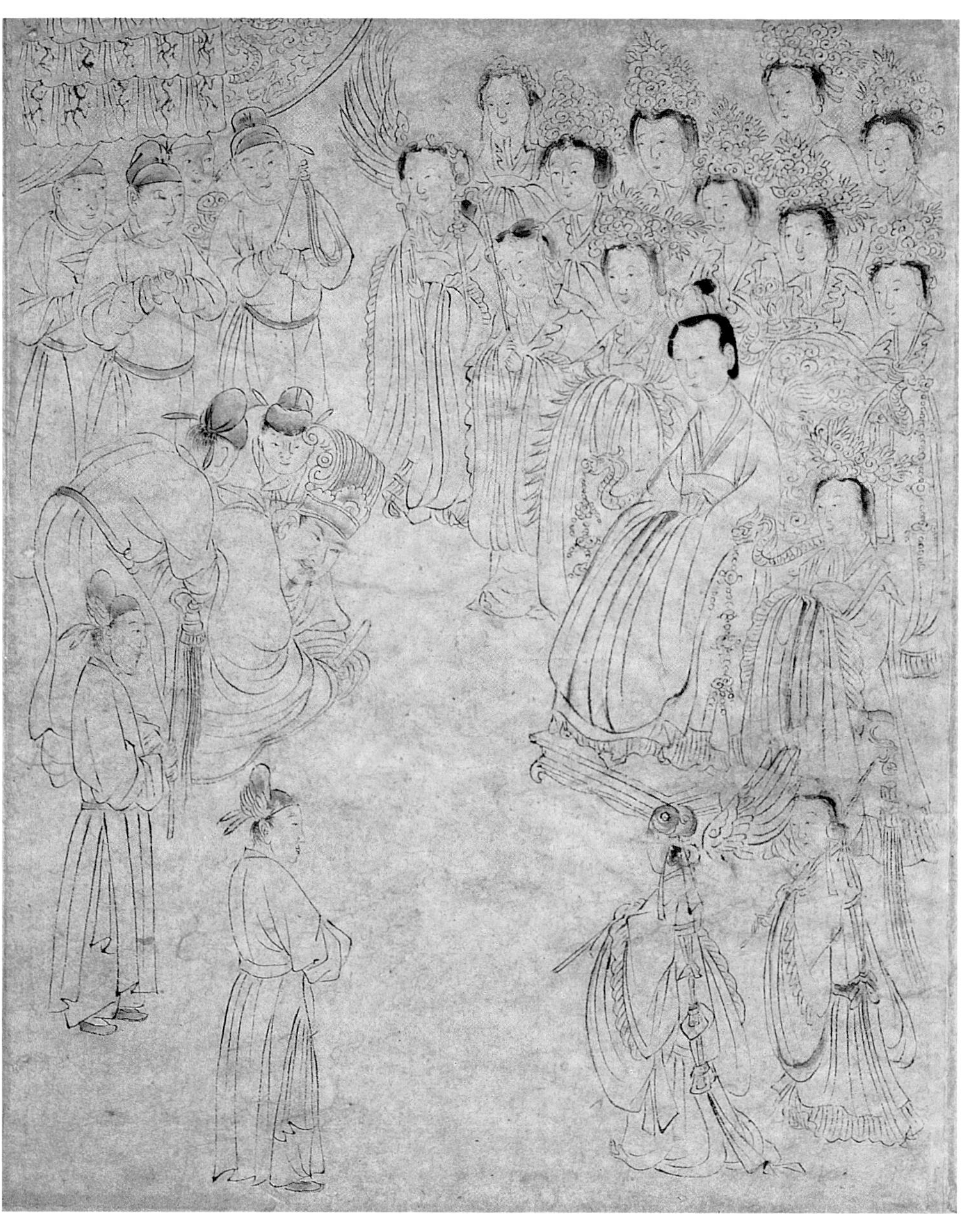

Figure 40. Unidentified artist (14th century?), after Li Kung-lin, chapter 2 of the *Classic of Filial Piety*. Handscroll, ink on paper, 8 1/16 × 276 3/8 in. (20.5 × 702.1 cm). National Palace Museum, Taipei

performance depicted here, observed by a sufficiently large audience to ensure that word of it would reach all necessary ears. The center of a vast network of bureaucratic organization, the emperor had to please many interests, and his every action was watched by a multitude for its potential implications.

It seems evident that what Li wished to convey by this illustration was the pretension and hollowness of such ceremony. His emperor, a fat, smirking aristocrat, is so overfed that he cannot even lower himself to the floor without assistance. His mother, elegant and infinitely patient, appears attentive to the humiliation to which he subjects himself. And pointedly, at the center of the composition, Li puts nothing. This hollow center is not the infinite space of Buddhism, but the emptiness of ostentatious display.

Li's style, in comparison, specifically represents an aesthetic of nonostentation. The corresponding term in Chinese is *p'ing-tan*, "bland," or, literally, "flat and pale." The term for his uncolored ink drawing, *pai-miao*, means plain, or uncolored, line. This style, invented by Li, stands in contrast to what was then the prevailing style of figural and dramatic narrative painting, which presented bold, pageantlike settings, rich color, and elaborate decorative details, as well as exaggerated expressions and melodramatic gestures.

The late Northern Sung period, beginning about the time Li painted the *Classic of Filial Piety*, in 1085, displayed a new fashion for simplicity and restraint in dress, furniture, decoration, design, and other areas of human activity.[22] A similar turn toward the aesthetic of *p'ing-tan* occurred in art and literature, and certainly calligraphers, painters, and poets began at this time to explore new directions characterized by the formal and stylistic simplification of the elaborate forms then prevalent.[23] Reforms of this kind affected nearly everything, from music and ritual to ceramics, essay writing, and court ceremonies. Reflecting a kind of neoclassicism then permeating Sung society, they were rooted in what were believed to be ancient orders of uncluttered simplicity.

Li Kung-lin's *Classic of Filial Piety* is among the works of art that first revealed this tendency, and clearly the underlying subject of his illustration for chapter 2 is the hollow center of ostentation and empty display at every level of society.

CHAPTER 3
Filial Piety in the Princes of State

When a prince is not proud and arrogant, he will not incur peril in spite of his high position. By exercising self-restraint he is judicious, ever keeping a proper balance between his need and use of material things. By such moderation his cup of wealth is full without wasteful overflow. And thus, preserving wealth and rank, he will be able to retain possession of his altars of the land and the grain and keep his subjects in peace. This is the filial piety of the prince of state. It is said in the Book of Songs:

Be apprehensive, be cautious,
As if on the brink of a deep abyss,
As if treading on thin ice.[24]

The princes of state in imperial China were the sons, adopted sons, brothers, and other chosen ones of the emperor, selected by the Son of Heaven to share, if only symbolically, the imperial blood, power, and privilege. Usually children of the emperor, they also represented him, playing important roles in the administration of civil and military control of the population. Each occupied a princely mansion or palace, received great wealth from the throne, and wielded financial, political, and military power second only to that of the emperor himself. In fact, the imperial princes were often profligate, greedy, destructive men, with excessive wealth and nearly unlimited power. In the imperially hieratic sequence of chapter subjects in the *Classic of Filial Piety*, the discussion of the filiality of the princes of state comes immediately following that concerning the emperor. This reflection of the socio-political and hereditary structures of China in the second or third century B.C. was still applicable to the ostensibly very changed structure of Sung China when Li Kung-lin painted these visual interpretations of the concepts and abuses of filial piety. This may suggest that the much-vaunted social, economic, and political advances often associated with the Sung period were not, in fact, what modern liberal humanists like to imagine they were.[25] Li Kung-lin's paintings appear to point quite directly to the terrible fracture that had long existed between hereditary wealth and privilege on the one hand and the lives and circumstances of the common people—including scholars—on the other. Li Kung-lin's position within this social dichotomy was ambiguous; he was descended from a great hereditary family, yet he lived his life in the company of artists, scholars, and poets.

In Li's illustration for chapter 3, a prince rides by a group of villagers—presumably, his subjects, all of whom are in the lower left corner of the composition (pl. 1). One of the villagers looks up reverently, while two others, with hands joined in respect, look down. One old man with a crutch ignores the passing procession altogether, however, and a crippled figure raises a fist in anger at his overlord. Formally, this small, helpless group is isolated from and nearly overwhelmed by the force, majesty, and strength of the prince and his retinue. In the face of this potential threat to the security of his altars and his privileges, the prince of state is apprehensive and cautious, "As if on the brink of a deep abyss,/As if treading on thin ice." He is surrounded and protected by a retinue of soldiers. The lead officer appears about to draw his sword as he stares suspiciously at the ragged group. Li Kung-lin makes it clear that they do not have the capacity to threaten their great lord; the prince, in his turn, "is not proud and arrogant"; on the contrary, he appears to be a man of keen and intelligent sympathy for the welfare of even the poorest of his people. Behind him sits an elderly, distinguished-looking man, who reinforces the ideal of human concern and dignity. But around them are gathered the badges and elements of power: soldiers, weapons, horses, carriages, banners, and uniforms—all of which have the single purpose of protecting the prince from the harm that may come from unexpected sources at any moment.

The rightness of the preservation of imperial power is the overriding message of the *Classic of Filial Piety*. In his paintings, Li Kung-lin appears to function not so much as a critic of the system but as a commentator on its abuses and excesses, illustrating the text in such a way as to emphasize the price paid in human suffering for the maintenance of hereditary privilege.

For his prince, Li drew upon representations of sages and philosophers of earlier times. Perhaps the most striking model was the idealized portrait of a wise man, either the Taoist philosopher Lao-tzu or the Buddhist saint Samanthabhadra, preserved in the Shinshōgokurakuji, Kyoto (fig. 41).[26] In such images, he would have found the prince's attitude of attentive concern and his position of leaning forward from the front of a carriage. The military entourage he surely would have known from his own daily observation, and the lives of the peasant population were visible to anyone who cared to look. There was, in fact, no reason for Li to have introduced such figures at all, unless he specifically wished us to understand them in the context of their relationship to power. He could simply have shown us a prince, practicing "moderation" and "restraint."

In this, the first of Li's original illustrations to have survived in the scroll, are all the essential elements of his art. The entire upper two-thirds of the composition is a dense mass of line and of ink tones that conveys the pageantry of the princely entourage. By creating this rich, heavy pattern above, Li isolates the figures below, creating a tension between the dramatically unequal groups. By thus emphasizing the poverty, frailness, and insignificance of the common people, the artist calls further attention to the excesses of wealth and power held by those who rest literally on top of them.

There is in the illustration to chapter 3 a spontaneity to the brush drawing that is, of course, lacking in the anonymous copies of the two lost illustrations for chapters 1 and 2. The sense that Li drew these figures slowly, spontaneously,

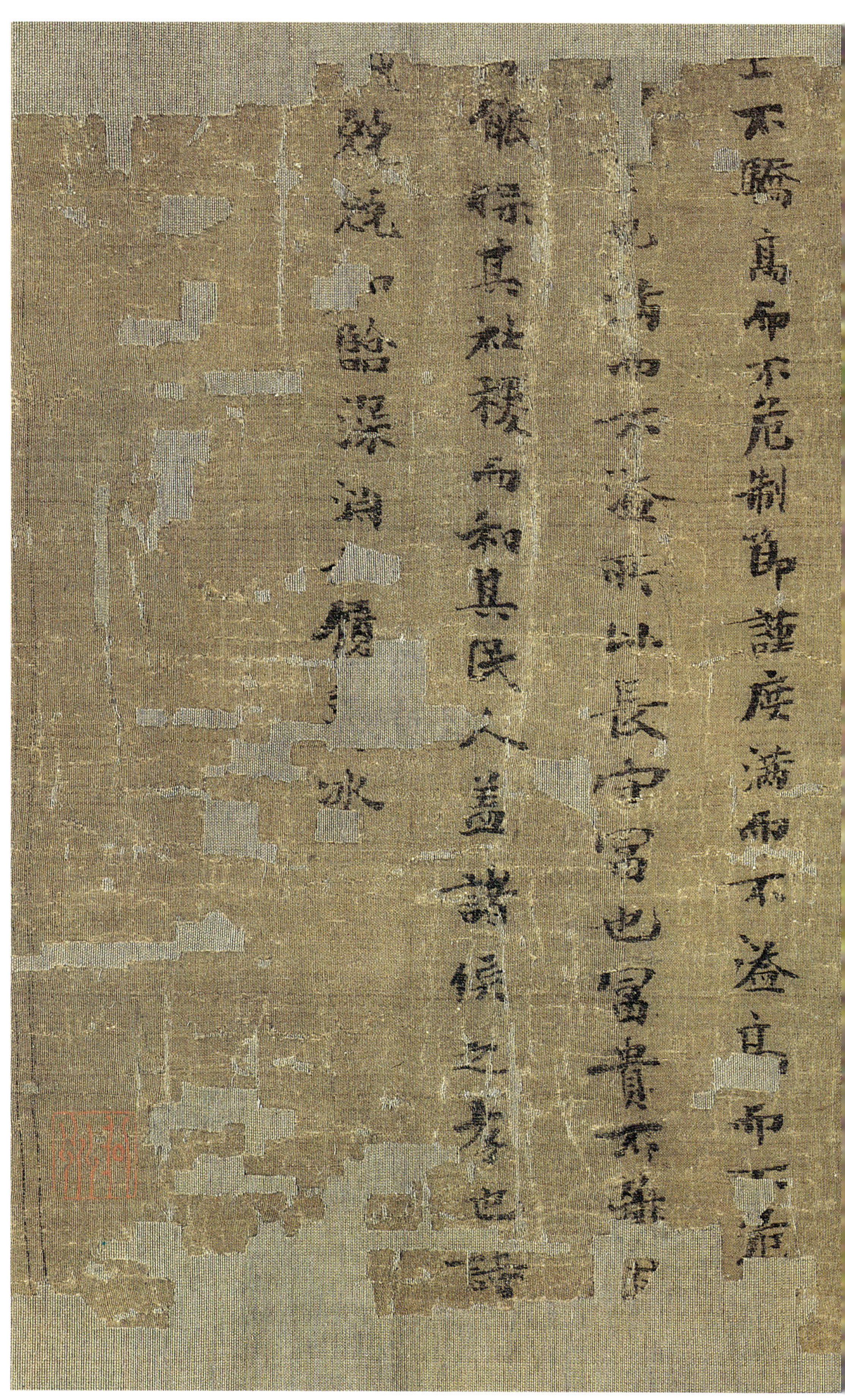

Plate 1. Li Kung-lin, chapter 3 of the *Classic of Filial Piety*, ca 1085. Handscroll, ink on silk, $8\frac{5}{8} \times 187\frac{1}{4}$ in. (21.9×475.5 cm). From the P. Y. and Kinmay W. Tang Family collection, Promised Gift of Jack C. Tang and Oscar L. Tang (L.1990.3.1)

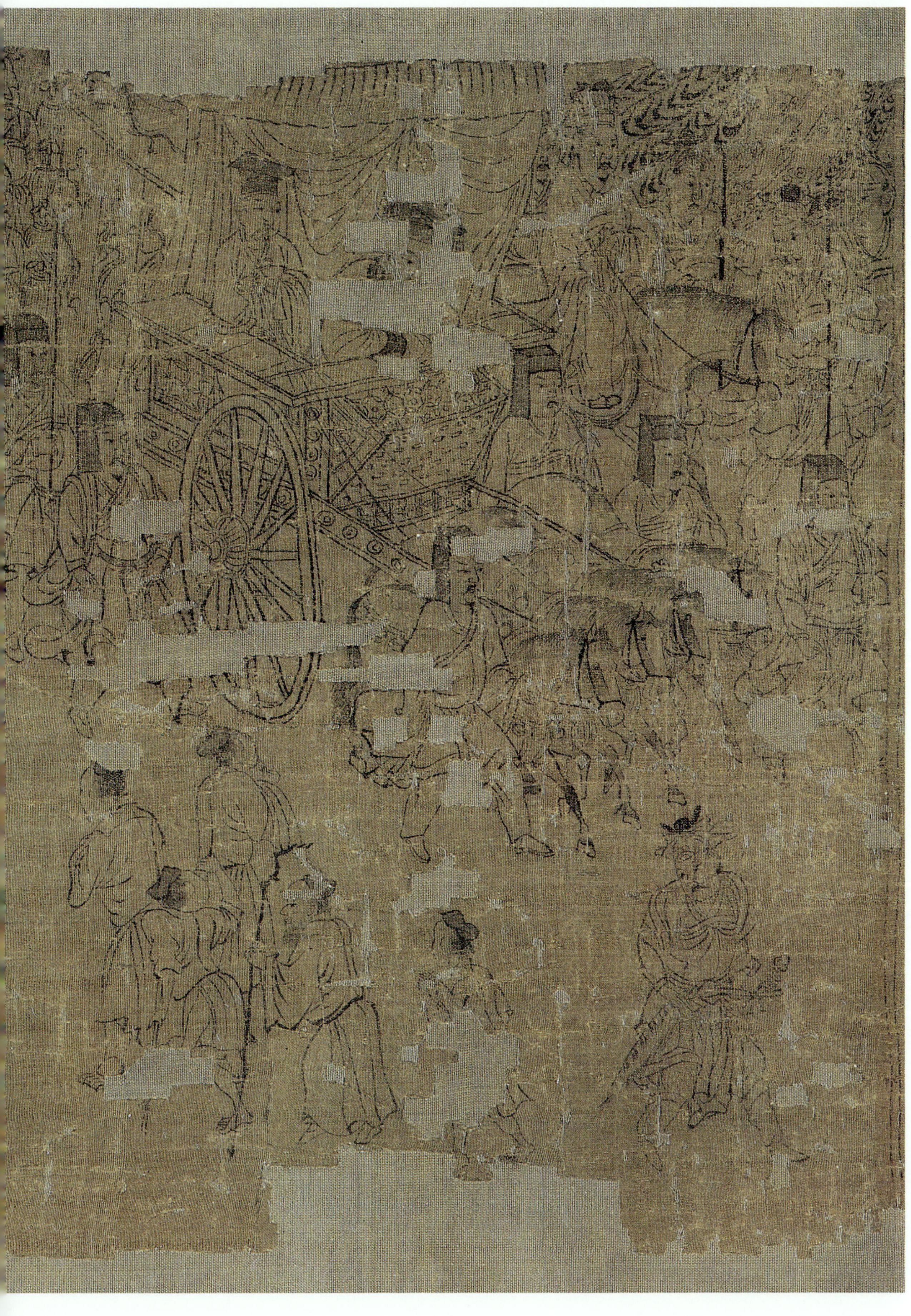

and quite easily is still vivid. All the more remarkable, then, is the sureness of his hand, since the drawing was done directly onto the raw silk, without preliminary sketches or other preparation. The picture is, in fact, more like a preparatory drawing than a finished painting, and we may begin to wonder whether it was a study for a later, more polished version, or for another form altogether—such as a book with wood-block print illustrations.

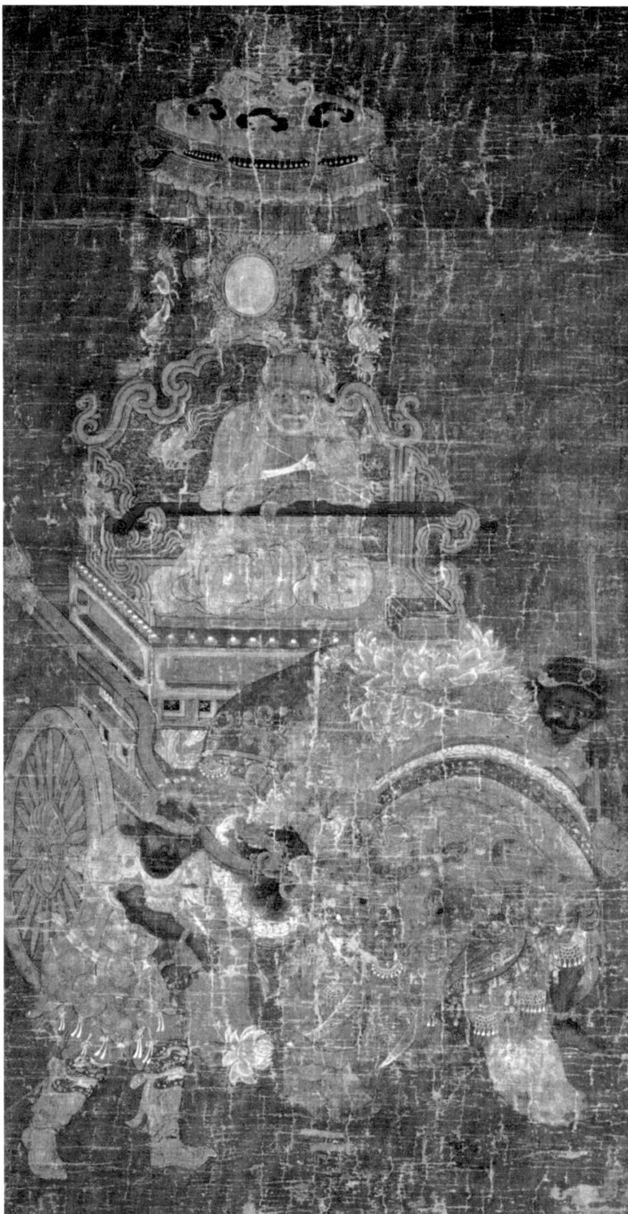

Figure 41. Unidentified artist (11th century?), *Samanthabhadra Bodhisattva*. Hanging scroll, ink and color on silk, 51 7/8 × 21 3/8 in. (131.8 × 54.4 cm). Shinshōgokurakuji, Kyoto

CHAPTER 4
Filial Piety in High Ministers and Great Officers

They do not presume to wear robes other than those appointed by the laws of the ancient kings, nor to speak words other than those sanctioned by them, nor to exhibit conduct other than that exemplified by their virtuous ways. Thus, none of their words being contrary to those sanctions, and none of their actions contrary to the Way, from their mouths there comes no objectionable speech, and in their conduct there are found no objectionable actions. Their words may fill all under heaven, yet no error of speech will be found in them. Their actions may fill all under heaven, yet no dissatisfaction or dislike will be awakened by them. When these three things are all complete, and as they should be, they can then preserve their ancestral temples. This is the filial piety of high ministers and great officers. In the Book of Songs *it is said:*

> *He is never idle, day or night,*
> *In the service of the One Man.*[27]

In his illustration of the filial piety of high officers and ministers of state (pl. 2), Li Kung-lin expands upon the image of teaching and learning with which his pictorial program began. Here, it is the emperor who sits upon the *k'ang*, with his high officials gathered behind him as attentively as the disciples of Confucius in the earlier image. Perhaps not incidentally there are, in fact, eleven officials and ministers here, just as there are eleven disciples in the first composition. Before the emperor kneels the Minister of the Right, who presumably addresses a memorial. His counterpart in the dualistic structure of ministerial power in traditional China, the Minister of the Left, stands to the left of the throne. What we see in this image of an ideal ruler and his ministers are the costumes sanctioned by the ancient kings. What we hear are the words of the ancient kings, and what we observe is the model conduct approved by the ancient kings for their ministers.

There is, nonetheless, a sense of danger, exposure, and fear, and there is every reason to believe that Li Kung-lin was entirely familiar with the tensions, personal and factional rivalries, scheming, and manipulative pursuit of personal gain that characterized Northern Sung court politics. Unlike the disciples of Confucius, who are shown sitting quietly and attentively around the sage, the high officials behind the emperor stand like a protective shield. One of them carries a halberd, which he is prepared to use should anything threaten his ruler. The kowtowing Minister of the Right is fully exposed to the power of the emperor and to the observant eyes of his fellow minister and the watchful body of officials. Among these men passed vicious slander and destructive innuendos, and any one of them could have been replaced in an instant at the whim of

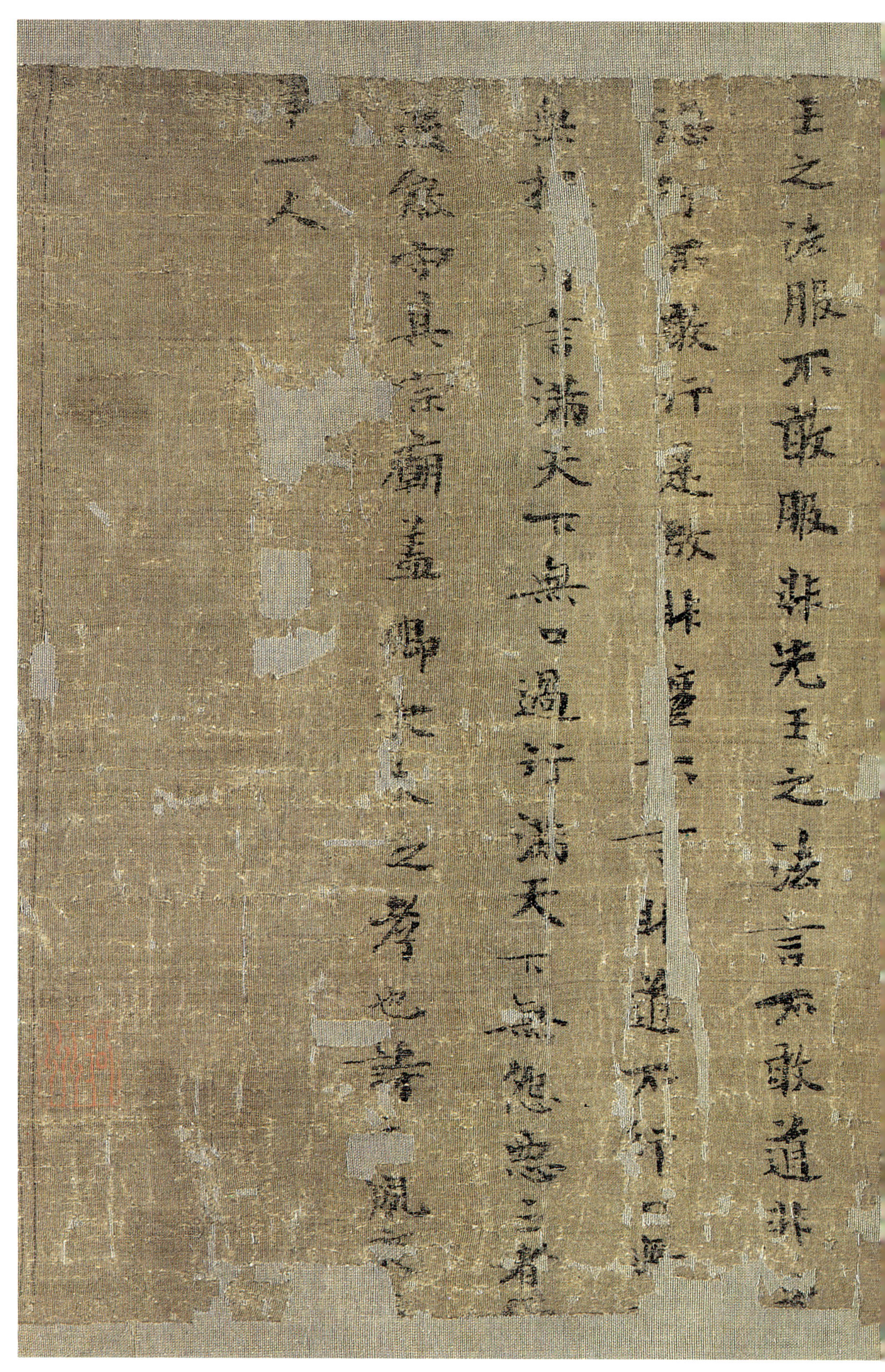

Plate 2. Li Kung-lin, chapter 4 of the *Classic of Filial Piety*

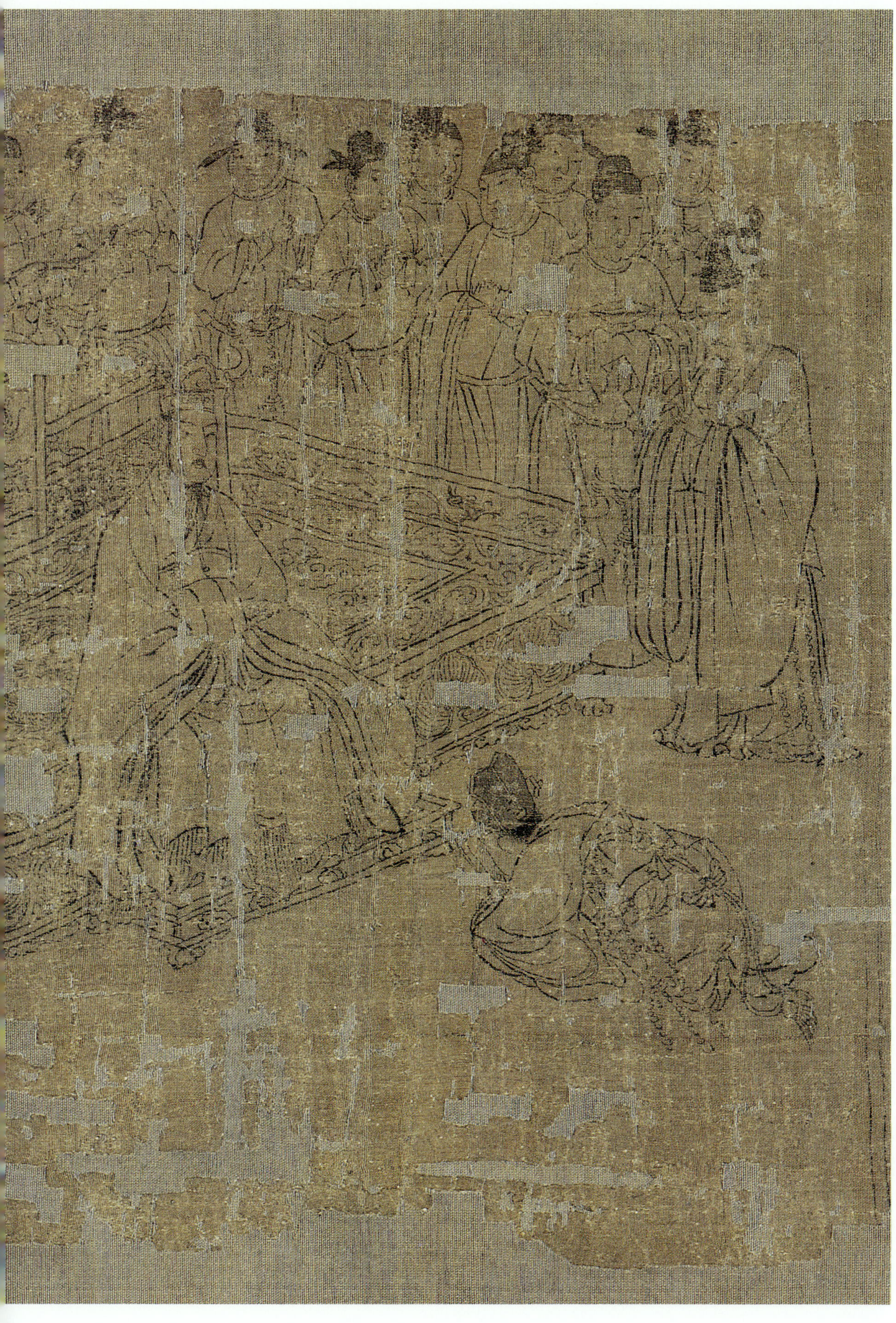

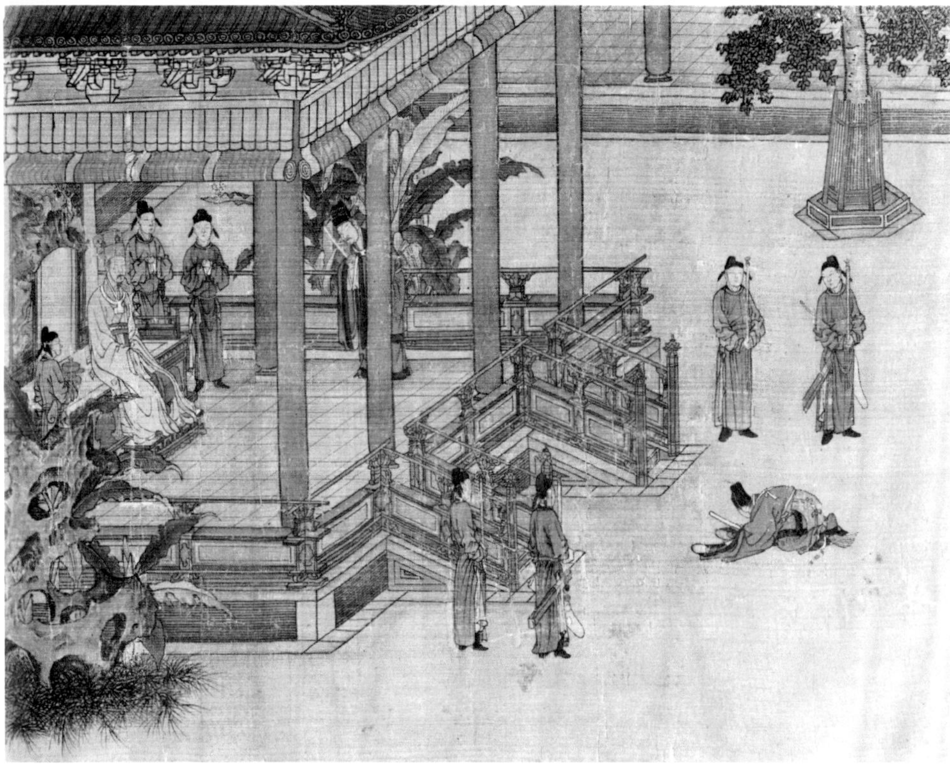

Figure 42. Attributed to Ma Ho-chih (active ca. 1130–ca. 1170), chapter 4 of the *Classic of Filial Piety*. Album of 15 paintings, ink and color on silk, sizes variable. National Palace Museum, Taipei

the emperor. Yet the foundations of the government depended on the honest functioning of opinion, recommendation, and criticism. This was a difficult requirement at best, and it often failed in the face of ambition and corruption. What Li helps us to see is the perilous balance maintained at court between effective government and factional disasters. He himself lived in the midst of that reality, and he counted among his friends both political reformers and their opponents, who sought to perpetuate the ideals of the ancient kings. How much of the true circumstances of political strife is actually embedded in the painting may be argued, but undoubtedly Li intended that we see the exposure to danger that confronted all officials in the figure of the Minister of the Right, who falls on his elbows at the feet of the emperor.

If we compare Li's painting with another version of the same subject by a very different kind of painter, we can see how effectively Li conveys this sense of confrontation and potential disaster. That version (fig. 42), painted by a twelfth-century court artist, traditionally has been attributed to Ma Ho-chih (active second half 12th century). Generally, if loosely, it follows the prototype established by Li. The twelfth-century painter draws a wider stage, however, and fills it with palatial architectural structures, with trees and rocks, and with garden plants. He also extends the stage back into space, adding a veranda and an open court beyond the foreground focus. But here we can scarcely speak of a focus; rather, we look upon a pageant set in an elaborate garden. Far to the left, back among the columns, sits the now nearly insignificant figure of the emperor. Four armed bailiffs stand casually before the raised throne chamber, as the Minister of the Right kowtows between them. Up on the porch, where the emperor sits, only three officials are in attendance, together with the bowing figure of the Minister of the Left.

Li's painting has a very different impact. Except for the couch, there are no accessories; nor is there any description of setting or place. There is no architecture, no garden, no indication of specific location. We are, quite simply, in the immediate presence of the emperor. And that is the only fact of place that matters. In this leap of imagination, Li dispenses with everything extraneous. The imperial presence, however, is not isolated; he joins a powerful company of officials and guardians, whose combined presence conveys a sense of claustrophobia and threat. To fall to one's knees before the imperial feet is to give one's life over to an unpredictable fate.

Here, again, we observe the casual, slow ease with which Li has drawn his images, the seeming carelessness even of the details—the elaborate but informal decoration, for example, over the imperial couch—and we may again suspect that this is not a finished painting but rather a sketch for a more polished, or formal, version that no longer exists—if it was, in fact, ever done.

CHAPTER 5
Filial Piety in Lesser Officials

As they serve their fathers, so they serve their mothers, and they love them equally. As they serve their fathers, so they serve their rulers, and they reverence them equally. Hence, love is what is chiefly rendered to the ruler, while both of these things are given to the father. Therefore, when they serve their ruler with filial piety they are loyal; when they serve their superiors with reverence they are obedient. Not failing in this loyalty and obedience in serving those above them, they are then able to preserve their emoluments and positions, and to maintain their sacrifices. This is the filial piety of the lesser officials. It is said in the Book of Songs:

> *Rising early and going to sleep late,*
> *Do not disgrace those who gave you birth.*[28]

Nearly all the human orders of relationship described in the *Classic of Filial Piety* are unequal. They form a society based on servitude and draw the picture of a pyramid, its greatest mass and weight at the base, in the common people, who serve and sustain those ever smaller groups above until we see alone at the top the emperor of China.

The family was a microcosm of that imperial structure, a model for the empire. In it, the father reigned supreme, like the emperor. But unlike the emperor, the father was owed not only respect but also love. Within this politicized social structure, the mother, interestingly, was owed only love, not respect.

In his illustrations, Li Kung-lin repeatedly calls our attention to the abuses of the structure of inequality that permeated Chinese society and to the heightened tensions that individual actions were subject to. He does this pictorially, and in many ways. At the same time, he consistently offers alternatives, most often in the ideal portrait of the family that he creates. His illustration for chapter 5 is typical (pl. 3). In it, we see a man and his wife serving a meal to (presumably) his father and mother. There are no servants here, only parents and children. The man and wife share responsibilities, he kneeling to prepare the food, she bringing a dish from the kitchen. Seated on a mat on the floor, in front of an enclosing folding screen, the father looks over at his wife and holds out his hand, as if to offer her first choice of the food they are served by their children. The many containers and utensils arrayed before the mat suggest that this is an elaborate feast, of many courses.

The mother and father are portrayed with exceptional sensitivity. He holds out his right hand, palm up, as he looks over at her. She, in turn, glances toward her husband, a faint smile on her lips as if she is speaking. Rarely in Chinese art had a husband and wife been depicted with such intimacy and apparent affection.

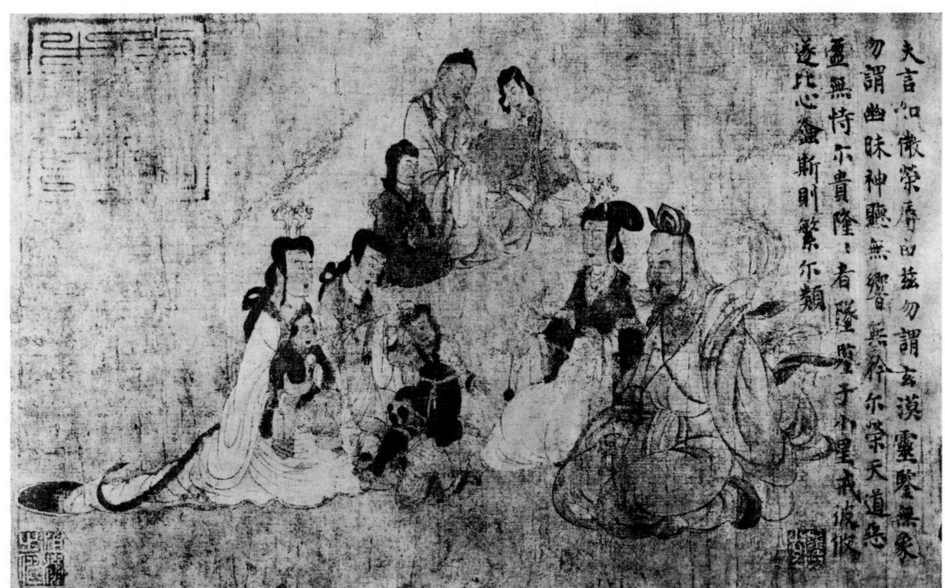

Figure 43. After Ku K'ai-chih (ca. 344–ca. 406), "Family Group," from *Admonitions of the Instructress to the Court Ladies*, possibly 8th century. Handscroll, ink and color on silk, $9\frac{13}{16} \times 137\frac{1}{16}$ in. (24.9 × 347.6 cm). Courtesy of the Trustees of the British Museum, London

The sensitivity of its expression would suggest that the essential relations among the mother, father, son, and daughter were a fundamental concern of the artist. And it might further suggest that he viewed those relations somewhat differently from the text he was illustrating and from the traditions it was intended to perpetuate.

Pictorial precedents for this painting are difficult to find, since portrayals of intimate family gatherings were not common in the artistic traditions of imperial China. Li's admiration for the ancient master Ku K'ai-chih (ca. 344–ca. 406), however, proves rewarding. In Ku's famed *Admonitions of the Instructress to the Court Ladies* there are several scenes of family life at court, including the one illustrated here, of an extended family of three generations (fig. 43). At the distant apex of the triangle that they form is the patriarch, while his son and the son's wife form the other two points. It was undoubtedly from such paintings as this that Li learned the principles of both composition and the depiction of human interaction. Both his painting and Ku's are formed upon a rhythmic, ongoing choreography of movement and human intercourse. Li rejects the hieratic triangle of the earlier master, however, for a more open, less structured form: the daughter enters from the right carrying a tray, the son kneels to prepare and serve the food, the father leans and gestures toward his wife, and she smiles and speaks to him in return. Movement is not arrested but continues like a slow dance to give life to the image.

It is impossible not to sense in such paintings Li's deep affection for the people he portrays. Surely they are visualizations of the reality of his own life and family. It seems likely that when he painted a father he was recalling his own father, and that when he painted a mother she was related somehow to his own. He then becomes the kneeling son, the wife approaching from the side, his own.

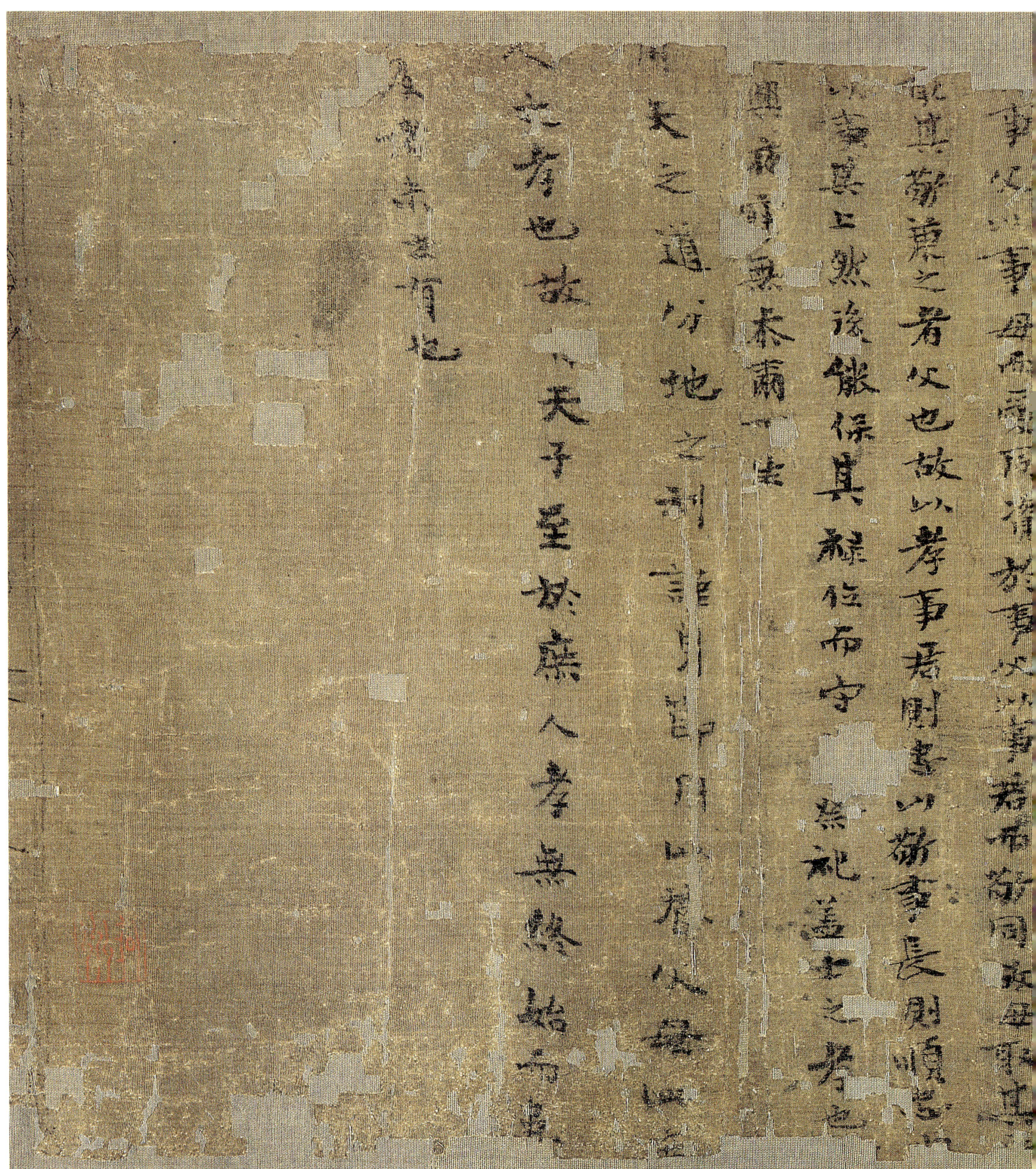

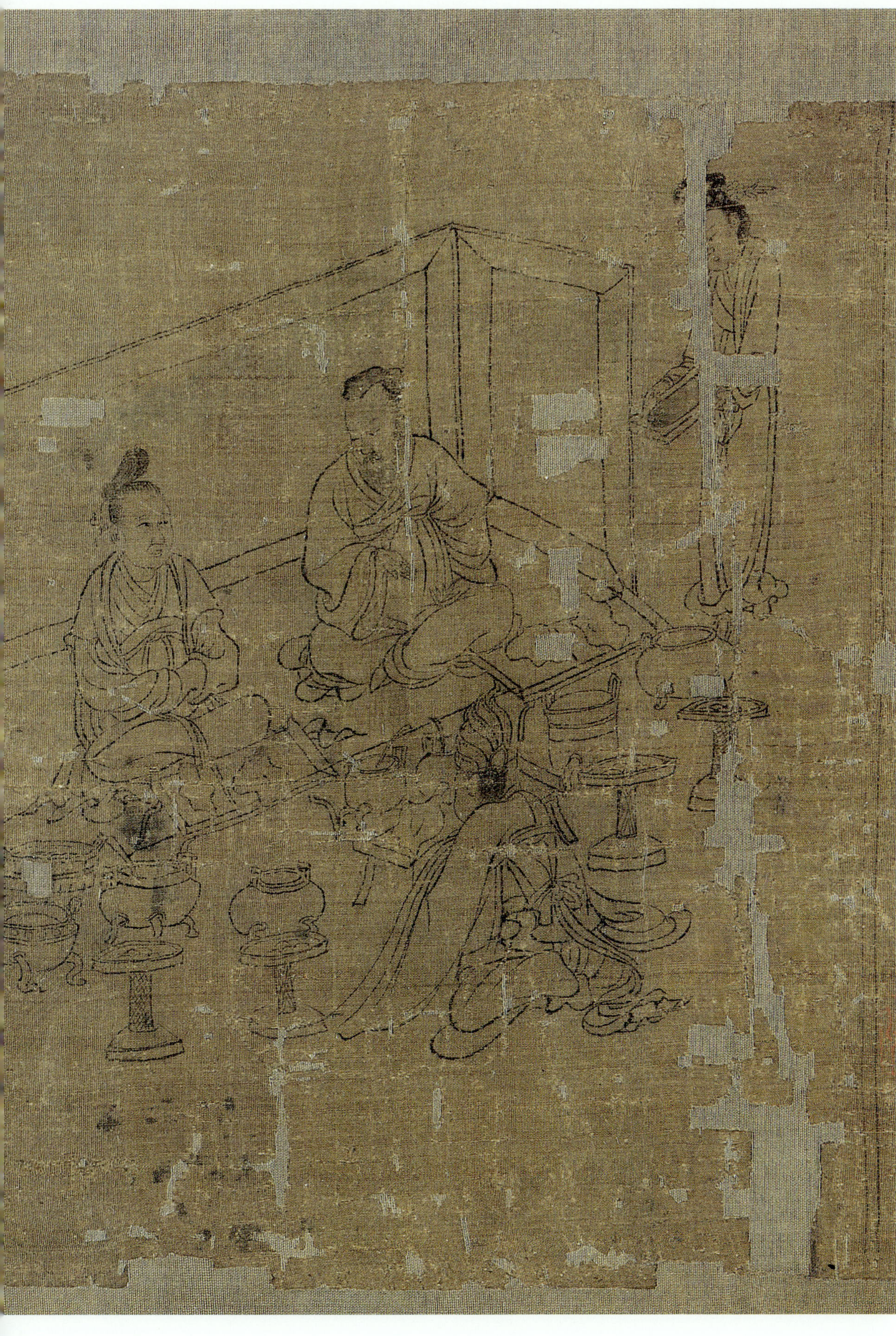

Plate 3. Li Kung-lin, chapter 5 of the *Classic of Filial Piety*

CHAPTER 6
Filial Piety in the Common People

They follow the course of heaven, and distinguish the advantages of the soil; they are careful of their conduct, and economical in their expenditure—all in order to nourish their parents. This is the filial piety of the common people. In this way, from the Son of Heaven down to the common people, there has never been one whose filial piety was without its beginning or its end upon whom calamity did not fall.[29]

Li Kung-lin's original illustration for this chapter is lost, and we again refer instead to the careful copy preserved in Taipei (fig. 44). The chapter on the filiality of the common people, as befits their position in traditional Chinese society, is the briefest in the classic, composed basically of only one sentence (the last sentence in the translation above is actually a summation of the import of the first six chapters). The view put forth in the *Classic of Filial Piety* on the responsibilities of the common people is the self-serving product of a hereditary aristocracy.

In his paintings, Li consistently presents a sympathetic perspective on peasant life. As far as we know, he did not endanger his own welfare to help them toward better conditions, and as a great landowner himself it was in his own interest to have a happy and contented peasantry. Nevertheless, his art seems to suggest that he sympathized with the many who suffered at the hands of those who enjoyed power and wealth, depicting them as victims, as beggars, cripples, and orphans—all at the mercy of the predatory and the arrogant.

Here, in a composition of three tiers or registers, Li illustrates—from top to bottom—plowing, harvesting, and looking after the parents. The stream between the low banks that winds through the middle of the composition continues into and through the following composition, illustrating chapter 7. The two illustrations appear to function as an extended, almost musical vision of a harmonious society, in which all classes live in peace and are mutually governed by filial respect and courtesy.

Because in this copy of the composition all nuance of expression and gesture is lost, we can only imagine from the illustrations to the other chapters the sensitivity with which the painter portrayed the peasants. In all likelihood, he portrayed them exactly as he did the family of the lesser officials—the class to which he himself belonged. These peasants are poor, and they dress more simply than their wealthier landlords, but the vignette is not very different from the intimate family scene that illustrates chapter 5. A nice contrast can be drawn between this Sung image of an extended family of three generations and the image introduced by Ku K'ai-chih (fig. 43). One obvious difference is that Li's peasant family is shown first plowing, then harvesting the fields, and only then enjoying the

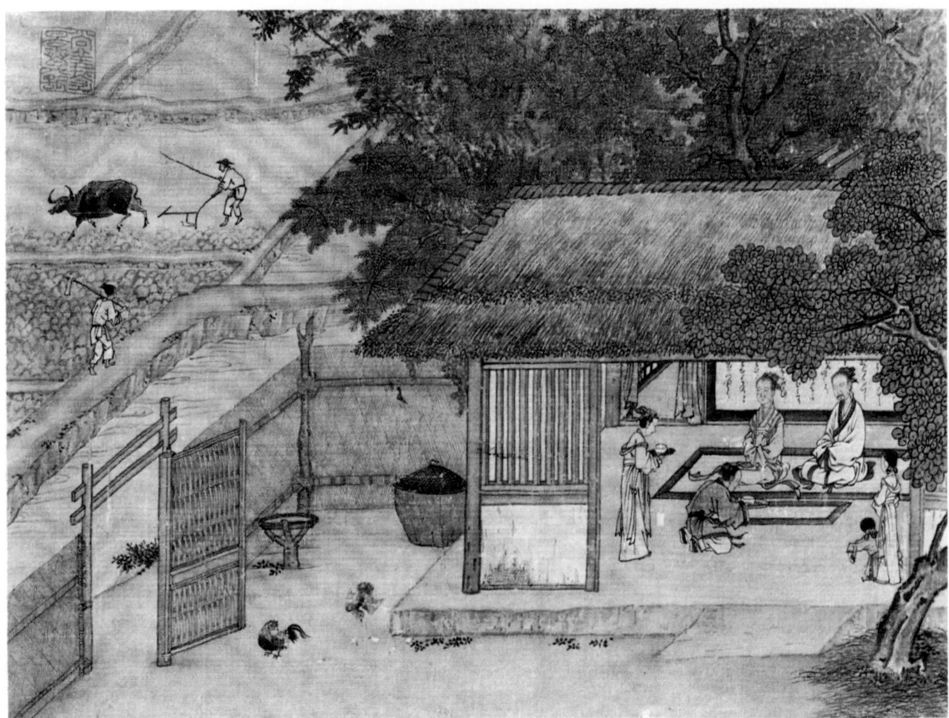

Figure 44. Unidentified artist (14th century?), after Li Kung-lin, chapter 6 of the *Classic of Filial Piety*. Handscroll, ink on paper, 8 1/16 × 276 3/8 in. (20.5 × 702.1 cm). National Palace Museum, Taipei

fruits of its labor, whereas Ku's scene shows only an aristocratic family enjoying the leisure of its wealth and power. Li Kung-lin was himself a careful, hard-working craftsman whose calligraphy and painting both reflect a disciplined and deliberate process of labor. We can at least imagine that he was sensitive to the reality of work and to the direct connection between labor and its reward.

What is clear is that Li was highly sympathetic to people as individuals rather than as groups. Not only do we see this sensitivity in his art, but we are told of it by his contemporaries. Often he would paint informal portraits of his friends that were so lifelike they would be used as substitutes for those friends when they could not themselves be present; and he was so attentive to nuances of class, region, personality, and even accent that his admirers could identify those characteristics from his paintings. Even horses, as was observed earlier, were regarded by Li as individuals.[30]

This sensitive appreciation of the individual personality was essential to the philosophy of art then taking form within the circles frequented by Li Kung-lin. Traditionally, art had served the will of the rulers by illustrating for the people the evils to be avoided and the good toward which to strive. It had that function still for Li Kung-lin in the *Classic of Filial Piety*, yet the entire spirit of the scroll is conveyed by nuances of individual character and by the human interaction within families, society, and the imperial court. The belief that the art of painting had the capacity to convey the individual "heart-print" (*hsin-yin*), or mind, was the central tenet of the theory of literati painting (*wen-jen-hua*) then taking shape within the brilliant coterie of scholars, philosophers, poets, calligraphers, and painters to which Li Kung-lin belonged. With this theory, Li and his friends claimed that painting should be invested with the same expressive capacity held by the sister arts of poetry and calligraphy. It was this theory that formed the basis of the later history of Chinese art. Li Kung-lin's *Classic of Filial Piety* was one of the first works of art to attempt the difficult task of giving human shape and reality to the traditional didactic texts, and the painstaking care given to nuances of human character is one of the essential ways that Li reveals his intentions. Another, of course, is the slow, natural, and spontaneous way he painted the entire scroll, creating an effect not at all like an official delivering a public speech, but rather like an old friend with whom one is having a quiet conversation on a subject of common concern.

Spontaneity, informality, and absence of pretension are a few of the features among the many that distinguished the new scholarly elite from the old aristocracy. Once all people were seen to have the capacity to achieve merit through talent, intelligence, and discipline—and to have no particular birthright of position or privilege—every individual was seen to have the same value, and all were deemed to be equally precious. We can thus view the present painting as a pictorial exploration of the human tensions and realities within a society still struggling to find a balance between established powers and new ideals.

CHAPTER 7
Filial Piety in Relation to the Three Powers

Tseng-tzu said, "Immense indeed is the greatness of filial piety!" The Master replied, "Yes, filial piety is the constant pattern of heaven, the righteousness of earth, and the duty of man. Heaven and earth inevitably pursue their course, and the people take it as their pattern. The ancient kings imitated the brilliant luminaries of heaven, and acted in accordance with the advantages afforded by the earth, and were thus in accord with all under heaven. Consequently, their teachings were successful without being severe, and their government secured perfect order without being repressive. The ancient kings, seeing how their teachings could transform the people, set before them therefore an example of the most extended love, and none of the people neglected their parents; they set forth to them the example of virtue and righteousness, and the people roused themselves to the practice of them; they went before them with reverence and yielding courtesy, and the people had no contentions; they led them by the rules of propriety and by music, and the people were harmonious and benign; they showed them what they liked and disliked, and the people understood their prohibitions. It is said in the Book of Songs:

> *Awe-inspiring are you, O Grand Master Yin,*
> *And all of the people look up to you."*[31]

In the center foreground of Li Kung-lin's composition for chapter 7 (pl. 4), a young boy listens respectfully to an old man who leans on a staff. Gesturing with his left hand, the old man appears to be instructing the boy, in illustration of the sentence "They set forth to them the example of virtue and righteousness, and the people roused themselves to the practice of them." In the lower right corner a plump, round-faced young man bows to an older man and a woman, as if about to depart on the horse being held for him nearby. The older couple must represent the parents of the young man, referring to the sentence "The ancient kings . . . set before them . . . an example of the most extended love, and none of the people neglected their parents." At the left, two friends meet and bow in greeting. One holds out his hand, inviting the other to pass, in illustration of the passage "They went before them with reverence and yielding courtesy, and the people had no contentions." In the upper left, on the opposite bank of the stream that divides the composition, a man lies sleeping, his shirt dropped carelessly beside him. A passerby, cold and shivering, dressed only in a loincloth, looks longingly down at the shirt that could warm his body. He walks on, however, resisting the temptation to pick it up. This incident illustrates the passage "They showed them what they liked and disliked, and the people understood their prohibitions." According to the text, "The ancient kings . . . led them by the

Overleaf
Plate 4. Li Kung-lin, chapter 7 of the *Classic of Filial Piety*

曾子曰甚哉孝之大也子曰夫孝天之經也地之義
民之行也天地之經而民是則之則天之明因地之利以
順天下是以其教不肅而成其政不嚴而治先王見
教之可以化民是故先之以博愛而民莫遺其親陳之以德
義而民興行先之以敬讓而民不爭導之以禮樂而民和
睦示之以好惡而民知禁詩云赫赫師尹民具爾瞻

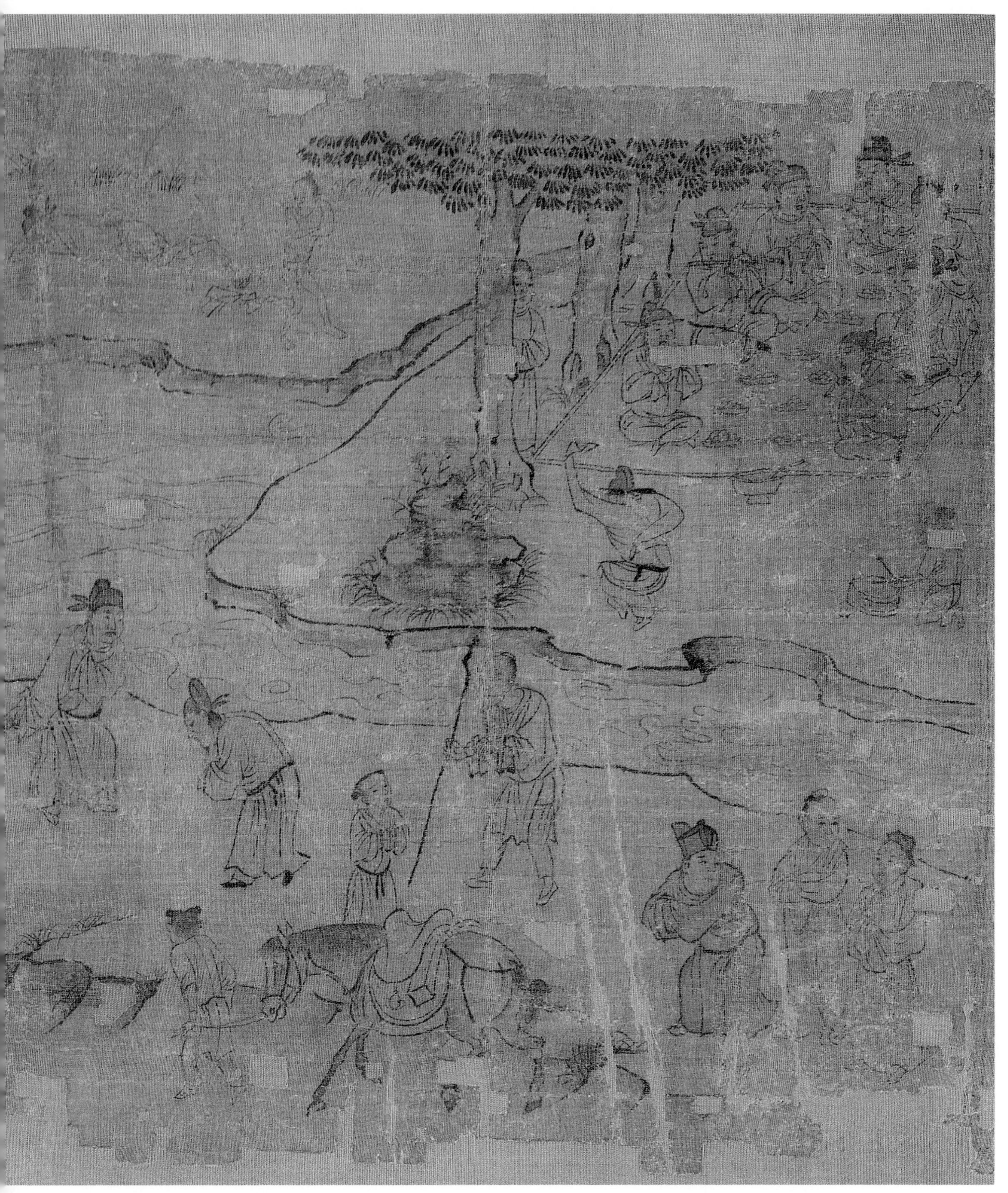

rules of propriety and by music, and the people were harmonious and benign." Accompanying these vignettes of a harmonious and peaceful populace is a group of musicians in the upper right. Seven men sit cross-legged beneath the trees; one plays a drum, one a flute, and another perhaps a set of clappers. At least one of the others appears to be singing. In front of them are a dancer and another drummer, the latter a curiously wizened-looking young boy. An onlooker stands partly hidden behind the nearest tree. And squarely in the center of the composition is a striking garden rock of the variety beloved of scholars. Thus, the painter illustrates literally each of the five sentences constituting the central paragraph of the chapter.

Throughout this unusually elaborate composition—which includes twenty human figures as well as a horse and a fairly elaborate landscape setting—Li Kung-lin's attention to nuances of figural gesture, expression, and interaction is remarkable. Especially in the foreground groups, where he depicts the human encounters and interactions he so delights in, we see a wide range of types, ages, and personalities, vividly portrayed with warmth and sensitivity. In the expression and bearing of the young boy who looks up at the venerable teacher, in the two friends who bow in greeting, and especially in the portraitlike group of three figures at the lower right, there would seem to be embodied memories of the actual people to whom his painting must be dedicated.

What seems most noteworthy, perhaps, is the fact that the composition has no traditional structure. That is, we cannot read it hieratically, or for its order or its symbolic message. Except, of course, that being without such order, it assumes a quite specific meaning. The elements of the composition are random, spread across the silk almost like chance encounters and connected somehow by the universal influence of filial piety, which is like the stream that wanders through, joining this to the preceding illustration. We are reminded of the lesson of Li Kung-lin's *Imperial Horses at Pasture*, that only the absence of overt control allows attainment of the natural Way. Principles are in operation, but they are unseen and unobtrusive.

CHAPTER 8
Filial Piety in Government

The Master said, "In former times, when the intelligent kings by means of filial piety ruled all under heaven, they did not dare to receive with disrespect the ministers even of small states. How much less would they have dared with dukes, marquises, counts, and barons! Thus it was that they got the myriad states to serve with joyful hearts their royal ancestors.

"The rulers of states did not dare to slight wifeless men and widows. How much less would they slight their officers and subjects! Thus it was that they got all the people to serve with joyful hearts the rulers, their predecessors.

"The heads of clans did not dare to slight their servants and concubines. How much less would they slight their wives and sons! Thus it was that they got the men in the service of their parents with joyful hearts.

"In such a state of things, the parents, while alive, reposed in their songs; and when sacrificed to, their disembodied spirits enjoyed the offerings made to them. Thus, everywhere under heaven, peace and harmony prevailed; disaster and calamities did not occur; misfortunes and rebellions did not arise. It is said in the Book of Songs:

To upright and virtuous conduct
In all the four quarters of the state,
render obedient homage."[32]

It is interesting that Li Kung-lin, with his dislike of coercion, force, and the abuses of power, chose to illustrate the passage about the unwillingness of rulers to slight widows and widowers, let alone their officers and subjects (pl. 5). Apparently he recalled, or invented, a symbolic occasion at which the emperor displayed his attentiveness to the common people by greeting a delegation from their ranks before his majestic palace. In front of him, then, in this imaginary ritual, are three stooped widows, two elderly widowers, and two children who must be orphans. Watched ominously by armed bailiffs, they are paraded before the emperor, who will most likely bestow some blessing or reward upon them. Arrayed beside and behind the ruler are his keen-eyed and attentive corps of elite officials, who look intently upon the ritual ceremony enacted before them.

The painter again isolates the common people from the majesty and power of the small minority who rule their every action. Especially telling is the young official to the ruler's left, who stands with a whip coiled at the ready over his forearm.

As we have seen him do before, Li deliberately chooses to show us the common people as they are herded and paraded, guarded against, looked upon with fear,

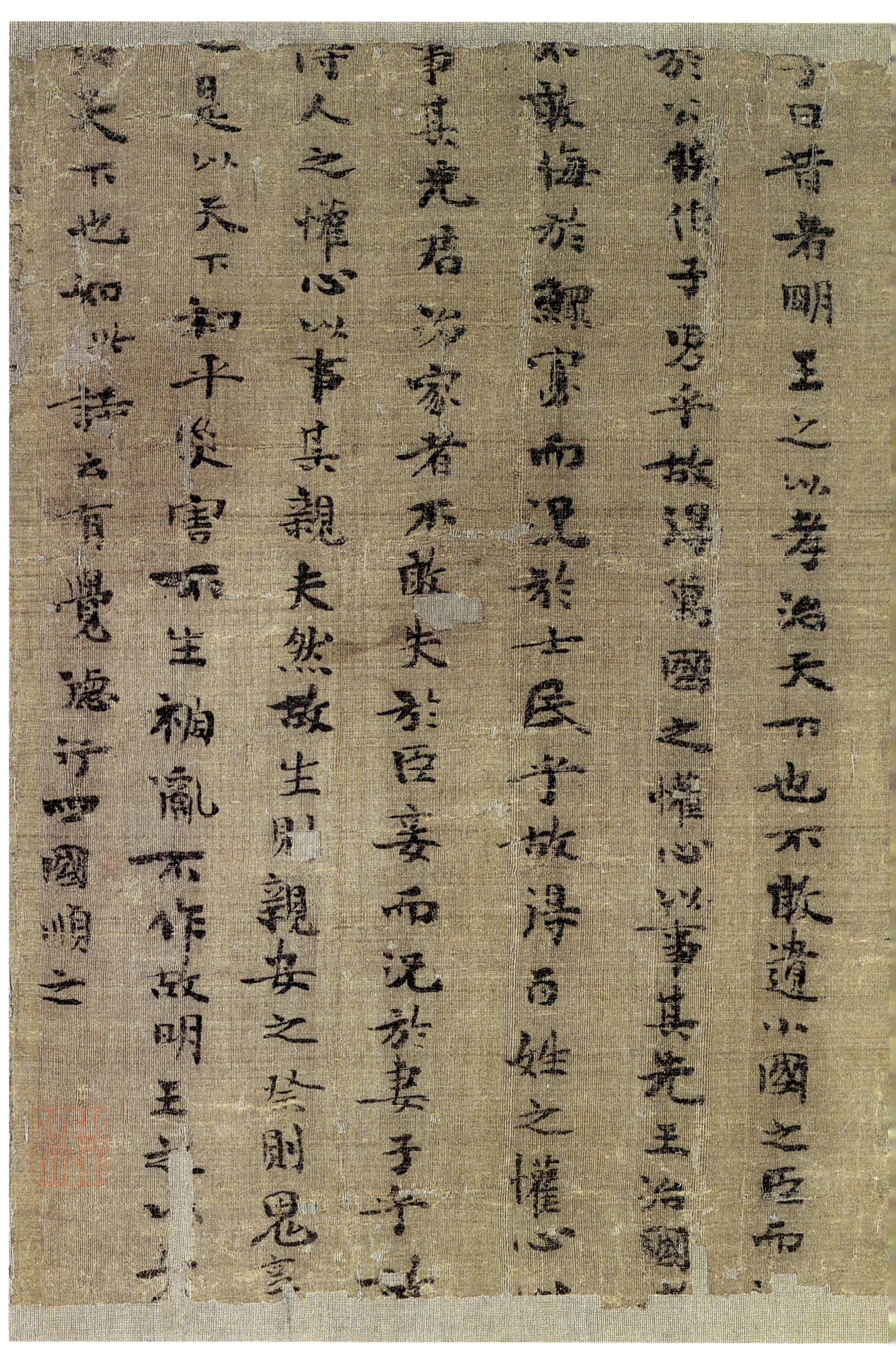

Plate 5. Li Kung-lin, chapter 8 of the *Classic of Filial Piety*

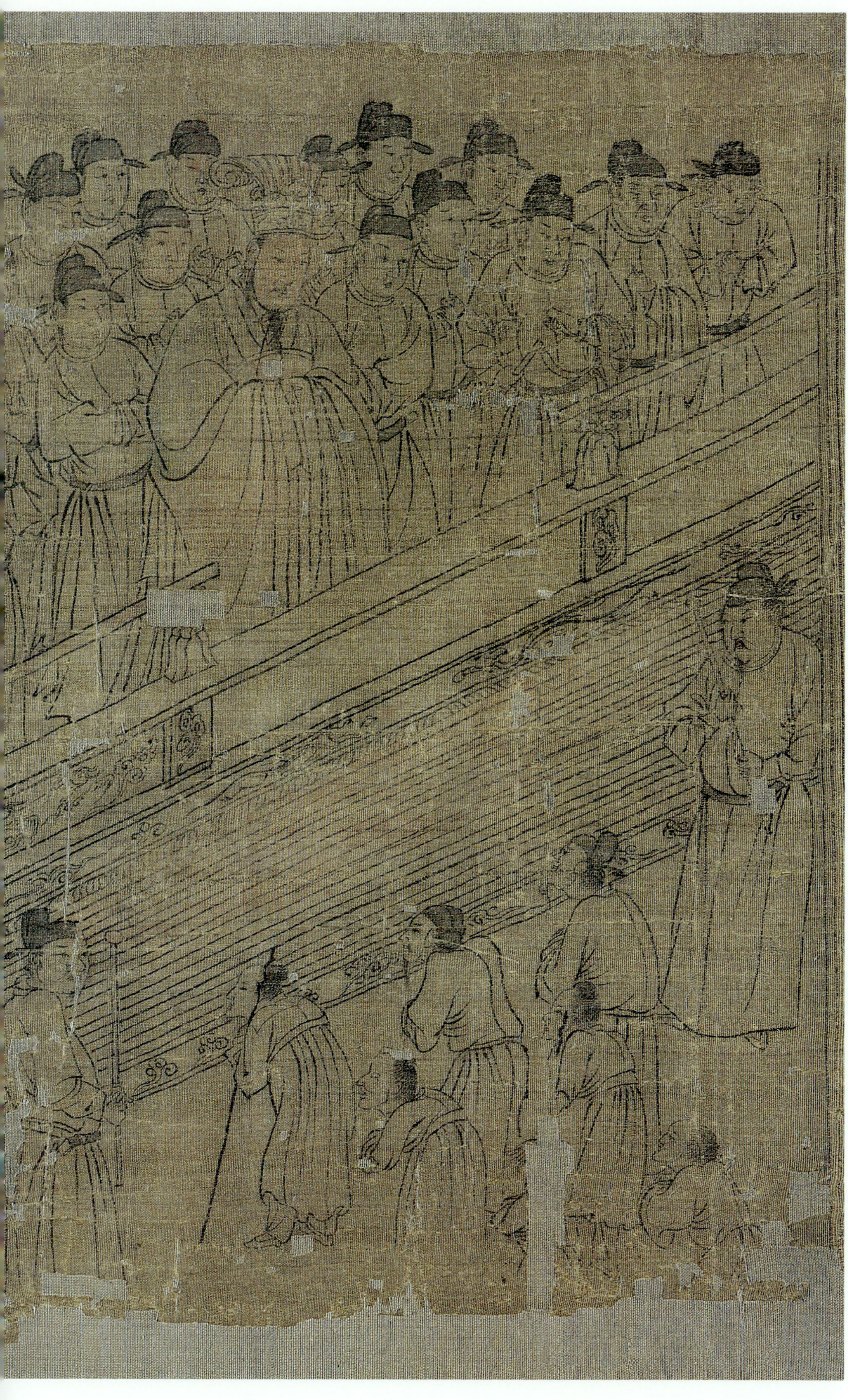

and kept at a distance from those who hold power. He did not have to illustrate such a confrontation; many other options were available to him. But he chooses once again to comment on the life of his own time by showing us the lives of those people made helpless in the face of power.

CHAPTER 9
The Government of the Sages

Tseng-tzu said, "I venture to ask whether in the virtues of the sages there was not something greater than filial piety." The Master replied, "Of all the living natures produced by heaven and earth, man is the noblest. Of all the actions of man, there is none greater than filial piety. In filial piety there is nothing greater than the reverential awe of one's father. In the reverential awe shown to one's father there is nothing greater than making him the companion of heaven. The duke of Chou was the man who first did this. Formerly, at the border altar, the duke of Chou sacrificed to Hou-chi as the companion of heaven, and in the Bright Hall he honored King Wen, and sacrificed to him as the companion of God. As a consequence, all of the princes within the Four Seas came to offer assistance in the performance of the sacrifices. In the virtue of the sages, what is there greater than filial piety? Now, the feelings of affection grow at the parents' knees, and as the nourishing of the parents is practiced those affections merge into awe. The sages proceeded from awe to reverence, and from affection to love. The teachings of the sages, without being severe, were successful, and their government, without being rigorous, was effective. What they proceeded from was the root of filial piety. The relationship and duties between father and son are of heaven-sent nature, and hold the principle of righteousness between ruler and subject. The son derives his life from his parents, and no greater gift can be transmitted. Ruler and parent in one, his father deals with him accordingly, and there is no generosity greater than this. Therefore, he who does not love his parents, but instead loves other men, is called a rebel against virtue. He who does not revere his parents, but reveres instead other men, is called a rebel against propriety. When a ruler himself thus acts contrary to that which should place him in accord with all men, he presents nothing for the people to imitate. He has nothing to do with what is good, but entirely and only with what is injurious to virtue. Though he may succeed, the superior man does not give him approval. It is not so with the superior man. He speaks, having thought whether the words should be spoken; he acts, having thought whether his actions are certain to give pleasure. His virtue and righteousness are such as will be honored; what he initiates and carries out is fit to be imitated; his deportment is worthy of contemplation; his movements in advancing or retiring are all according to the proper rule. In this way does he present himself to the people, who both revere and love him, imitate and become like him. Thus he is able to make his teaching of virtue successful, and his government and orders to be carried into effect. It is said in the Book of Songs:

> *The virtuous man, the princely one,*
> *Has no flaw in his deportment."*[33]

Overleaf
Plate 6. Li Kung-lin, chapter 9 of the *Classic of Filial Piety*

曾子曰敢問聖人之德無以加於孝乎子曰天地之
性人為貴人之行莫大於孝孝莫大於嚴父嚴父莫大
配天則周公其人也昔者周公郊祀后稷以配天宗祀
文王於明堂以配上帝是以四海之内各以其職來祭夫聖
人之德又何以加於孝乎故親生之膝下以養父母日嚴聖人
因嚴以教敬因親以教愛聖人之教不肅而成其政不嚴
而治其所因者本也父子之道天性也君臣之義也父母
生之續莫大焉君親臨之厚莫重焉故不愛其親而
愛他人者謂之悖德不敬其親而敬他人者謂之悖禮
以順則逆民無則焉不在於善而皆在於凶德雖得之
君子不貴也君子則不然言思可道行思可樂德義可
尊作事可法容止可觀進退可度以臨其民是以
其民畏而愛之則而象之故能成其德教而行其政令
詩云淑人君子其儀不忒

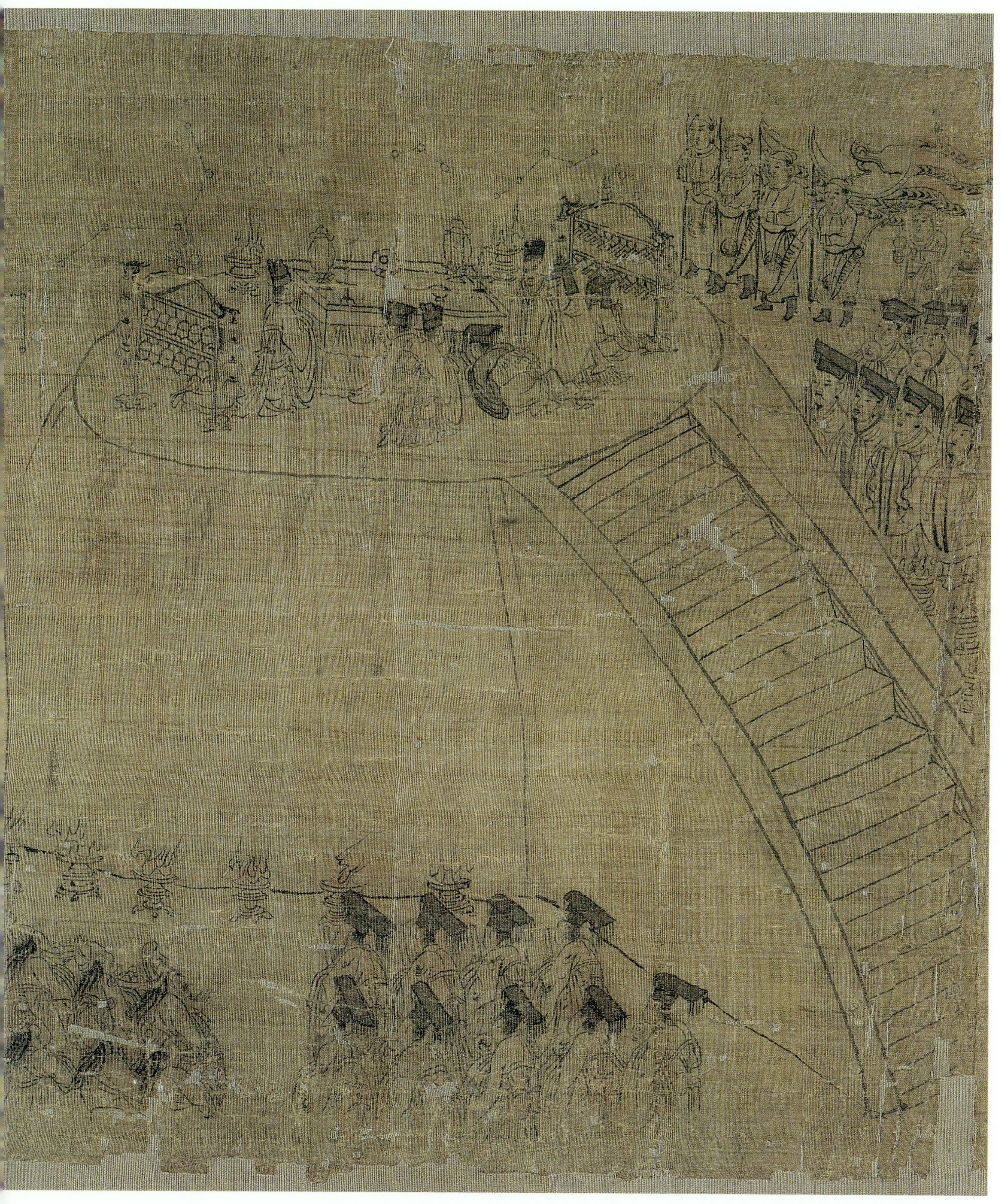

This unusually long chapter propounds the argument that within the operation of the ideal of filial piety, which is the supreme action of mankind, the ultimate possibility is to elevate the object of one's reverential, filial awe to the position of companion, coadjutor, or correlate (*p'ei*) of heaven. According to Confucian tradition, the creator of this practice was the duke of Chou, who first offered sacrifice to Hou-chi, and thus made him companion to heaven. Hou-chi was the original ancestor of the Chou rulers, and also the mythical inventor of agriculture. By elevating his ancestor to the position of a companion of God, the duke of Chou made his ancestor into the equivalent of a god. It is clear that the sponsors of the original text wished all of those who served them to elevate them to the position of a god through ceaseless, selfless service and sacrifice.

Whatever his view of this argument may have been, Li Kung-lin chose to illustrate the sacrifice to Hou-chi by the duke of Chou. Imperial sacrifice was a continuing issue, even in Li Kung-lin's time, and the nature and point of the sacrifice were always being debated. It is impossible to know, however, the reaction to this particular illustration by proponents of the various points of view discussed at the time.

The text of the *Classic of Filial Piety* was the product of several very different ages and political systems. Certainly it was not written by Confucius but constructed by members of successive systems of self-interest to serve their own purposes. The first six chapters were evidently written during a period when the hereditary aristocracy vigorously controlled Chinese society and could still promote a fictitious text with sufficient authority to ensure its acceptance. What they promoted, of course, was the view that members of the hereditary aristocracy were the natural, heaven-mandated rulers of the world and that all others had their respective inferior places within this well-ordered society. The later chapters, however, were added by later interest-systems, in an attempt to validate other priorities. By the time chapter 9 was somehow added to the first six chapters and whatever else may have been appended to them then (and it is impossible at present to know how the entire text was put together and over what expanse of time), the purpose was simply to perpetuate the social structure that kept the mass of the population in a state of happy servitude, so eager to serve their masters that they could take it on faith that their supreme goal in life was to elevate to the position of a god their own supreme ancestors by never ceasing to serve them, even long after their deaths.

In the illustration (pl. 6), the duke of Chou is shown at the top of a long stairway on the southern altar, bowing before a table on which are placed several ritual objects. With the duke are five attendants. At the right and left, two musicians kneel before their bells. Two fires burn in pots behind the table, and other pots are placed around the mound-shaped altar. In the sky are cosmic symbols. And around the altar are arrayed the princes of state who have come to assist in the sacrifice, flag-bearing soldiers, and a group of non-Chinese worshipers.

The story of Hou-chi's miraculous birth and life is the subject of a long poem in the *Classic of Poetry*. Another ode, one of the sacrificial chants of the Chou state, records the words to be spoken at the sacrifice, the scene that is illustrated:

> *Mighty are you, Houji,*
> *Full partner in heaven's power.*
> *That we, the thronging peoples,*
> *were raised up is all your doing.*
> *You gave us wheat and barley*
> *In obedience to God's command.*
> *Not to this limit only or to that frontier,*
> *But near, far, and forever throughout*
> *these lands of Hsia.*[34]

Li Kung-lin's conception of the border altar is a primitive one. The mound seems to be no more than piled earth, against which a long flight of stairs has been constructed; a single table with a few plain implements suffices for the ritual. Whatever the contemporary concerns and implications of imperial sacrifice may have been—and the one certainty is that these were highly charged, vitally important political issues—what Li seems to be asserting is a spirit of sacrifice from a time and a place long past. A pile of dirt and a few stepladders were already far removed from the altars of the Sung dynasty, which probably more closely resembled the present-day Temple and Altar of Heaven in Beijing. As in so much that he did, the artist appears to be rejecting the corrupt, dubious present in favor of a simpler, more honest, less complicated, and more attractive mythical past. Li's almost mystical belief in his own personal understanding of that remote past is a touching element in his biography, and is surely lodged as well in these illustrations of a nonexistent world.

CHAPTER 10

An Orderly Description of the Acts of Filial Piety

The Master said, "The service which a son renders to his parents is as follows. In his general conduct toward them he manifests the utmost reverence. In his nourishing of them, his endeavor is to give them the utmost pleasure. When they are ill, he feels the greatest anxiety. In mourning for them, he exhibits every manifestation of grief. In sacrificing to them, he displays the utmost solemnity. When a son is complete in these five things, he is able to serve his parents. He who thus serves his parents, in a high situation, will be free from pride; in a low situation, will be free from insubordination; and, among his equals, will not be quarrelsome. In a high situation pride leads to ruin; in a low situation insubordination leads to punishment; among equals quarrelsomeness leads to the wielding of weapons. If those three things be not put away, even though a son every day contribute beef, mutton, and pork to nourish his parents, he is not filial."[35]

Li Kung-lin in chapter 10 illustrates the sentence "In his nourishing of them, his endeavor is to give them the utmost pleasure" (pl. 7). Seated in armchairs on a raised platform, an elderly couple watches the entertainment that has been prepared for them by their children. The entertainers consist of a magician, a woman—perhaps the magician's wife—who accompanies him on a drum, and a dancer. Between them are seated the two young grandchildren of the old couple. From the right, their son and daughter-in-law approach, bearing trays of refreshment. The attention of the adults, however, is fixed on the tiny bird that flies from the cone held out by the magician. The grandmother appears to have started in surprise, her mouth slightly open in a faintly alarmed gasp. The more phlegmatic grandfather smiles gently. Their son and his wife, momentarily forgetting the trays they carry, watch the entertainment as well. The young grandchildren, seated with the entertainers, are also caught up in the excitement: the girl, seated to the left, holds tightly to the hand of her bare-bottomed baby brother and leans intently toward the drummer.

The entire scene is characterized by a wonderful warmth and intimacy, an intimacy reflected in the composition, a loose circle around which the figures are arrayed. Two vases of flowering plants placed in the center of the circle provide a superb touch of artistry. The plants are a study in contrast. In the larger, heavier arrangement to the left, the flowers and leaves are done entirely in outline. In the elegant, slender group to the right, each leaf is rendered in a soft, sure impression of the full brush tip. But, as always, it is in the characterization of the figures that Li is most persuasive. The gentleness with which the old couple is portrayed and their obvious pleasure at the entertainment provided by their children speak more clearly than could any words of the spirit of filial piety and its ideal purpose.

A possible iconographic parallel to Li's illustration might be found in the popular story of one of the paragons of filial piety, Lao Lai-tzu. As a middle-aged man, Lao played the role of a young boy—dressing like a child and pretending to trip and fall down—so that his parents would not realize they were growing old. Presumably, Li's illustration evoked echoes of Lao and his childlike entertainments.[36]

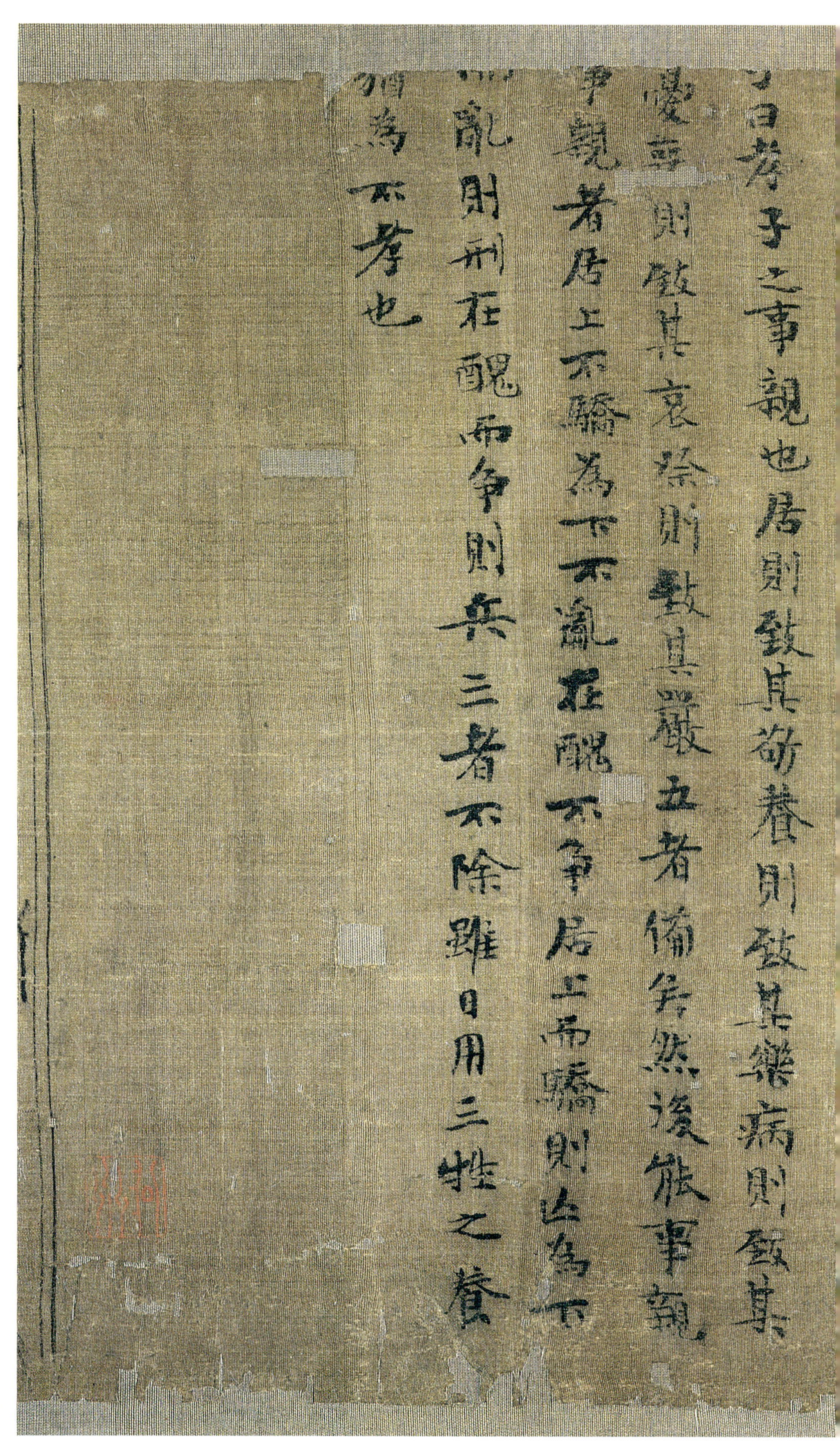

Plate 7. Li Kung-lin, chapter 10 of the *Classic of Filial Piety*

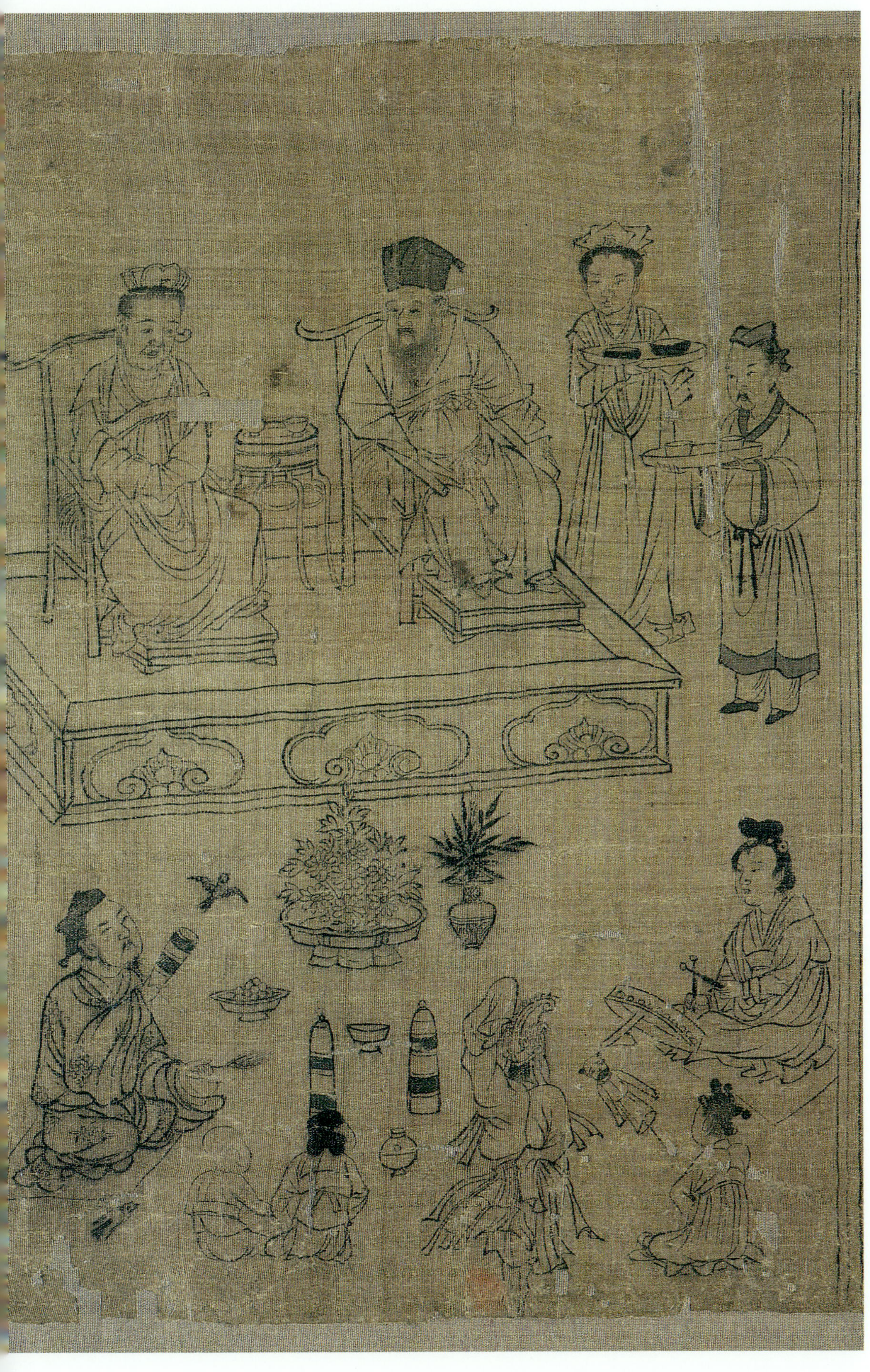

CHAPTER 11
Filial Piety in Relation to the Five Punishments

The Master said, "There are three thousand offenses against which the five punishments are directed, and there is not one of them greater than being unfilial. When constraint is put upon a ruler, that is the disowning of his superiority. When the authority of the sages is disallowed, that is the disowning of law. When filial piety is put aside, that is the disowning of the principle of affection. This paves the way to anarchy."[37]

The illustration for this chapter is out of place. It would seem that Li Kung-lin mistakenly reversed the positions of the illustrations for chapters 11 and 14, so that his depiction of chapter 14 appears with the text of chapter 11 and vice versa. In the illustration of the impartial operation of justice and punishment (pl. 11), a magistrate sits at a small table on the raised open porch of an official building, judging a criminal case. Three officials stand behind him, and a fourth, to the left, holds a scroll on which, presumably, the particulars of the case being heard are written. Immediately below, it appears that two men and a woman are presenting testimony on the crime for which one or more of them is being tried. A fourth man, evidently distraught, is closely restrained by two constables. A vehement argument is taking place.

In the lower right, meanwhile, the guilty parties in the previous case are being led away by two other constables or bailiffs. The man is pilloried, his wrists manacled, and he is pulled at roughly by a tall, stick-bearing constable. Behind him, his wife is treated only slightly less severely. A constable pulls her along by the hair with his right hand, while in his left hand he holds a coiled whip. She wrings her hands in distress. The artist makes no effort to gloss over the unpleasantness of the situation.

Compositionally, this is among the more interesting and ambiguous of the illustrations. Dividing the fifteen figures into three groups and distributing them fairly widely over the picture plane, Li avoids the impression of an overwhelming force acting against specific individuals. Authority is typically shown in an elevated position in Li's compositions, as is the local magistrate here. Only three assistants stand behind him, however, and the four constables below are busy with their duties. One hearing has concluded, and another is well under way. The composition, in other words, creates in an orderly and impartial manner the impression of an ongoing process. The natural functioning of justice is thus depicted as unmediated and inevitable, the legal system in its ideal condition.

What is especially interesting about this relationship between subject, composition, and probable meaning is its very close similarity to another key chapter of the text, chapter 15 (pl. 12), which focuses on the necessity for honest, unhin-

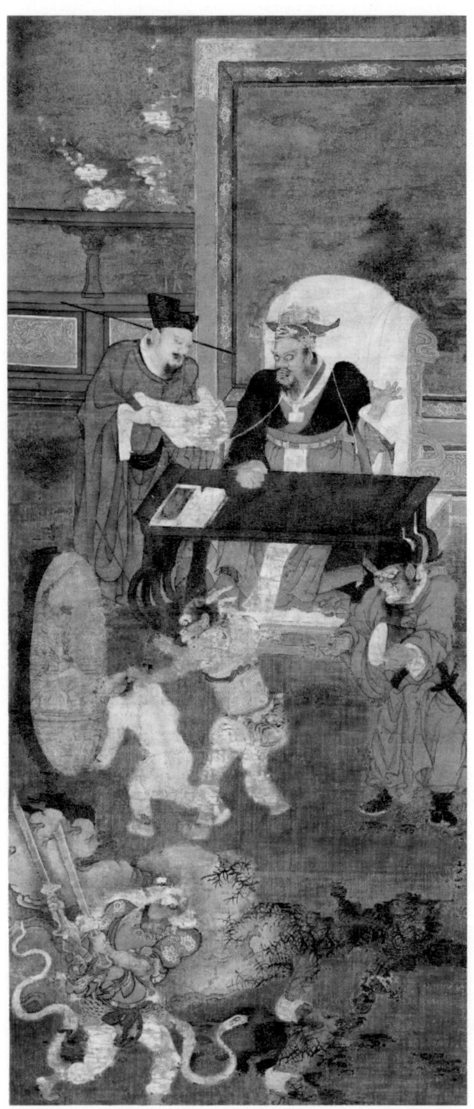

Figure 45. Chin Ch'u-shih (late 12th century), "The Fifth King, Yama," from *Ten Kings of Hell*, before 1195. One of a set of ten hanging scrolls, ink and color on silk, 44 × 18¾ in. (111.8 × 47.6 cm). The Metropolitan Museum of Art, New York. Rogers Fund, 1930 (30.76.293)

dered remonstrance in the functioning of imperial society. Just criticism and just punishment would thus seem to be two of Li Kung-lin's essential prescriptions for a humane state based on the principles of filiality.

Li's duties as a local official would certainly have provided for him a rich experience in precisely such activities as are taking place in his illustration. No doubt, he sat more than once in the position of the presiding magistrate and dispensed local justice. We may presume that here, as elsewhere, he was reflecting upon the experiences of his own life as he sought to give contemporary shape to the words of an ancient text.

In Li's time, there was current a very vivid imagery of criminal trials, one Li certainly knew very well. Paintings of the Ten Kings of Hell (fig. 45) functioned at the popular level to instruct the people in the punishments that awaited criminals in the next world.[38] Compared with such violent and bloody scenes of terror, Li's criminal hearing epitomizes restraint and humaneness in the administration of justice.

Plate 8. Li Kung-lin, chapter 11 of the *Classic of Filial Piety*

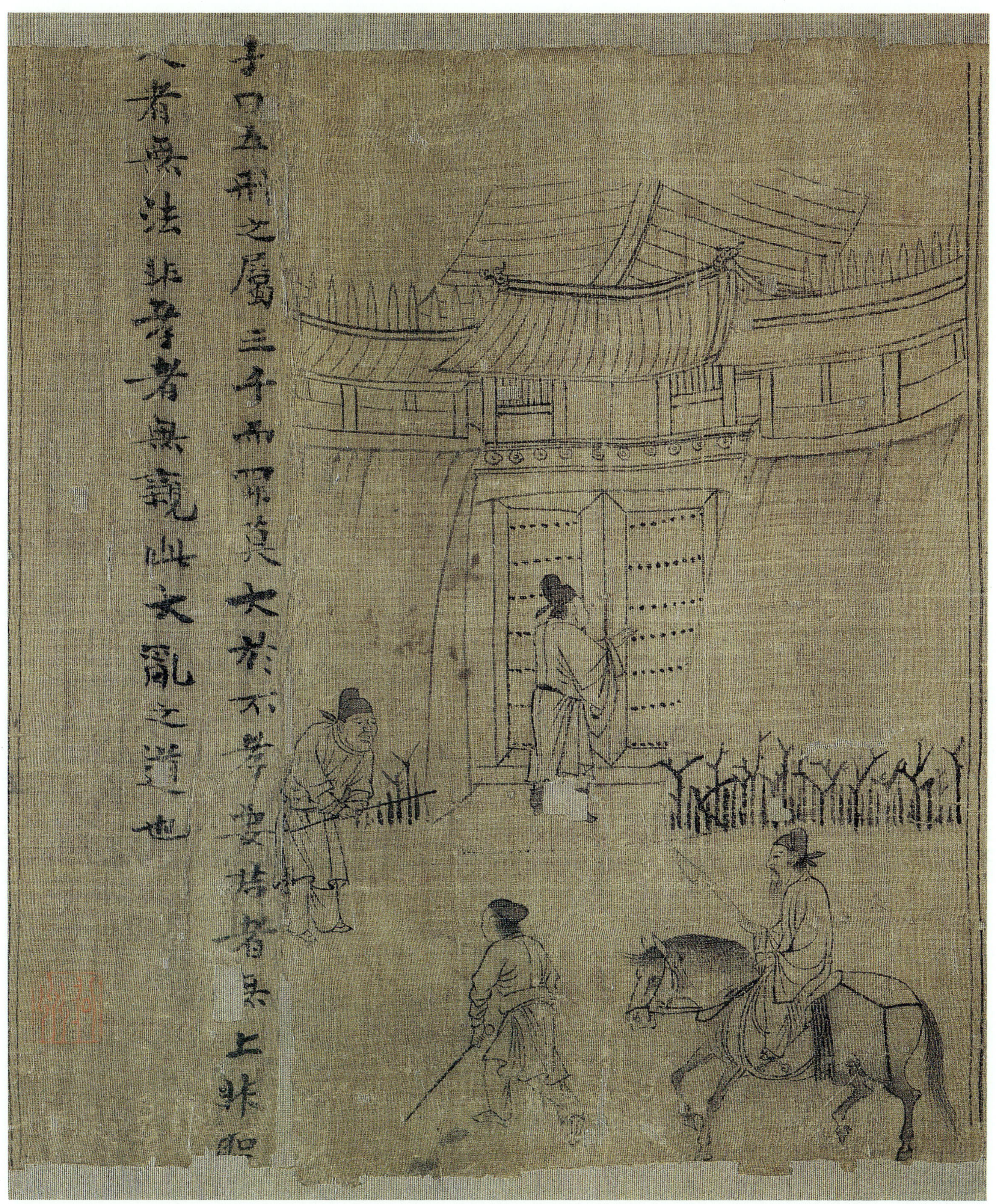
子曰五刑之屬三千而罪莫大於不孝要君者無上非
人者無法非孝者無親此大亂之道也

The fact that the illustration for this chapter is out of place may suggest certain assumptions about the making of the scroll. What evidently happened is that the artist first made all the paintings, beginning with the illustration for chapter 1 and proceeding with the following illustrations one by one. He did this quite spontaneously, almost as if he were making a series of sketches for paintings. On both sides of each picture he drew in double or triple lines, like a simple frame, leaving room to the left for the text. It is clear that the texts were not written while the paintings were being done, because there is very little correspondence between the length of the text and the width of the space left for it. Only after the paintings were finished, therefore, did Li write in the text beside each illustration. Apparently, even though, like every schoolboy in China, he had memorized the entire text, he seems to have mistakenly reversed the illustrations for chapters 11 and 14. Later, when he inscribed the texts, he simply corrected his mistake by writing the appropriate, correct text beside each picture. That he left them reversed, without any note or other indication that he had done so (the original silk is so damaged and broken that, in fact, we cannot be quite certain that there was never such a notation), may further support the view that this was not the finished version, or form, of the painting. That is, Li may have believed that another painting—or printed reproduction—was going to replace this one and that his mistake would easily be corrected at the next stage.

CHAPTER 12
Amplification of "The All-Embracing Rule of Conduct" in Chapter 1

The Master said, "For teaching the people to be affectionate and loving there is nothing better than filial piety. For teaching them propriety and submissiveness there is nothing better than fraternal duty. For changing their manners and altering their customs there is nothing better than music. For securing the repose of superiors and the good order of the people there is nothing better than propriety. Propriety is simply respect. Therefore, the respect paid to one's father pleases all sons; the respect paid to one's elder brother pleases all younger sons; the respect paid to one's ruler pleases all subjects. The respect paid to one man pleases thousands and myriads of men. The respect is paid to a few and the pleasure extends to many—this is what is meant by the Essential Way."[39]

Once again, Li Kung-lin surprises us with his choice of subject. For chapter 12, on the "Essential Way" (*yao-tao*), two men so close in age and in appearance they can only be brothers are depicted in a garden setting (pl. 9). The younger of the two bows deeply to his older brother, who slowly returns the gesture of respect. Two younger friends or disciples stand behind the older of the brothers. Beyond them geese and reeds are seen on an island in a pond, while the two main figures are echoed by a dramatic Lake T'ai garden rock with bamboo growing thickly behind it. There is in the painting a vivid sense of contemporary life, and there can be little doubt that Li is conveying his thoughts in the form of representations of people of his own time.

The two most famous brothers in Li's lifetime were Su Shih (1037–1101) and Su Ch'e (1039–1112), both of whom were close friends of the painter. Portraits of Su Shih and other informal representations of him by members of Li Kung-lin's circle (fig. 46) make clear that he is the subject of this illustration.[40] A large, big-boned, rather heavy man, Su Shih had a strong, handsome face; his brother, Su Ch'e, resembled him and was two years younger. The prominence given to the garden setting, the geese and reeds, and the rock and bamboo supports the contemporary reference, since ink bamboo was a new subject in painting and one particularly associated with Su Shih and his cousin Wen T'ung. The two of them virtually invented the subject of ink bamboo painting, which would thereafter be associated specifically with scholar-painters. That Li Kung-lin, the classicist, includes it prominently and with pointed symbolism in his illustration suggests the fresh, living spirit of contemporary life that he brought to all his work.

Possibly related to these observations is the fact that—though no longer extant—the only recorded contemporary colophon to the *Classic of Filial Piety* was written by Su Shih; it is included in his collected works.[41] Su does not say that he noticed

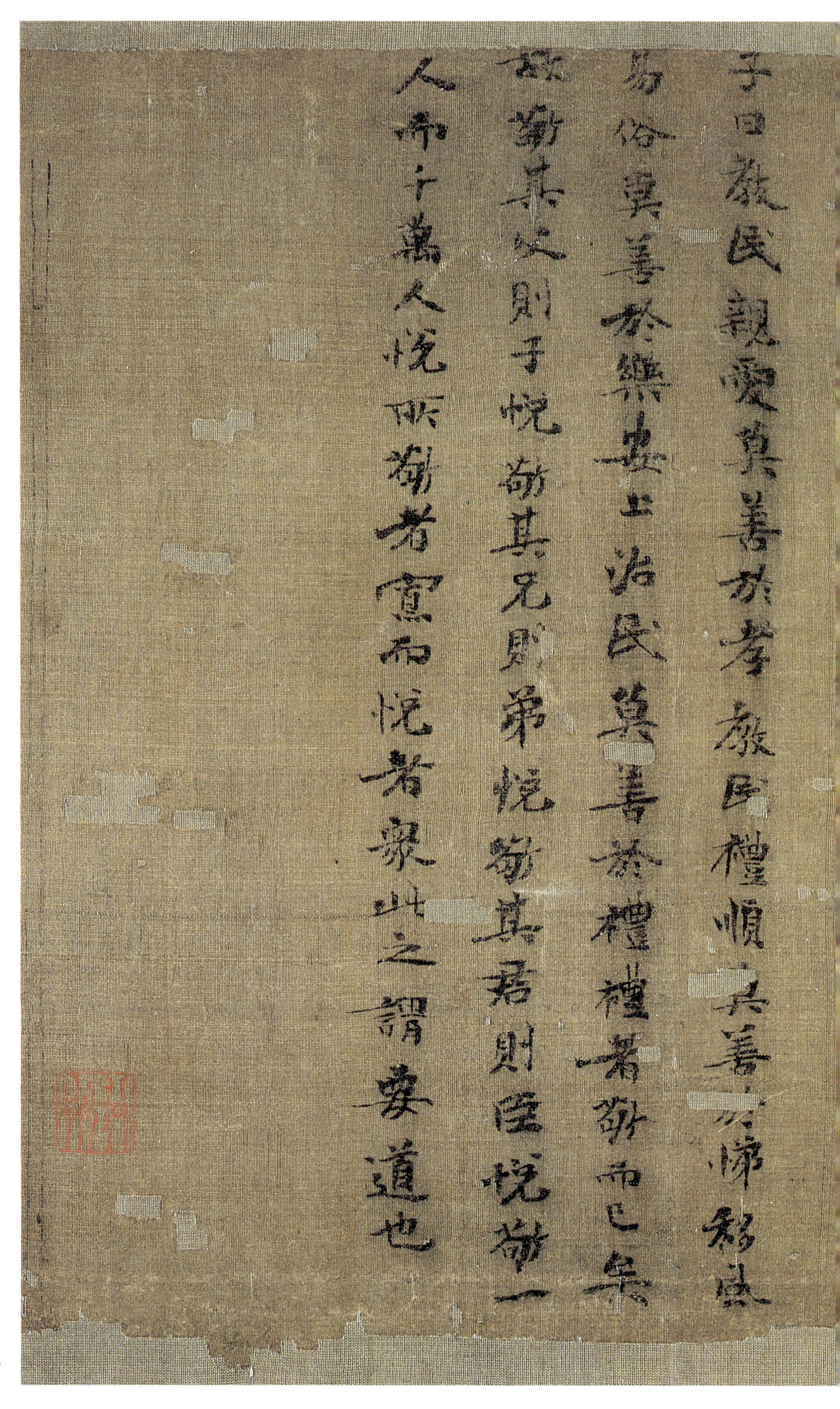
子曰教民親愛莫善於孝教民禮順莫善於悌移風
易俗莫善於樂安上治民莫善於禮禮者敬而已矣
故敬其父則子悅敬其兄則弟悅敬其君則臣悅敬一
人而千萬人悅所敬者寡而悅者衆此之謂要道也

Plate 9. Li Kung-lin, chapter 12 of the *Classic of Filial Piety*

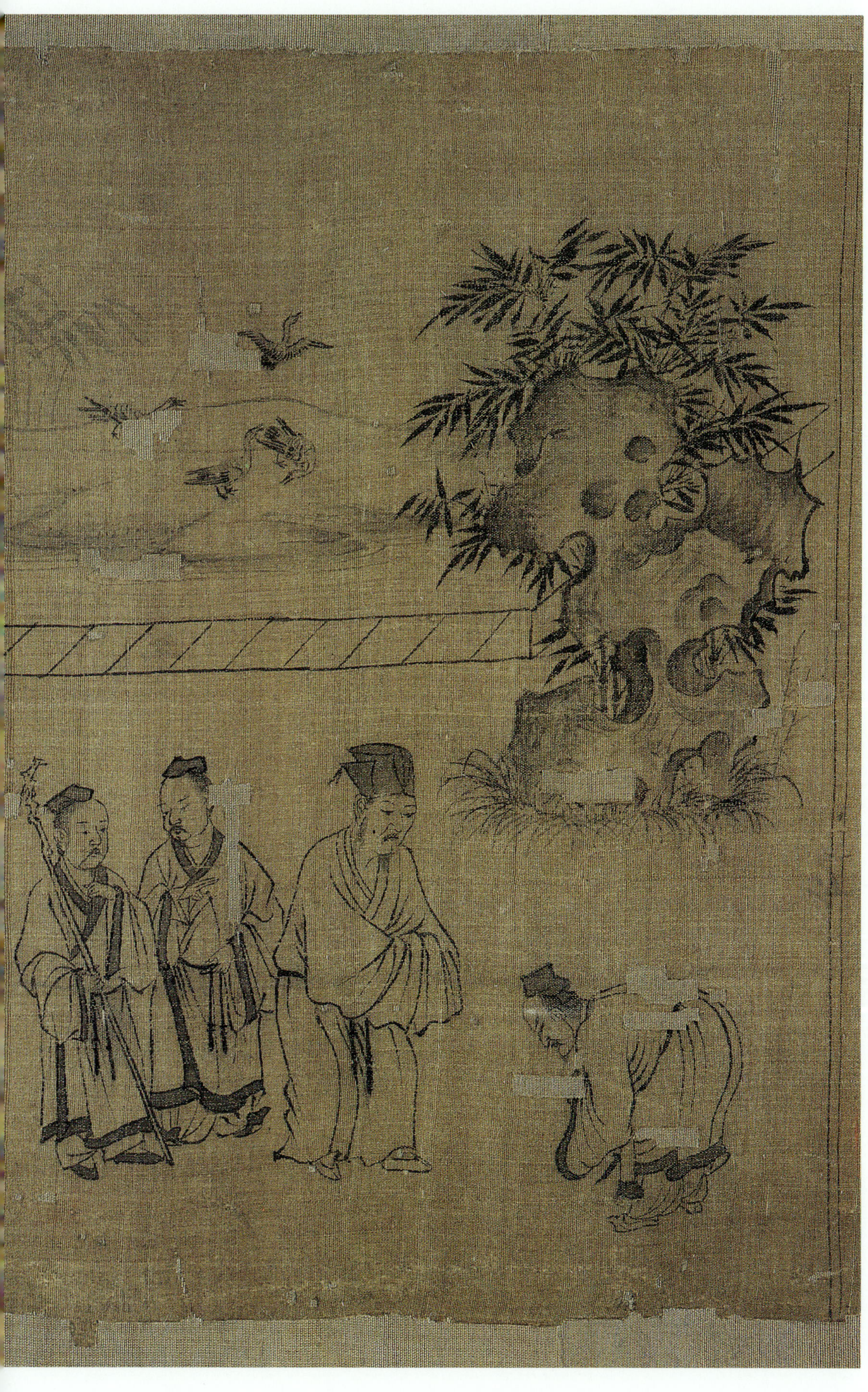

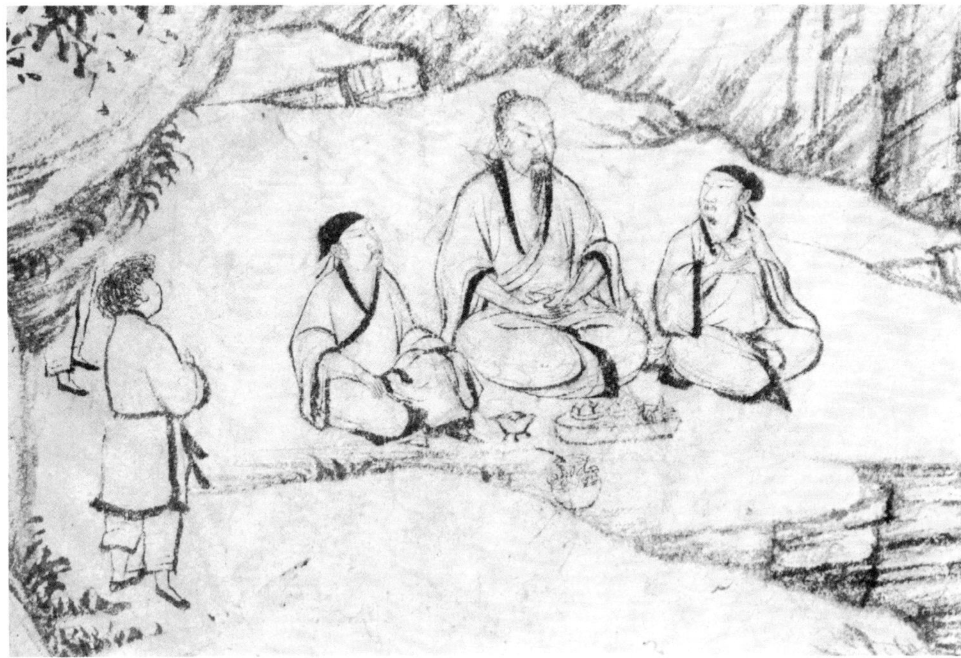

Figure 46. Ch'iao Chung-ch'ang (early 12th century), detail from *Su Shih's Second Ode on the Red Cliff*. Handscroll, ink on paper, 11⅝ × 220⅝ in. (29.5 × 560.4 cm). The Nelson-Atkins Museum of Art, Kansas City, Missouri. Nelson Gallery Foundation Purchase

himself among the numerous figures in the scroll, but we may nonetheless suspect with good reason that he did recognize himself there, just as Li's other contemporaries undoubtedly saw other people and other references to contemporary events and personalities that are now too remote to be understood. It should be assumed, as we have suggested, that when the artist painted a father he had in mind his own father, as well as other fathers he knew; that his ministers reflected ministers who passed before his eyes; that brothers recalled brothers numbered among his friends; that mothers or sisters somehow embodied his own; and that in his compositions people high and low were representations, however indirect, of the men and women of Sung China around the year 1085.

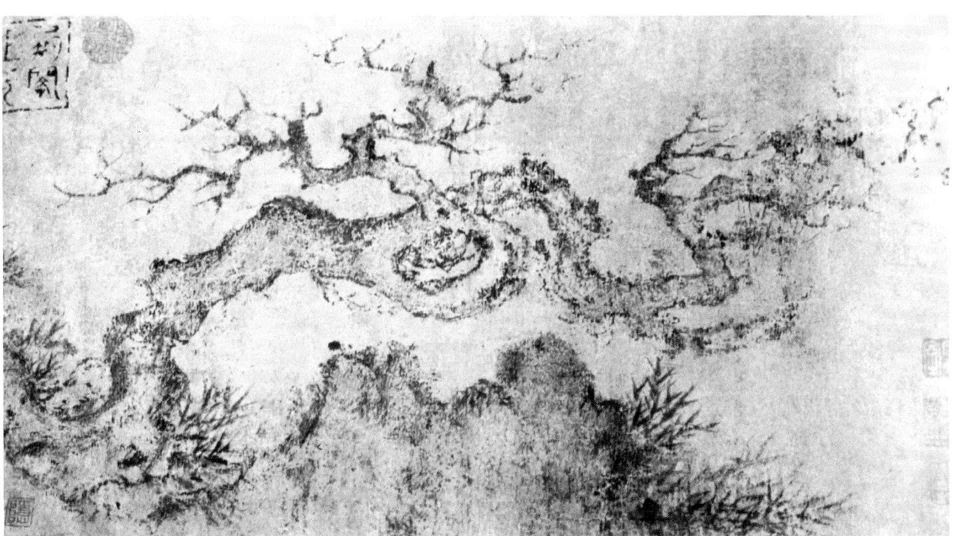

Figure 47. Attributed to Su Shih (1037–1101), detail from *Old Tree, Bamboo, and Rock*. Handscroll, ink on paper, 9¼ × 20 in. (23.4 × 50.9 cm). Shanghai Museum

A painting by, or attributed to, Su Shih of bamboo in a garden setting of the type seen in Li's painting (fig. 47) suggests the kind of image associated with Su Shih that Li's contemporaries surely would have had in mind when they studied his illustrations. The graphic projection of the great Sung poet, painter, and calligrapher is one of symbiosis—bamboo, rock, and tree—and echoes brightly in Li's picture. Moreover, the symbiosis of painted motifs parallels the symbiosis of brotherly love and respect that is at the heart of Li's composition.

There are records of earlier paintings in which contemporary personalities were seen in depictions of philosophical or religious subjects. Certainly it is significant that Li's good friend and rival Mi Fu was fond of thinking that he had occasionally discovered such loosely disguised portraits—quite possibly because he was fully aware of what his friend Li was doing in his own paintings of classical subjects.[42] It is also significant that, by the late twelfth century, even professional painters, such as Chou Chi-ch'ang and Lin T'ing-kuei, commonly included actual portraits of living people in their religious icons, since they were in other important ways followers of Li.[43] It thus seems highly likely that Li was among the first Chinese painters to present philosophical, religious, and classic texts through the personae of living contemporaries whose lives embodied the ideals celebrated and recounted in the texts. This is a stage in the evolution of Chinese narrative painting vaguely similar to Benjamin West's depiction of such heroic events as Wolfe's death with figures in contemporary costume rather than in the clothing of ancient Greece and Rome.[44]

CHAPTER 13
Amplification of "The Perfect Virtue" in Chapter 1

The Master said, "The teaching of filial piety by the superior man does not require that he should go to family after family, and daily see the members of each. His teaching of filial piety is a tribute of reverence to all the fathers under heaven. His teaching of fraternal submission is a tribute of reverence to all the elder brothers under heaven. His teaching of the duty of a subject is a tribute of reverence to all the rulers under heaven. It is said in the Book of Songs:

The happy and courteous sovereign
Is the parent of the people.

"If it were not a perfect virtue, how could it be recognized as in accordance with their nature by the people so extensively as this?"[45]

The first part of the passage that constitutes chapter 13 is annotated by the T'ang emperor Hsüan-tsung: "He merely practices filial piety within his home, and the transforming power of his example will of itself be extended abroad."[46]

Li Kung-lin centers his illustration on the father, seated in an armchair before a great landscape screen (pl. 10). He is surrounded by the members of his family—in all probability, two sons, two daughters, and a brother—and four servants. In the foreground, two men carry in a mesh-covered table to set before him and a maidservant brings a tray of food. The table is evidently heavy, for the servant turned toward the viewer grimaces at the effort. Another maidservant appears from behind the screen at the left carrying a large container, perhaps of wine, and she, too, shows the exertion of bearing its weight. The father speaks to a stooped, older man, presumably his uncle. Behind the older man, standing at the right against the screen and listening, is a woman, the daughter or daughter-in-law of the central figure. On the opposite side stand the two sons, the younger of whom is going to address his father. Behind them is another woman, probably a second sister. She and her elder brother both look affectionately at the younger brother, who prepares to speak. All the figures thus converge on the father, seated in the center.

The fourth and last of the intimate family scenes that Li offers in this set of eighteen chapters, the illustration for chapter 13 focuses closely on the father as the central and symbolic perpetuator and recipient of the network of filial piety as it was practiced within the extended family. As in Ku K'ai-chih's portrayal of an extended family seven hundred years earlier (fig. 43), the oldest living male takes a position inferior to the current father. Ku K'ai-chih put that figure in the rear, teaching a grandchild how to read, while the prevailing male figurehead sits prominently at the front. Here, the older man defers to the seated father, who is literally king in his own home. The parallel, socially, politically, and economically, between father and emperor is drawn again and again both in the text and in the illustrations. The four women shown here serve, needless to say, in even more subsidiary roles; they are literally at the edges, behind the various generations and ranks of men.

Nonetheless, we must not fail to note the truly unusual nature of these intimate depictions of family life. It is nearly impossible to find elsewhere in early Chinese art other family vignettes in which men and women interact so closely and privately as they do in these paintings. Ku K'ai-chih's *Admonitions* scroll is an important exception, and this is another way in which Li connects himself and his art to the earlier master.

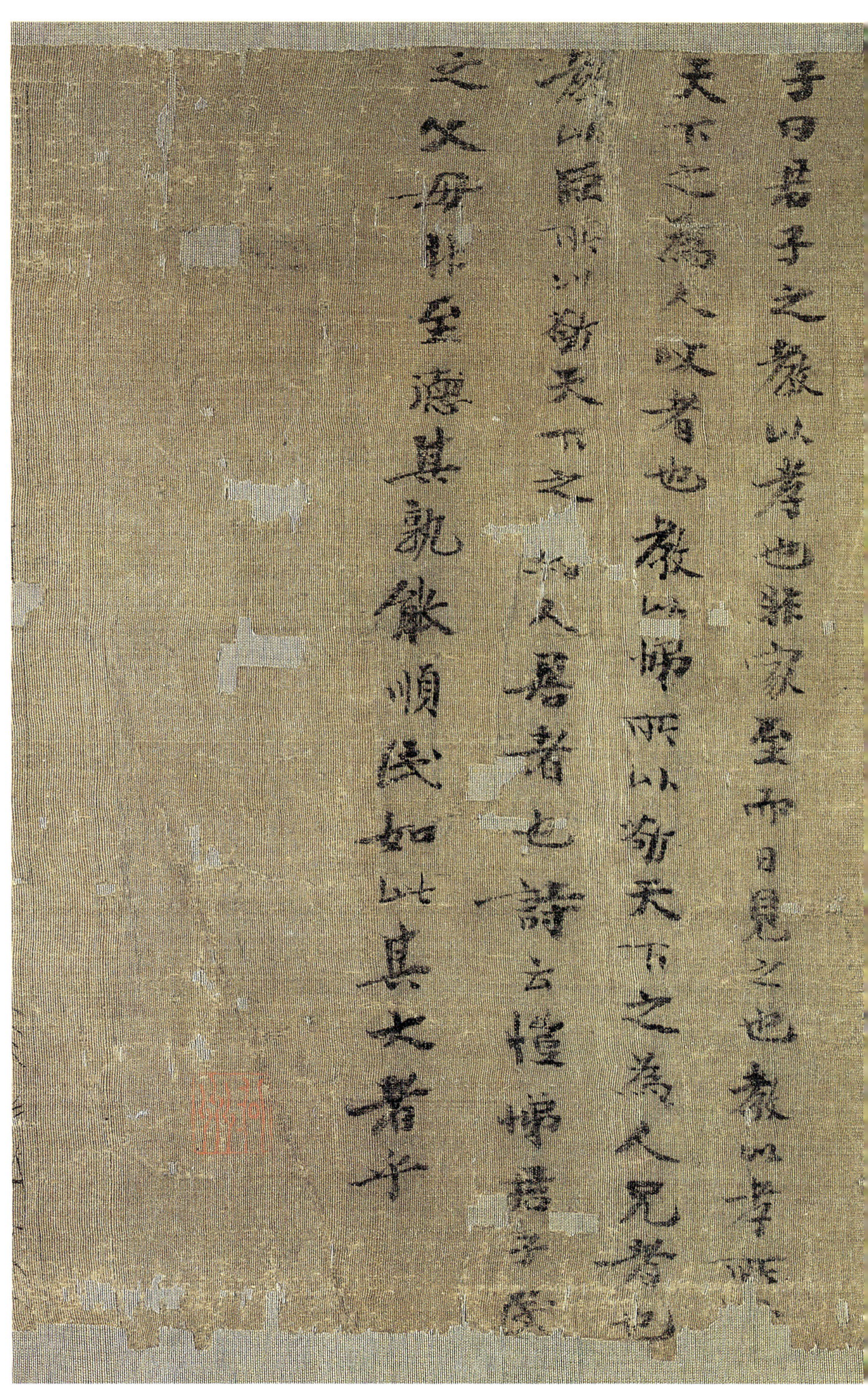

Plate 10. Li Kung-lin, chapter 13 of the *Classic of Filial Piety*

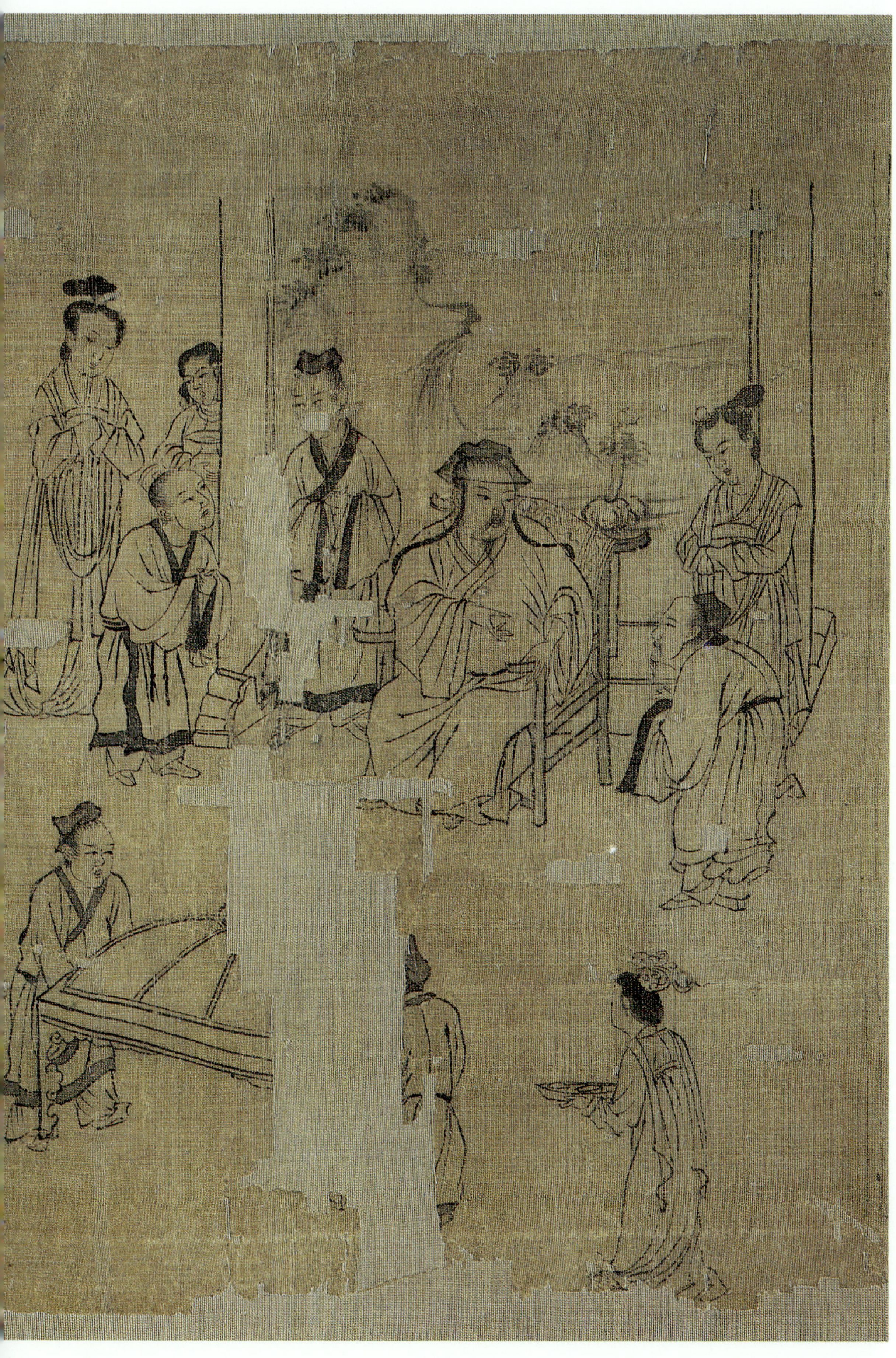

CHAPTER 14

Amplification of "Making Our Name Famous" in Chapter 1

The Master said, "The filial piety with which the superior man serves his parents may be transferred as loyalty to the ruler. The fraternal duty with which he serves the eldest brother may be transferred as submissive deference to elders. His regulation of his family may be transferred as good government in any official position. Therefore, when his conduct is thus successful in his inner circle, his name will be established for future generations."[47]

As noted in the discussion for chapter 11, the illustrations for chapters 11 and 14 are reversed. The illustration for this chapter (pl. 8) follows the passage "His regulation of his family may be transferred as good government in any official position." An official on horseback is seen approaching the gate of a government compound, where he will take up the duties of a new position; his servant walks ahead. The rider is greeted by a tough-looking, but smiling, local functionary. A second man unlocks the gate.

Within the oddly personal world he constructs in his art, Li Kung-lin obviously held in highest esteem those men of his own scholar-bureaucrat class. Here, as elsewhere in the *Classic of Filial Piety* whenever he focuses on them, he portrays them as the essential foundation of a humane society. In that same world, just as clearly, those who wield power are often villains and the common people are typically victims. Li does not seem to have held those close to the throne in esteem. They seem, instead, to epitomize the excesses to which even minor functionaries who hold power succumb: put a whip in a man's hand, and all others become a threat to him.

From the Sung period on, the common practice for officials of all ranks was a change of post every three years and no assignment of a post in the home region. The reason for this practice was simply the avoidance of entanglements caused either by too long a residence in one place or by favoritism toward family, friends, and neighbors. *Kuan-hsi*, or the special favors granted through personal relationship, has been one of the traditional vices of Chinese society, as it still is today. Regular changing of assignments theoretically helped to prevent such alliances from forming and also allowed a variety of experiences to contribute to the education, maturity, and wisdom of the individual official. It was literally upon the decency of those thousands of government officials, moving every three years to a new post in a new region, that the decency of government in traditional China depended.

Like all the others of his class, Li himself had experienced the life of an itinerant official, going from post to post at regular two- or three-year intervals. He had undoubtedly been greeted many times by local clerks and runners like the ones depicted here. He does not seem to glamorize the experience; another town, he may be remembering, another job.

CHAPTER 15

Filial Piety in Relation to Reproof and Remonstrance

Tseng-tzu said: "I have heard your instructions on the affection of love, on respect and reverence, on giving repose to our parents, and on making our names famous. I would venture to ask if simple obedience to the orders of one's father can be pronounced filial piety?" The Master replied: "What words are these! What words are these! In former times, if the Son of Heaven had seven ministers who would remonstrate with him, although he had not right methods of government, he would not lose possession of his kingdom; if the prince of a state had five such ministers, though his measures might be equally wrong, he would not lose his state; if a great officer had three, he would not, in a similar case, lose his clan; if an inferior officer had a friend who would remonstrate with him, a good name would not cease to be connected with his character; and the father who had a son that would remonstrate with him would not sink into the gulf of unrighteous deeds. Therefore, where a case of unrighteous conduct is concerned, a son must by no means keep from remonstrating with his father, nor a minister from remonstrating with his ruler. Hence, since remonstrance is required in the case of unrighteous conduct, how can simple obedience to the order of a father be accounted filial piety?"[48]

Another of the key elements in the social, political, and moral structure of filiality that Li Kung-lin visualized for us in his scroll is the subject of this chapter: reproof, remonstrance, and open, honest criticism. The concept is essential to the entire structure of filiality, since without its constant presence and living spirit the nature of government and of social order becomes purely totalitarian. The long passage discussing this is of fundamental importance to the entire text.

In Li's illustration for this chapter he chose the figure of the "great officer" to represent authority (pl. 12). Following the text quite literally, he shows the officer attended by three officials, one of whom remonstrates with him. The composition is open and relatively unthreatening, and the presence of the great officer's wife and two female attendants behind him further civilizes and softens the confrontation. The composition is very much like the compositions that illustrate the five punishments and the several domestic settings of family gatherings. There is little difference between the great officer and his officials. All four men dress alike and appear more like brothers than superior and inferiors. The picture says to us that great leaders depend upon the frankness of their officers; honest remonstration is a fundamental requirement of government.

It was, of course, men of Li's class who were placed in the position of remonstrator and critic of public policy. In his time, this was a difficult responsibility,

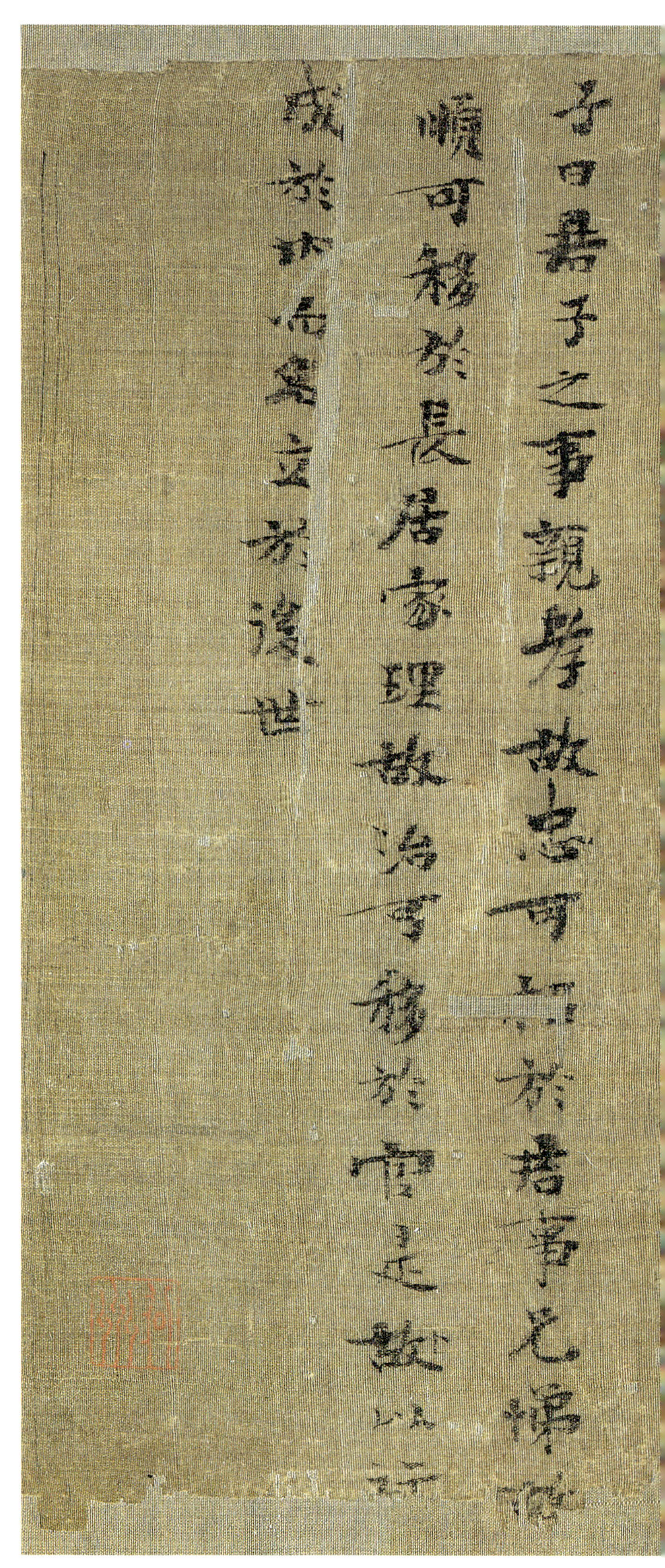

Plate 11. Li Kung-lin, chapter 14 of the *Classic of Filial Piety*

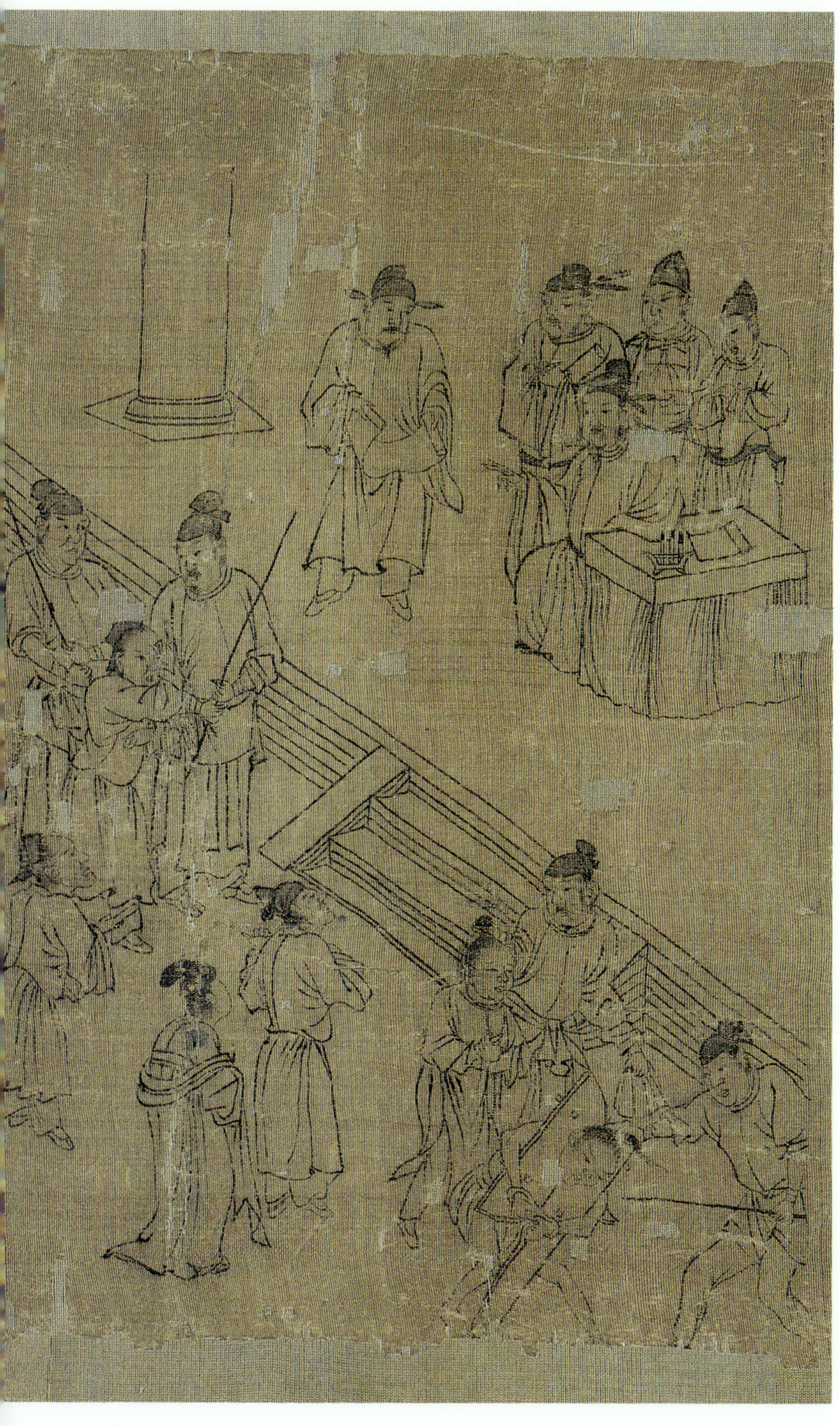

從父之令可謂孝乎子曰是何言與是何言與昔者
天子有爭臣七人雖無道不失其天下諸侯有爭臣五
人雖無道不失其國大夫有爭臣三人雖無道不失其家
士有爭友則身不離於令名父有爭子則身不陷於不義
故當不義則子不可以不爭於父臣不可以不爭於君故
當不義則爭之從父之令又焉得為孝乎

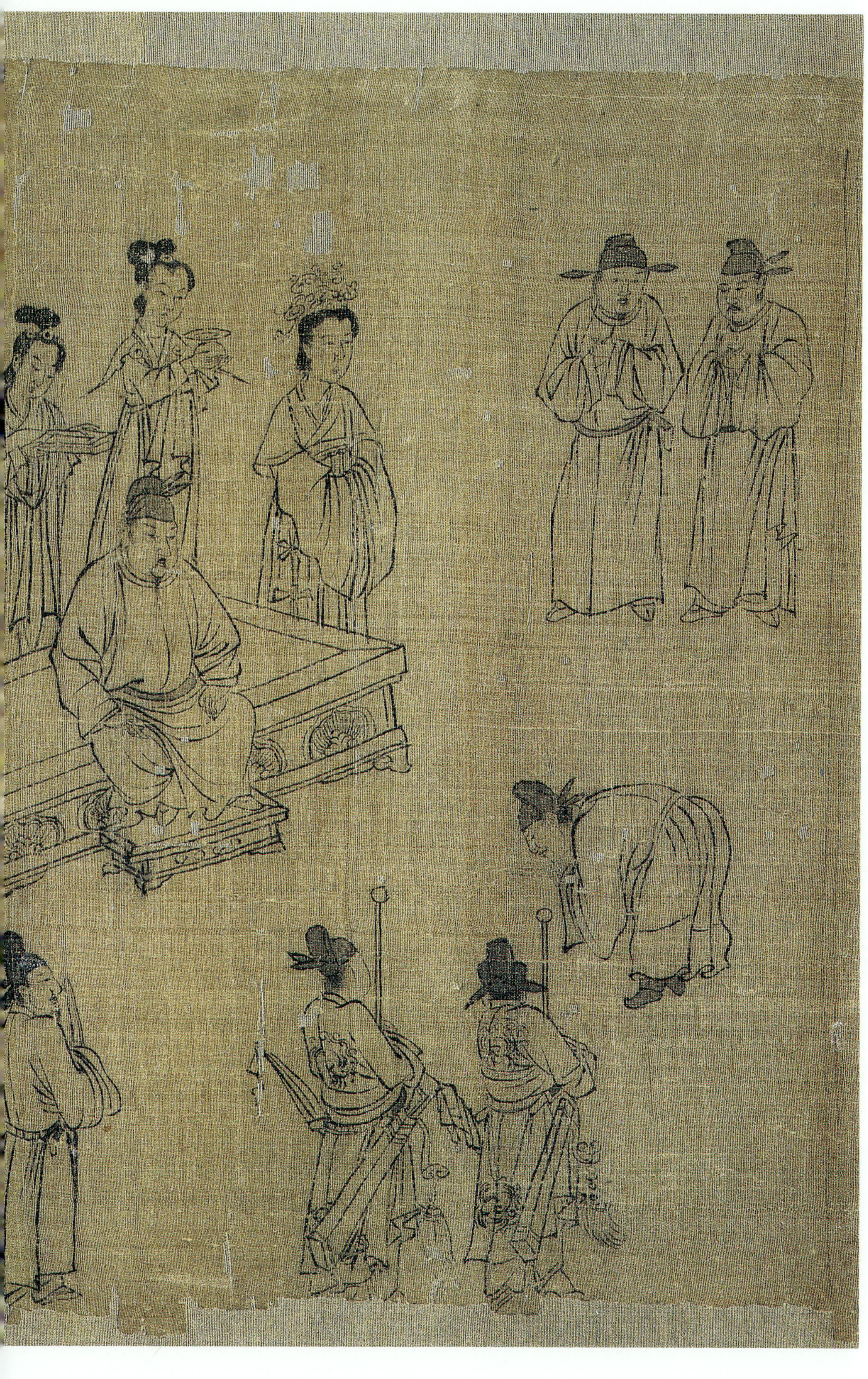

Plate 12. Li Kung-lin, chapter 15 of the *Classic of Filial Piety*

especially because of the uncertainties of political favor. Two powerful factions that vied for control of the throne could never be quite certain which of them would prevail in a given year, and those out of favor were often demoted, banished, or exiled. Li was not especially courageous in the sphere of political infighting, and surely he would have wished for the kind of tolerant, and basically benevolent, forum he creates for us here. In fact, however, even during the humane and enlightened Sung period, it probably did not exist.

Nearly every one of Li's most intimate friends experienced demotion, imprisonment, banishment, or exile—often repeatedly—during the politically troubled and deeply factionalized years of his lifetime. Some died in exile. The toll on human life was heavy, and the actual results of honest remonstrance were more likely to be painful than rewarding. Li probably saw this system in operation every day of his official life, yet he chose to illustrate this chapter on remonstrance as if the ideal were attainable. Perhaps—though the day-to-day reality was generally far from perfection—it was that continued belief which allowed the Sung dynasty finally to appear to be honest, humane, and decent in comparison with every other dynasty in Chinese history.

CHAPTER 16

The Influence of Filial Piety and the Response to It

The Master said, "In former times, the intelligent kings served their fathers with filial piety, and therefore they served earth with discrimination. They pursued the right course with reference to their seniors and juniors, and therefore they secured the regulation of the relations between superiors and inferiors everywhere. When heaven and earth were served with intelligence and discrimination, their spiritual intelligences displayed themselves. Therefore, even the Son of Heaven must have some whom he honors; that is, he has his uncles of his surname. He must have some to whom he concedes precedence; that is, he has his cousins, who bear the same surname, and are older than himself. In the ancestral temple he manifests the utmost reverence, showing that he does not forget his parents. He cultivates his person and is careful of his conduct, fearing lest he should disgrace his predecessors. When in the ancestral temple he exhibits the utmost reverence, the spirits of the departed manifest themselves. Perfect filial piety and fraternal duty reach to the spiritual intelligences, and diffuse their light on all within the Four Seas. They penetrate everywhere. It is said in the Book of Songs:

> *From the west to the east,*
> *From the south to the north,*
> *There was not a thought but did him homage."*[49]

It is, as always, interesting to see which passage Li Kung-lin chose to illustrate. The element of choice was a crucial factor in conveying the artist's concerns and intentions, because in most cases he selected his focus from a broad range of possibilities. In the long chapter above, for example, one can imagine any number of possible choices. Li chose the brief passage that begins, "In the ancestral temple he manifests the utmost reverence, showing that he does not forget his parents" (pl. 13).

The sacrificial rituals performed by the emperor ensured the welfare of his state and the continuance of his mandate. In addition to the ritual sacrifices to heaven and earth performed on the winter solstice, which Li had illustrated in his painting for chapter 9, the emperor also regularly sacrificed to his ancestors, a ritual that symbolized the national cult of ancestor worship. Imperial sacrifices to the ancestors took place in a ritual hall called the Ming T'ang, or Bright Hall, a traditional place of imperial prerogative described in the ancient books and built anew for every ruling house. It is the setting for Li's illustration.[50]

The Son of Heaven, the principal sacrificer, stands just outside the sacrificial altar to the east. Opposite is his wife. The officer of prayer, the young man who kneels near the entrance to the stagelike altar, sacrifices just inside the temple

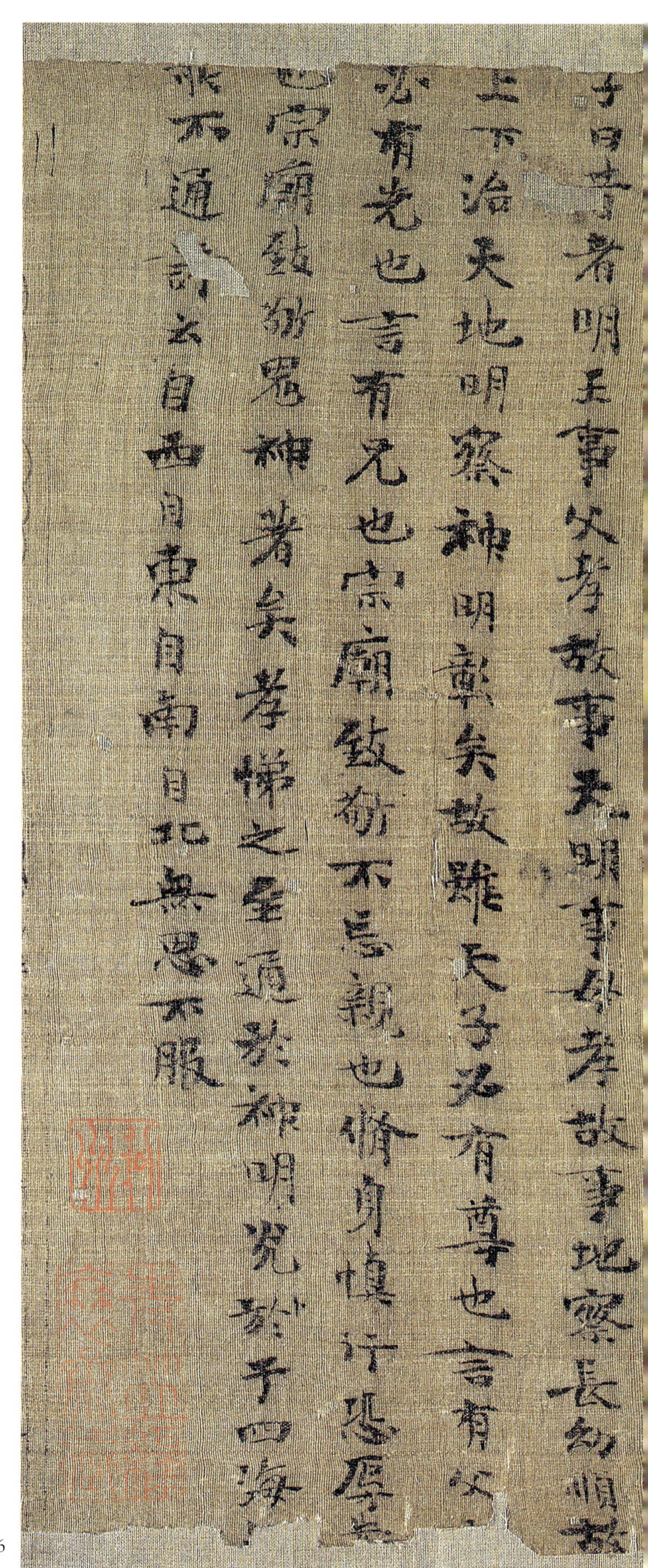

Plate 13. Li Kung-lin, chapter 16 of the *Classic of Filial Piety*

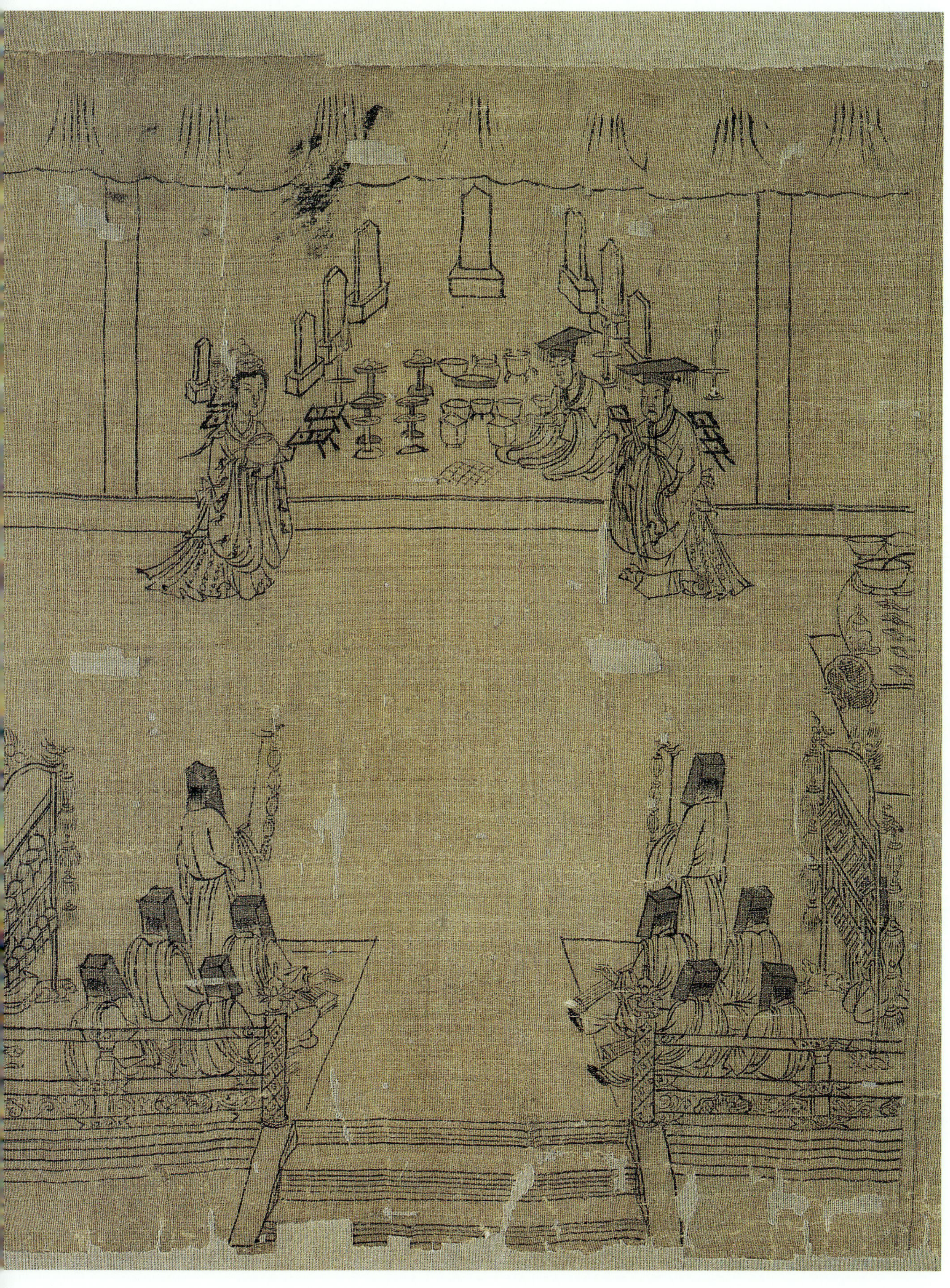

gate. According to a commentary to the *Classic of Poetry*, "The filial son does not know where the spirits are, and therefore sends the officer of prayer to seek them inside the entrance while he waits outside." To attract the spirits, the kneeling officer pours fragrant wine into libation cups. Lining the altar are the ancestral tablets, while outside are the prepared offerings. After the officer of prayer has communicated with the ancestral spirits, he goes to the principal sacrificer to report: "Fragrant has been your filial sacrifice. And the spirits have enjoyed your spirits and viands. They confer on you a hundred blessings, each as it is desired." The ritual concluded, "The bells and drums give their warning," and the officer of prayer announces, "The spirits have drunk to the full!"[51] The spirits of the dead then depart to the music of the bells and drums, and the service is concluded. A banquet for the participants follows.

Here, the composition is symmetrical and hierarchical. It proceeds from the stairs below, past the musicians to the principal sacrificer and his consort, up to the altar proper, where the officer of prayer kneels, and to the ancestral tablets, which are arranged like the composition as a whole, in lines converging toward the central tablet. This approximation of Western perspective is a common feature of early Chinese painting in depictions of religious subjects. The symmetry of this form perhaps suggested the systematic ritual disposition of the solemn act depicted. It is the Chinese state in miniature.

CHAPTER 17
The Service of the Ruler

The Master said, "The superior man serves his ruler in such a way that, when at court in his presence, his thought is how to discharge his loyal duty to the utmost; and, when he retires from it, his thought is how to amend his errors. He carries out with deference the measures springing from his ruler's excellent qualities, and rectifies him only to preserve him from what is evil. Hence, as superior and inferior they are able to have affection for one another. It is said in the Book of Songs:

In my heart I love him so,
And why should I not say so?
In the core of my heart I keep him,
And never will forget him."[52]

Li Kung-lin chose to illustrate the first sentence of chapter 17. In the lower portion of the illustration (pl. 14), a man is seated on a veranda beneath a willow tree. His hands folded in his lap, he gazes off into space. Above him is a cloud of mist that cuts the composition into two parts and above which the same man stands before his prince, who is seated on a couch listening to him. The intent is clearly to indicate by the cloud, in a manner common to Buddhist art, two realms of existence. Above is the world of the mind, below the world of the body or, in Confucian terms, above is the active realm and below it the contemplative. The man is sitting in retirement from his duties at court, considering "how to amend his errors" when he returns. He imagines himself approaching his sovereign with new plans and new ideas, as he will do when he returns to service.

It is likely that Li was engaged in some degree of wishful thinking when he painted this image. He himself was evidently quite content to absent himself from public duty, as we know from his long avoidance of official service and his early retirement. He was intelligent, talented, and extremely learned, and his interests lay in the sphere of the mind, in learning and the creative imagination. His twenty years of reluctant and undistinguished governmental service must have been necessitated by financial considerations, and the life he actively wished for himself is probably most clearly suggested in his famed composition that depicts his country retreat, the *Lung-mien Mountain Villa* (see figs. 6–8). Probably in 1085, when he painted the *Classic of Filial Piety*, he imagined himself sitting by a garden on a willow-shaded veranda. Indeed, the details of the picture that occupy him most are the willow, the clouds, and the garden rock, filling the center of the composition. Each wisp of cloud, each precise, delicate willow leaf engaged his hand and mind like elements in a dream of his retirement from official life that he was creating for himself.

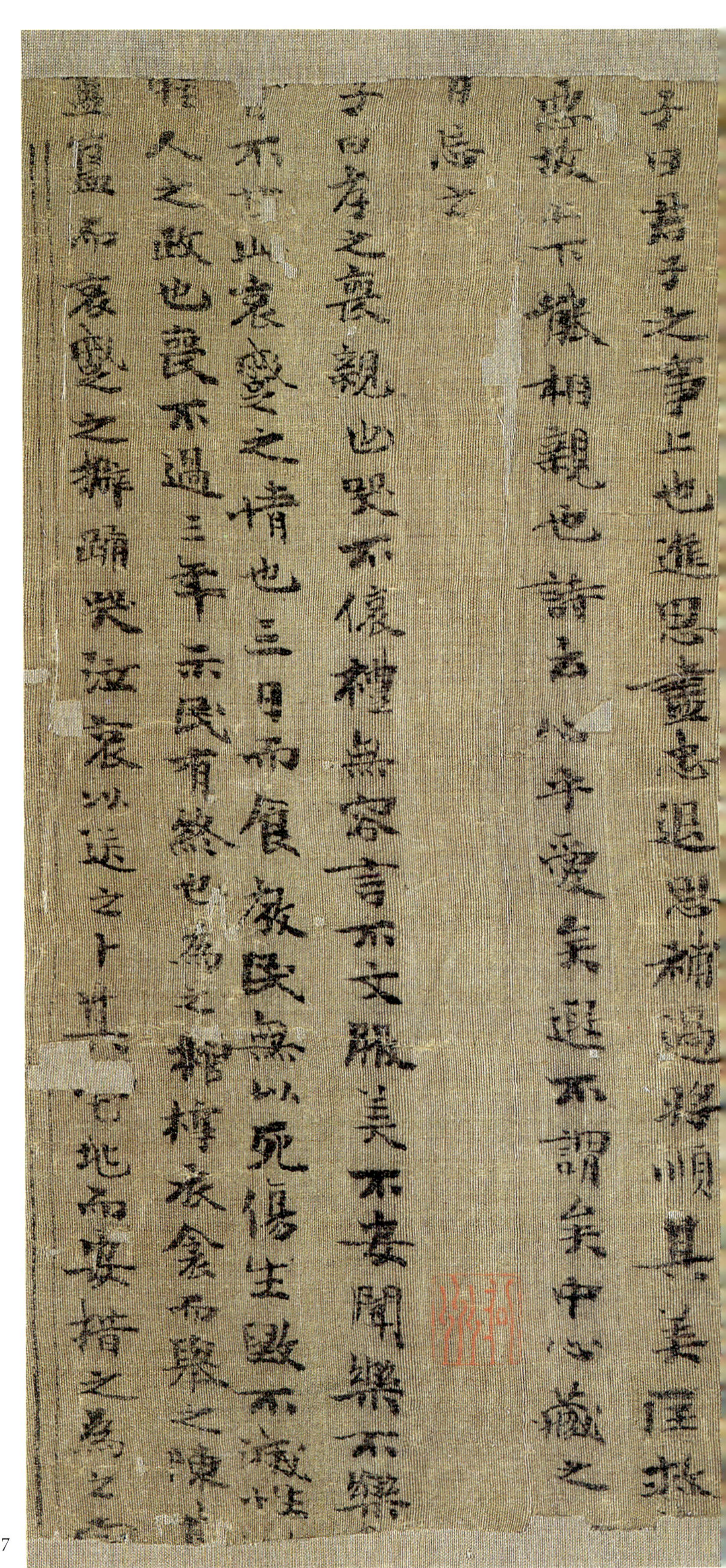
子曰君子之事上也進思盡忠退思補過將順其美匡救
其惡故上下能相親也詩云心乎愛矣遐不謂矣中心藏之
何日忘之
子曰孝子之喪親也哭不偯禮無容言不文服美不安聞樂不樂
食旨不甘此哀戚之情也三日而食教民無以死傷生毀不滅性
此聖人之政也喪不過三年示民有終也為之棺槨衣衾而舉之陳其
簠簋而哀戚之擗踊哭泣哀以送之卜其宅兆而安措之為之宗

Plate 14. Li Kung-lin, chapter 17 of the *Classic of Filial Piety*

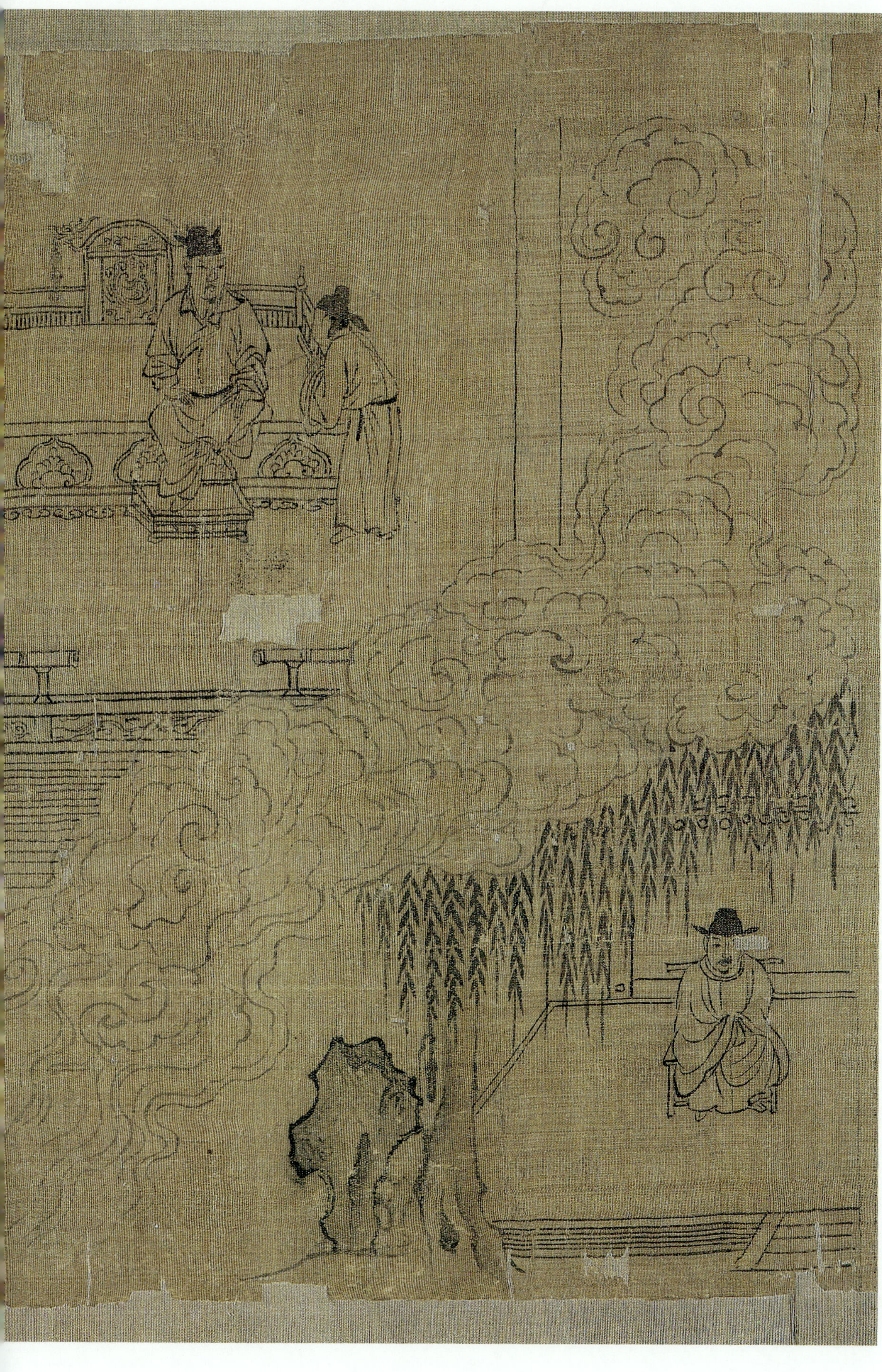

CHAPTER 18
Filial Piety in Mourning for Parents

The Master said, "When a filial son is mourning for a parent, he wails, but not with a prolonged sobbing; in the movements of ceremony, he pays no attention to his appearance; his words are without elegance of phrase; he cannot bear to wear fine clothes; when he hears music, he feels no delight; when he eats a delicacy, he is not conscious of its flavor. Such is the nature of grief and sorrow.

"After three days, he may partake of food; for thus the people are taught that the living should not be injured on account of the dead, and that emaciation must not be carried to the extinction of life. Such is the rule of the sages. The period of mourning does not extend beyond three years, to show the people that it must have an end.

"An inner and an outer coffin are made; the grave clothes also are put on, and the shroud; and the body is lifted into the coffin. The sacrificial vessels, round and square, are set forth, and cause further distress. The women beat their breasts, and the men stamp their feet, wailing and weeping, while they sorrowfully escort the coffin to the grave. They consult the tortoiseshell to determine the grave and the ground about it, and they lay the body in peace. They prepare the ancestral temple, and there present offerings to the disembodied spirit. In the spring and autumn they offer sacrifices, thinking of the deceased as the seasons come round.

"The services of love and reverence to parents when alive, and those of grief and sorrow when they are dead—these completely discharge the fundamental duty of living men. The righteous claims of life and death are all satisfied, and the filial son's service to his parents is completed."[53]

Instead of choosing to depict a scene of mourning or burial or even sacrifice, Li Kung-lin creates an image not even suggested in the text (pl. 15). A lone boat drifts by mist-shrouded mountains, as if lost in emptiness. Indeed, emptiness is the metaphor of the image, the emptiness of loss and of mourning, the emptiness of death's aftermath.

It is likely that the source for this image was another great classic text, the *Book of Songs*, or the *Shih-ching*, a text quoted often in the *Classic of Filial Piety* itself. In the *Book of Songs* is an ancient poem of mourning for one's parents, "The Two of You Went Off in a Boat":

> *The two of you went off in a boat,*
> *Floating, floating far away.*
> *Longingly I think of you;*
> *My heart within is pained.*

The two of you went off in a boat,
Floating, floating you sped away.
Longingly I think of you.
Oh may you come to no harm![54]

If the subtle beauty of this reference was lost on some later interpreters of the *Classic of Filial Piety*, it was the one extraordinary achievement that Su Shih, in his colophon, chose to praise:

> When we look at these pictures, feelings of warm, loving duty and loyalty toward our parents well up within us. The superb brushwork is not inferior to that of Ku K'ai-chih and Lu T'an-wei. As for the final chapter, in which all that a son finds unbearable is described, the painter conveys these meanings in only the faintest suggestion of form. None but a truly superior man possessing the Way could achieve his level.[55]

Su Shih was the most distinguished poet of the Sung dynasty and the most influential art critic of his time. It is likely, as was noted above, that Li Kung-lin included an informal portrait of Su in his illustration for chapter 12. Su's colophon may have been in part some form of acknowledgment of that fact. Li, in any case, painted Su's portrait several other times, and Su was a frequent commentator on Li's painting. On another occasion, Su wrote appreciatively about the qualities of realism and authenticity in Li's figure painting and about the vivid topographical plausibility of his landscape composition the *Lung-mien Mountain Villa* (figs. 6–8). From among the eighteen paintings that constitute the *Classic of Filial Piety*, he singles out the last for particular admiration. The others, he tells us, draw from the viewer feelings of loving duty toward one's parents. The final image, however, expresses the sadness and pain one feels at their death, communicating that deep anguish with only the faintest suggestion of form. According to Su, only someone of the loftiest character and knowledge of the Way could have conceived of such subtlety.

What a contemporary commentator writes about a work of art for the people of his own time is probably always guarded. But it seems likely that Su Shih was suggesting that within Li's images were many profound and important meanings, that they were subtly and imaginatively conveyed, and that they were the product of a superior mind—a mind concerned with morality, justice, and decency, and capable of seeing an ideal and of informing us of the ways in which that ideal was yet far from reality.

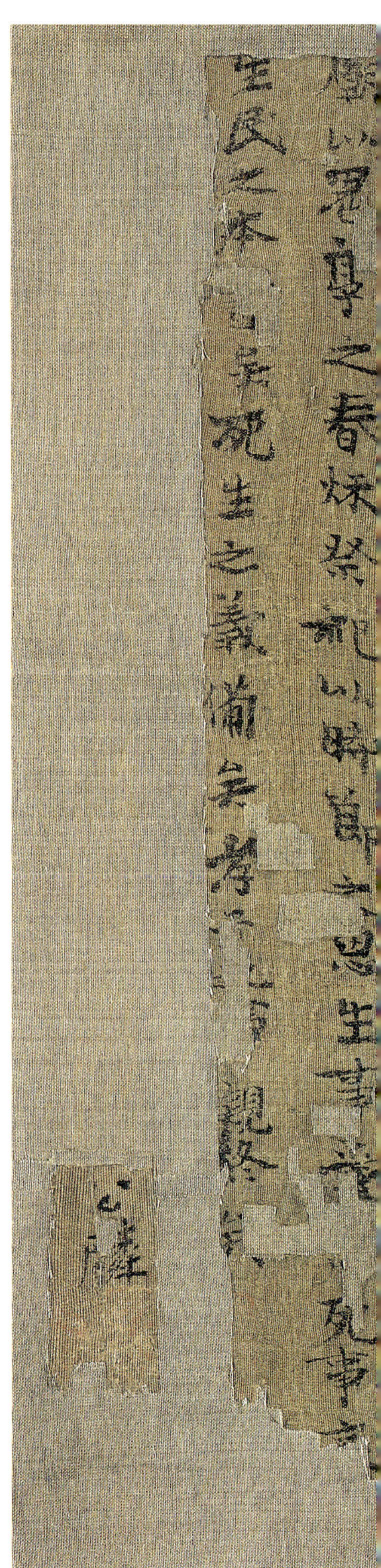

Plate 15. Li Kung-lin, chapter 18 of the *Classic of Filial Piety*

1. The basic translation and annotation of the *Classic of Filial Piety* in English is James Legge, *The Hsiao King*, in *The Sacred Books of China: The Texts of Confucianism*, pt. 1 (Oxford, 1879). For other discussions of filial piety, see Mary Lelia Makra, trans., *The Hsiao Ching*, ed. Paul K. T. Sih (New York, 1961), especially the preface by Sih; and Richard M. Barnhart, "Li Kung-lin's *Hsiao Ching T'u*: Illustrations of the 'Classic of Filial Piety'" (Ph.D. diss., Princeton University, 1967), pp. 63–66. The role of filial piety within Confucian thought and society is discussed most fully in Fung Yu-lan, *A History of Chinese Philosophy*, trans. Dirk Bodde, 2 vols. (Princeton, 1952–53), vol. 1, pp. 357–61.
2. *Lun-yü* 1:2; translation from Fung, *History of Chinese Philosophy*, vol. 1, p. 361.
3. This passage from the *P'ei-wen-chai shu-hua p'u* (1708) is cited in Barnhart, "Li Kung-lin's *Hsiao Ching T'u*," p. 66.
4. The Hsieh Chih version is listed by Chang Yen-yüan in his biography of Hsieh in his *Li-tai ming-hua chi* (reprint, Shanghai, 1963), *chüan* 5, p. 121. The Liang dynasty copy is recorded in the *Sui Shu* and cited in Wu Ch'eng-shih, *Hsiao-ching t'ung-lun* (Shanghai, 1934), p. 85.
5. Since its publication in Barnhart, "Li Kung-lin's *Hsiao Ching T'u*," Li Kung-lin's *Classic of Filial Piety* has been published many times; for example, Hironobu Kohara, ed., *Bunjinga Suihen* (Tokyo, 1976), vol. 2, pp. 82–83; Kei Suzuki, *Chūgoku Kaigashi* (Tokyo, 1981), vol. 1, pp. 320–21; Richard M. Barnhart, *Along the Border of Heaven: Sung and Yüan Paintings from the C. C. Wang Family Collection* (New York, 1983); and Wen C. Fong, *Beyond Representation: Chinese Painting and Calligraphy, 8th–14th Century* (New York, 1992).
6. *Ku-kung shu-hua lu* (Taipei, 1965), vol. 4, *chüan* 8, p. 31. See also Barnhart, "Li Kung-lin's *Hsiao Ching T'u*," figs. 23–40.
7. Reproduced in *Chung-kuo ku-tai shu-hua t'u-mu* (Beijing, 1987), vol. 2, p. 127.
8. Recorded in *Ku-kung shu-hua lu*, vol. 4, *chüan* 6, pp. 164–66.
9. The former Yen Li-pen version, now in the Liao-ning Provincial Museum, proves not to be earlier than the twelfth century in date and unconnected to anything earlier than the Sung dynasty. This invalidates the assumptions made in Barnhart, "Li Kung-lin's *Hsiao Ching T'u*," note 110, and removes the most likely link between Li Kung-lin and any known earlier version. For a color reproduction, see *Chung-kuo mei-shu ch'üan-chi, Hui-hua pien* (Beijing, 1988), vol. 4, no. 33, pp. 50–51.
10. Reproduced as a facsimile album; see National Palace Museum, *Chao Meng-fu Hsiao-ching t'u-chuan* (Taipei, 1956). Both the painting and the calligraphy appear to be copies after a lost version by Chao Meng-fu.
11. Kuan Yun-shih, *Hsin-k'an ch'uan-hsiang Ch'eng-chai Hsiao-ching chih-chieh* (Beijing, 1308; reprint, Beijing, 1938).
12. Recorded in *Ku-kung shu-hua lu*, vol. 2, *chüan* 4, pp. 297–98.
13. The Chin T'ing-piao scroll is recorded in *Shih-ch'ü pao-chi, hsü-pien* (1793; reprint, Taipei: National Palace Museum, 1969–71), p. 1474.
14. Chou Mi, *Yun-yen kuo-yen lu* (*Mei-shu ts'ung-shu* ed.), reprinted in *I-shu ts'ung-pien* (Taipei, 1962), p. 45.
15. *Hsüan-ho hua-p'u* (original preface 1120), translated into modern Chinese and annotated by Yü Chien-hua (Beijing, 1964), p. 132.
16. Recorded in Pien Yung-yu, *Shih-ku-t'ang shu-hua hui-k'ao* (reprint, Taipei, 1958), *chüan* 12 (Li Kung-lin), pp. 1a–2a. See also Barnhart, "Li Kung-lin's *Hsiao Ching T'u*," pp. 38–39.
17. Translation, with slight modifications, from Legge, *Hsiao King*, pp. 465–67.
18. Used, for example, in the T'ang court's commemorative portraits of distinguished officials and in Northern Sung portraits of distinguished scholars. See *Wen-wu*, no. 4 (1960), pp. 61–69, for the former; and Mary Gardner Neill, *The Communion of Scholars* (New York, 1982), pp. 97–100, for the latter.
19. Osvald Siren, *Chinese Painting, Leading Masters and Principles*, 7 vols. (New York, 1956–58), vol. 3, pl. 199.
20. The version by Tu Chin, a fifteenth-century artist, now in the Metropolitan Museum, preserves this composition; see Christie's, New York, *Fine Chinese Paintings*, sale cat., June 5, 1985, lot 8.
21. Translation based upon Legge, *Hsiao King*, pp. 467–68; and Makra, *Hsiao Ching*, p. 5.

22. Su Pai, *Pai-sha Sung-mu* (Beijing, 1975), p. 80.

23. For late Northern Sung aesthetic theory, see especially the discussion of the term *p'ing-tan* ("flat and pale") in Jonathan Chaves, *Mei Yao-ch'en and the Development of Early Sung Poetry* (New York and London, 1976), pp. 114–32, where the term is translated as "even and bland." See also Susan Bush, *The Chinese Literati on Painting: Su Shih (1037–1101) to Tung Ch'i-ch'ang (1555–1636)*, Harvard-Yenching Institute Studies 27 (Cambridge, Mass., 1971), pp. 22–28, 67–74.

24. Translation based upon Legge, *Hsiao King*, pp. 468–69; and Makra, *Hsiao Ching*, p. 7.

25. Patricia Ebrey, "The Dynamics of Elite Domination in Sung China," *Harvard Journal of Asiatic Studies* 48, no. 2 (1988), pp. 493–519. See also an unpublished paper by Valerie Hansen, "Using Art as Evidence: What the *Qingming Shanghetu* Scroll Reveals about Twelfth-Century China," read at the Association of Asian Studies annual meeting in New Orleans, 1991.

26. *Sodai no kaiga: Tokubetsuten/Song Paintings from Japanese Collection*[s] (Nara, 1989), cat. 58, p. 93.

27. Translation, with slight modifications, from Legge, *Hsiao King*, pp. 469–70.

28. Ibid., pp. 470–71.

29. Ibid., pp. 471–72.

30. Agnes E. Meyer, *Chinese Painting as Reflected in the Thought and Art of Li Lung-mien, 1070–1106* (New York, 1923), pp. 287–88, for example.

31. Translation, with slight modifications, from Legge, *Hsiao King*, p. 474.

32. Ibid., pp. 474–75.

33. Ibid., pp. 476–80.

34. Arthur Waley, *The Book of Songs* (New York, 1960), p. 160.

35. Translation, with slight modifications, from Legge, *Hsiao King*, pp. 480–81.

36. Barnhart, "Li Kung-lin's *Hsiao Ching T'u*," p. 107.

37. Translation, with slight modifications, from Legge, *Hsiao King*, p. 481.

38. Lothar Ledderose, "A King of Hell," in the volume of essays written in honor of Kei Suzuki's sixtieth birthday, *Suzuki Kei sensei kanreki-kinen: Chūgoku kaigashi ronshū* (Tokyo, 1981), pp. 31–42.

39. Based upon Legge, *Hsiao King*, pp. 481–82.

40. For a discussion of Li's portraits of Su, see Barnhart, "Li Kung-lin's *Hsiao Ching T'u*," pp. 118–19.

41. The colophon is translated below and discussed in Barnhart, *Along the Border of Heaven*, note 55.

42. For a discussion of this practice, see Barnhart, "Li Kung-lin's *Hsiao Ching T'u*," p. 117. Mi Fu, *Hua-shih*, in *Mei-shu ts'ung-k'an* (Taipei, 1956), p. 87, discusses a self-portrait by Wang Wei.

43. An example by Lin T'ing-kuei is reproduced in Kojiro Tomita, *Portfolio of Chinese Paintings in the Museum: Han to Sung* (Cambridge, Mass., 1933), pl. 83.

44. Simon Schama, *Dead Certainties* (New York, 1991), pp. 3–39.

45. Legge, *Hsiao King*, pp. 482–83.

46. Juan Yüan, *Hsiao-ching chu-shu, chüan* 7, p. 1a, in Juan Yüan, *Shih-san ching chu-shu* (1816; reprint, Taipei, n.d.).

47. Translation, with slight modifications, from Legge, *Hsiao King*, p. 483.

48. Ibid., pp. 483–84.

49. Ibid., pp. 484–86.

50. Fong, *Beyond Representation*, pp. 51–54.

51. Translation, with slight modifications, from Legge, *The Religious Portions of the Shih King*, in *Sacred Books of China*, p. 367.

52. Translation, with slight modifications, from Legge, *Hsiao King*, p. 486.

53. Ibid., pp. 487–88.

54. Waley, *Book of Songs*, p. 41.

55. Author's translation of Su Shih's "Colophon to Li Kung-lin's *Hsiao-ching t'u*," which is found in *P'ei-wen-chai shu-hua p'u* (1708; reprint, Shanghai, 1883), p. 1a.

APPENDIX 1
Colophons and Documentation

Richard M. Barnhart

The only evidence of ownership earlier than Tung Ch'i-ch'ang (1555–1636) now on the Metropolitan scroll is a long colophon written on fine Sung paper by an unidentified "Han-man-weng" (fig. 49b).* The style of the calligraphy is close to that of the thirteenth-century poet and calligrapher Chang Chi-chih (1186–1266). The writer's seals are of wood, another feature of the Southern Sung or Yüan period. One seal reads: "Han-man-weng"; the other gives the cyclical date *keng-yin*. The text of the colophon is a biography of Li Kung-lin based on the account in Teng Ch'un's *Hua-chi* of 1167. The date *keng-yin* could therefore refer to 1230 or 1290. On the evidence of the style of the calligraphy, it could not be very much later.

Of the four colophons by Tung Ch'i-ch'ang, only the last of them, written in 1609, is dated. Tung certainly owned the scroll before 1603, when he had the complete text of chapter 9 reproduced in his collection of model calligraphy, *Hsi-hung-t'ang fa-t'ieh* (fig. 50). Tung's seals are also impressed on the present mounting, and on the silk itself. Tung's first colophon (fig. 49a) reads:

> In the *Hsuan-ho hua-p'u*, it is said that in his calligraphy Li Lung-mien revered the masters of the Wei and Chin periods. In this scroll, he took as his model the "Memorial Recommending Chi Chih" [*Chien Chi Chih piao*], by Chung Yu [151–230]. At the end of the scroll is the signature "Kung-lin." This is not seen in other works by him. I have had the calligraphy reproduced in the first *chüan* of my collection of model calligraphy, *Hsi-hung-t'ang* [*fa-t'ieh*]. As to the subtle beauty of his painting technique, it directly follows Ku Hu-t'ou [Ku K'ai-chih]. Together, his painting and calligraphy are worthy of being called "The Two Nonpareils."

*Because inscriptions and colophons are discussed in the chronological order in which they were added to the *Classic of Filial Piety* rather than in the order of their appearance on the scroll, figure references in Appendix 1 are occasionally out of sequence.

In his second note (fig. 49c), Tung points out the characters in the text that were written incompletely to avoid the taboos of the Sung imperial family. He mistakenly wrote *yin* (as in Yin dynasty) for *jang*, "to yield," as the character *yin* does not occur in the text:

> The characters *yin* and *ching* ["to respect"] are written incompletely in this scroll in order to avoid offending the Sung imperial family. The same taboos are observed in the calligraphy of Mi Fei.

Tung's third colophon (fig. 49d) suggests that the present scroll is the same as that recorded by Chou Mi about 1300:

> In his *Yun-yen kuo-yen lu*, Chou Mi records a *Hsiao-ching t'u* with both painting and calligraphy by Li Po-shih. That is this scroll. Whereas none of Po-shih's other paintings are signed, this one has the signature "Kung-lin," which suggests that it was painted for the emperor.

In his colophon dated 1609 (fig. 49e), Tung records the exchange made that year with the Han-lin academician Liu Yu-chen of the *Hsiao-ching t'u* for Chao Meng-fu's *Strumming a Lute in the Autumn Forest*.

From Liu Yu-chen, the painting passed into the hands of the noted authority on the *Hsiao-ching*, Hsu Yüan-wen (1634–1691), chief editor of the *Hsiao-ching Yen-i*, a voluminous compendium of extended interpretations of the *Classic of Filial Piety*. Hsu wrote and sealed a short colophon (fig. 49n) recording Tung Ch'i-ch'ang's note accompanying the reproduction of chapter 9 in *Hsi-hung-t'ang fa-t'ieh*, and affixed another seal to the painting proper.

The next known owner was Wang T'ing-chang, or Wang Ling-wen, a wealthy merchant from Hsi-hsien, Anhwei Province. So highly did he prize the scroll that he built a Hall of the *Classic of Filial Piety* (*Hsiao-ching T'ang*) in which to house it,

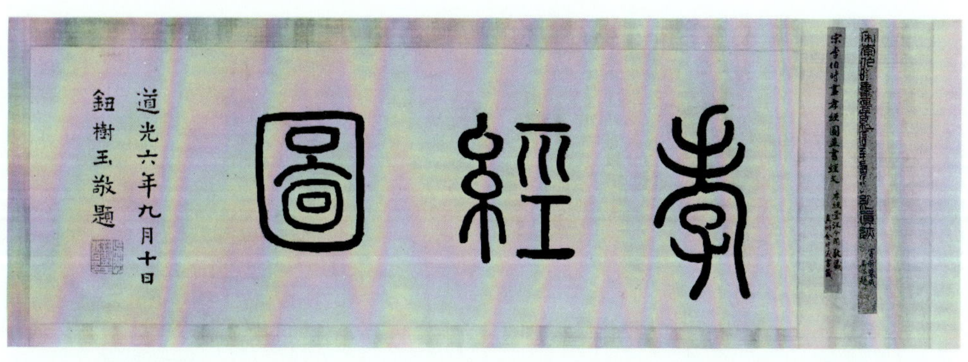

c b a

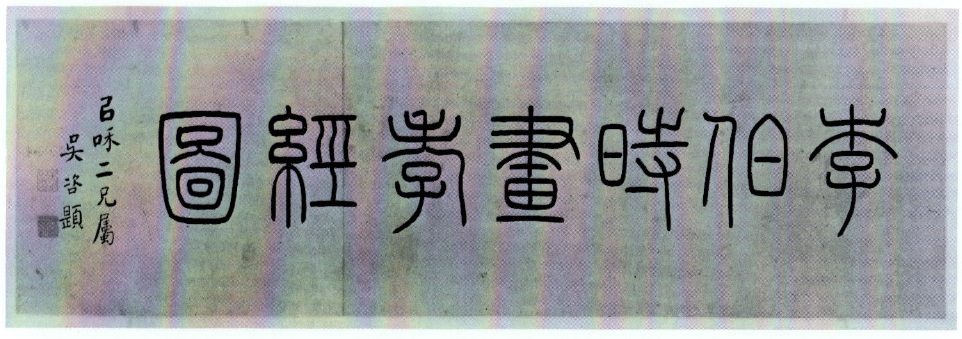

d

Figure 48a–d. Label strips and frontispieces to Li Kung-lin, *Classic of Filial Piety*

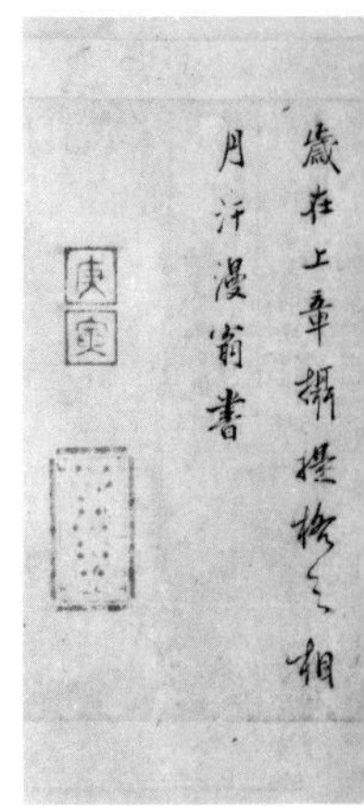

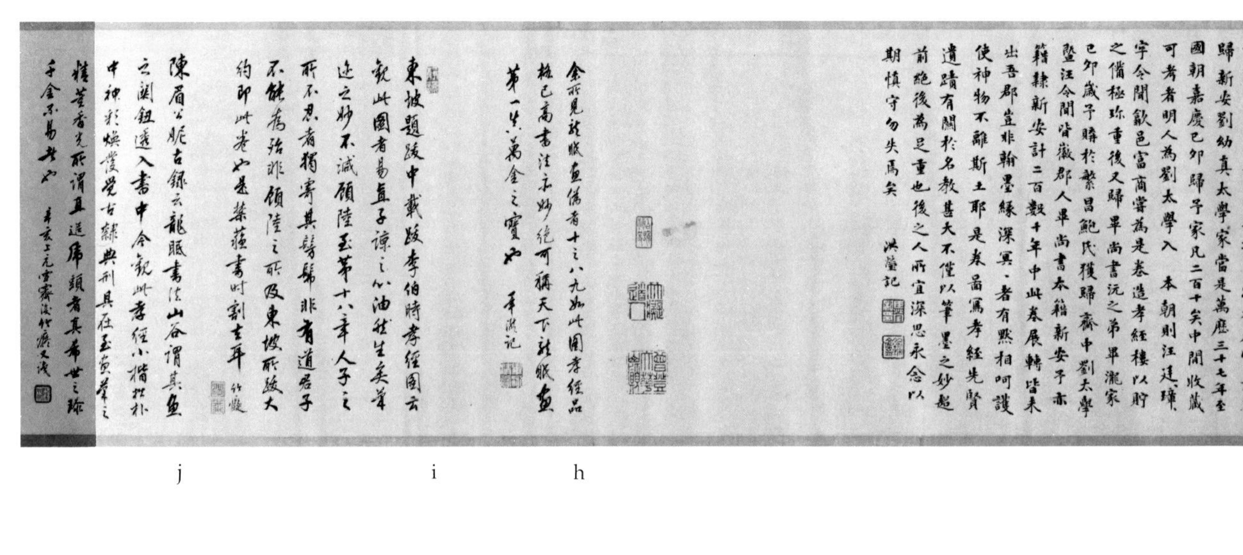

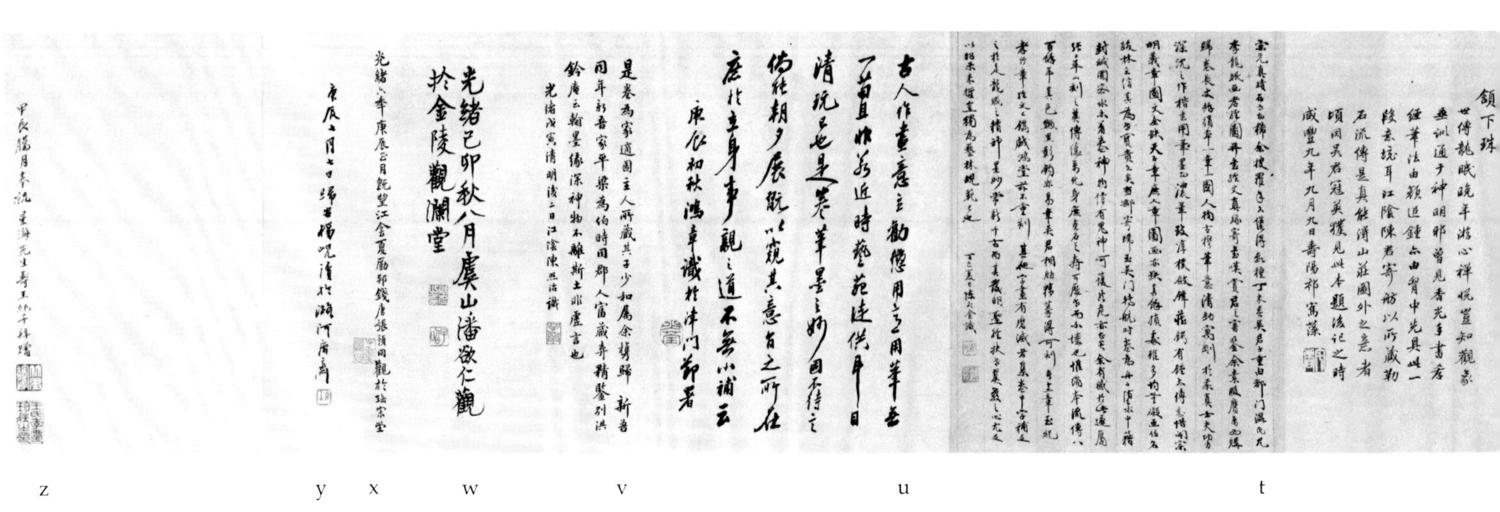

Figure 49a–z. Colophons to Li Kung-lin, *Classic of Filial Piety*

b a

f e d c

r q p o n m l k

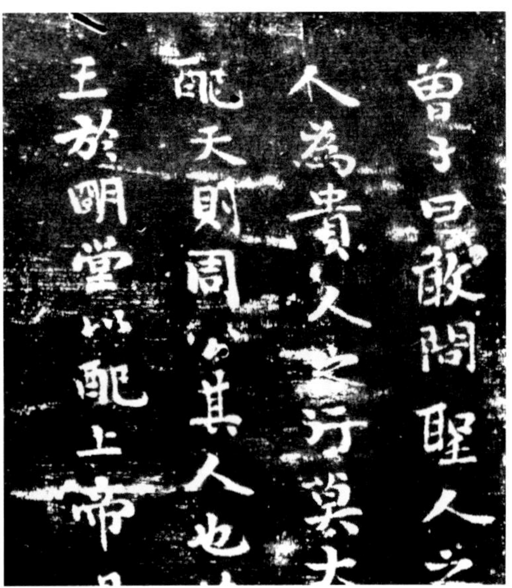

Figure 50. Tung Ch'i-ch'ang (1555–1636), colophon from a rubbing of chapter 9 of the *Classic of Filial Piety*. Marquand Library, Princeton University

using only rare and expensive cedarwood. A label strip still on the scroll reads: "*Hsiao-ching t'u*, painted by Li Po-shih of Sung, who also wrote the text. Respectfully treasured by Wang Ling-wen in his Hall of the *Classic of Filial Piety*. This label written by Chin Shih-i [active ca. 1736–96]" (fig. 48b). The painter Fang Shih-shu (1692–1751), like Wang a native of Hsi-hsien, saw the painting sometime before 1747, probably while it was owned by the merchant. His signature, along with those of Fang Chen-kuan (1679–1747) and Wu Wen-chih, records the viewing (fig. 49f). Fang Shih-shu also mentions the painting in his collection of miscellany, *T'ien-yung-an pi-chi*.

During this period, the scroll had already come to be veiled in mystery. Evidently, it was widely known but seldom seen. Among its admirers was Pi Lung, a brother of the governor-general of Hu-kuang (the present provinces of Hunan and Hupei). Finally, in 1788, after the death of Wang T'ing-chang, it was obtained by a certain Lu Meng-chao, who sold it to Pi Lung the following year for 50,000 cash. During the next decade, Pi Lung wrote six colophons that not only reveal his deep love for the painting but supply interesting historical background as well. They are given here in the sequence in which they were written:

1. (fig. 49m)
   Hsiao-ching t'u, a genuine work by Li Lung-mien of Sung. A rare treasure of the highest class. In the year *wu-shen* [1788] of the Ch'ien-lung period Lu Hsiao-lien, Meng-chao of Wu-men obtained it from the Wang family of Yang-chou. In the year *chi-yu* [1789], fifth intercalary month, I bought it from Meng-chao for a price of 50,000 cash.

   Recorded by the Master of Ching-i Studio, Pi Lung.

2. (fig. 49l)
   Wang T'ing-chang of Hsi-hsien, also called Ling-wen, was a wealthy merchant of Yang-chou, a man of considerable culture and elegance. Among his retainers was a certain Ch'iu Yu-kao, who once wrote an account of a long handscroll by Li Lung-mien transcribing and illustrating the *Classic of Filial Piety* that was owned by Wang. He obtained it for a price of 1,200 gold, and then built a Hall of

the *Classic of Filial Piety* in his garden using only precious cedarwood. He was one who truly guarded and cherished his precious possessions! I too knew from afar of the fame of the scroll, but I was never able to see it. In only a few years, however, Wang had passed away, and now the painting has unexpectedly come to me. One can only say that objects gather about those who love them. This painting, moreover, is a supernatural thing, and I will guard and preserve it with all my power. . . .

Recorded again by Chu-ch'ih.

3. (fig. 49k)
In the third month of the year *chi-yu* [1609], Tung Wen-min exchanged this scroll with Liu T'ai-hsueh of Hsin-an. I obtained it in the fifth month of the year *chi-yu* [1789], a difference of 180 years. I, too, am a native of Hsin-an. A remarkable thing indeed! This is evidently a case of a mysterious destiny.

Chi-yu [1789], autumn, eighth month, on a snowy day, recorded by Chu-ch'ih.

4. (fig. 49j)
In Ch'en Mei-kung's [Ch'en Chi-ju's] *Ni-ku-lu* it says: "Of Li Kung-lin's calligraphy, Huang T'ing-chien said, 'He penetrated the secrets of calligraphy through the doorway of painting.'" As we look now at the small *k'ai* script of the *Hsiao-ching,* a spiritual brilliance radiates from the primitive brushstrokes, and we can perceive the pattern of the ancient *li* [clerical] script still preserved in it. As to the excellence of the brushwork of the painting, as Tung Ch'i-ch'ang said, it directly follows Ku K'ai-chih. Truly, it is one of the rarest treasures of the age! I would not exchange this scroll for a thousand in gold!

Hsin-hai [1791], fifteenth day of the first month, after the snow cleared, again recorded by Chu-chi'ih.

5. (fig. 49i)
In the *Collected Colophons of Su Shih* [*Tung-p'o t'i-pa*], there is a colophon to Li Po-shih's *Hsiao-ching t'u*: "When we look at these pictures, feelings of warm, loving duty and loyalty toward our parents well up within us. The superb brushwork is not inferior to that of Ku K'ai-chih and Lu T'an-wei. As for the final chapter, in which all that a son finds unbearable is described, the painter conveys these meanings in only the faintest suggestion of form. None but a truly superior man possessing the Way could achieve this level. Ku and Lu did not reach it." The painting that Su Shih inscribed was in all probability this one. His colophon was simply cut off during the period of Emperor Hui-tsung's ban on his calligraphy.

[signed] Chu-ch'ih

6. (fig. 49h)
Of the paintings attributed to Li Kung-lin that I have seen, eight or nine out of every ten have been forgeries. As for this *Hsiao-ching t'u*, not only is the quality of the painting itself lofty but the calligraphy, too, is of unsurpassed excellence. It deserves to be called the finest Lung-mien painting in the world; a treasure worth 10,000 gold.

Recorded by Pi Lung.

The property of the Pi family was confiscated in 1799, following the discovery of what appeared to be scandalous misuse of government funds by Pi Lung's brother Pi Yüan. It was probably at that time that the *Hsiao-ching t'u* was acquired by a certain Pao of

Fan-ch'ang, who in turn sold it to the scholar Hung Ying. In his colophon (fig. 49g), Hung, too, remarks on the mysterious fate that had seemed to guide and preserve the painting within the borders of Anhwei for over two centuries:

> Is there not a deep and mysterious destiny of brush and ink, protected by a guardian deity who will not permit this holy thing to leave this land? This scroll, which illustrates the *Classic of Filial Piety*, is a legacy from the worthies of old. Its affinity to the renowned teachings of Confucius is great indeed! It is worthy of esteem therefore not merely because the excellence of brush and ink is unsurpassed through all time. Those who follow me should think deeply and long on this that they might guard and protect it without remiss.

On the day following the Tuan-yang Festival (observed on the fifth day of the fifth lunar month), 1826, the distinguished Confucian scholar Niu Shu-yü (1760–1827) viewed the scroll with two friends (fig. 49o). Later that year, on the tenth day of the ninth lunar month, Niu also wrote a title frontispiece (fig. 48c), one of two still attached to the painting. The second was written by the noted calligrapher Wu Tzu (1813–1858; fig. 48d), who also contributed a label strip (fig. 48a).

The great teacher and literary figure Yao Nai remarked before his death in 1815 that he had lived all his life in the Lung-mien Mountains, near the birthplace of Li Kung-lin, but had never seen a painting by the Sung master. Yao Nai's student Kuan T'ung, in the colophon he wrote twelve years after his master's death, addresses him to report that his sons had now acquired not one but three paintings by Li Kung-lin, and that he might rest more easily knowing that his lifelong desire had been fulfilled, albeit only in death (fig. 49p):

> Li Po-shih's *Hsiao-ching t'u*. From each chapter, he selected one or two words to be illustrated. Its dreamlike images are astonishingly fine, far superior to the other two paintings [attributed to Li Kung-lin], *Immortals* and *Pig Hunt*. As for the calligraphy, an earlier writer has said that it vigorously pursues the model of Chung Yu, and the comment is not an empty one. Yao Hsi-pao once said that though he lived in Lung-mien, in his entire lifetime he had never seen Po-shih's painting. Now this inequity has been corrected. In the space of a few years, three precious paintings by Li Po-shih have been acquired. The Master should feel contented now.

Twenty years later the scroll was in Beijing, in the possession of a family named Wen. Through the good offices of the painter and connoisseur Wu Chun, or Wu Kuan-ying, it was brought to the attention of another, wealthier painter, Ch'en Shih-chin. Ch'en was at that time in mourning, and following Wu Chun's advice he bought the scroll, as much, it seems, for its subject matter, so meaningful to him just then, as for its artistic merit. A deeply filial son, he immediately set about having the entire scroll engraved on stone so that through rubbings it could be more widely circulated. The painting he apparently guarded jealously and let scarcely anyone see. His long colophon, written in 1857, recounts the story and well illustrates the almost tangible aura of immortality that surrounded the painting during the entire period of its known history (fig. 49t). Ch'en Shih-chin, like its other owners, regarded it as a holy object:

> Extant authentic works of the Sung and Yüan periods are extremely rare. I have been searching for them for many years, and have succeeded in finding only a few. In the spring of the year *ting-wei* [1847], Wu Tzu-chung [Wu Chun] saw at

the home of Shi Wen in the capital Li Lung-mien's *Hsiao-ching t'u*, the transcription and illustration of the *Classic of Filial Piety*, an authentic work. He sent me a letter praising the work, and as I had long been impressed by Master Wu's connoisseurship, I asked him to buy it and have it brought back to me. The scroll is well over ten feet long, on silk; each chapter of the text is accompanied by an illustration. The figures are antique and respectful, the brushwork pure and vigorous, embodying strength in pliancy—truly a work that reveals the artistic merit and profound thought of a scholar. In his calligraphy in the *k'ai*, or model, script he used very thick ink. The effect he achieves with the brush is pure and unsophisticated; the tip of the brush is withdrawn, its edge concealed. It follows the concepts of Chung T'ai-fu [Chung Yu]. Unfortunately, both the text and the illustration of chapter 1 are lost, and the illustrations of the chapters on the emperor and the common people are lost as well. Although there are numerous other areas of loss and damage, none is excessive. As for the transmission of the painting, the forest of colophons by famous men suffices to prove that it has long been treasured and esteemed. When the boat on which the scroll was sent me by post was turning around at Wu-men, a boatman accidentally dropped it into the water. Thanks to the strength and firmness of the wrapping, however, the water did not penetrate through to the painting itself. Truly, holy things are protected by the gods! And yet they can still encounter grave danger! I was moved by this, and decided to entrust the scroll to Master Chang Ts'ui-shan to make an engraving so that it might be transmitted through numberless transformations. The longevity of hard, white stone will enable it to pass through future ages without harm. The silk, however, having survived over eight hundred years, had turned very dark and it was not easy to trace the painting. Fortunately, Master Wu assisted in the work, and a fine copy was made. We obtained a version that could be engraved consisting of twelve chapters. Chapter 10 [a mistake for chapter 9] had already been reproduced in *Hsi-hung-t'ang*, and we did not repeat it. As for the rest, wherever the calligraphy or painting had been rubbed off or lost, we repaired it with material drawn from elsewhere in the scroll. With this, Lung-mien's spirit and the excellence of his art will be fresh and new forever; and his mind, which illumines the sage's classic and thereby assists the world in spreading his teaching, will still be able to clearly explain the meaning of filial piety to philosophers of the future. It is certainly not merely a model for the world of art and nothing more!

Ting-ssu [1857], a summer day, recorded by Ch'en Shih-chin.

During the long period in which the painting was owned by Ch'en Shih-chin and subsequently by his son Ch'en Shao-ho—from 1847 to 1878—it was evidently rarely seen. No colophons written for the painting itself are now attached to it. Rubbings of the engraving, however, circulated widely, and three colophons now attached to the Metropolitan Museum scroll were written in appreciation of these reproductions. The rubbings were seen in each case through Wu Chun, who had been instrumental in the purchase of the work by Ch'en Shih-chin. One colophon was written by the eminent scholar, poet, and official Ch'i Chun-tsao (1793–1866; fig. 49s); another by the celebrated painter and martyr Tai Hsi (1801–1860; fig. 49r); and the third by a Buddhist monk, Chueh-an (fig. 49q). Ch'i Chun-tsao, himself a rigorous Confucianist who served four emperors in his long career, emphasized in his colophon the essentially Confucian philosophy of Li Po-shih. His poem reads:

How can "emptiness" compare to imitating the mirror of reality!
When the myriad Buddhist fates are swept away, the true Confucian scholar is revealed.
The customs of the family are preserved in *Moral Lessons at the Mountain Home* [another painting by Li Kung-lin].
But *this* is a pearl beneath the jaws of a dragon [i.e., a treasure almost impossible to obtain]!

In his colophon, now attached to the painting but originally written for one of the reproductions shown him by Wu Kuan-ying, Tai Hsi tells of the reputation of the painting and of the influence of Li Kung-lin's calligraphy on the famous eighteenth-century calligrapher Liu Yung (1719–1804):

> Lung-mien shan-jen's *Hsiao-ching t'u*, together with the text of the classic written in the small *k'ai* script. Ssu-weng [Tung ch'i-ch'ang] was completely bowled over by it. He had the calligraphy engraved in the first chapter of *Hsi-hung-t'ang*. Through that reproduction I was already familiar with its general appearance. As for the painting itself, I had no idea by whom it was owned and enjoyed. Recently, however, I met the Chung-ch'eng [Counselor of the Center] Hsu Hsun-ch'en [Hsu Nai-chao], and our talk turned to this painting. He spoke with the greatest admiration of the lofty antiquity of the style of painting and the freedom and purity of the calligraphy. He also told me that Liu Wen-ch'ing [Liu Yung], who lived early in this dynasty, had completely based his own style of calligraphy on it. I thirsted for even a glimpse of the scroll, but my wish was never fulfilled. Then, in the fifth intercalary month of *ting-ssu* [1857] in the Hsien-feng era, Master Wu Kuan-ying of Chiang-yin came to visit me, bringing with him a rubbing made from a stone engraving of the entire scroll made by Master Ch'en Chi-fang, and at long last I had the privilege of seeing this holy object. Stunned with awe and admiration, I realized that everything Hsun-weng [Hsun-ch'en] had said of it was indeed true!

In 1878, the scroll was given by Ch'en Shao-ho, the son of Ch'en Shih-chin, to Hsin-wu of P'ing-liang via Ch'en Chao-chih, another relative of Ch'en Shih-chin. A colophon by Ch'en Chao-chih records the transaction and points out that, thanks to the deities who guarded its fate, the painting had still not left Anhwei (fig. 49v). The last colophon of any interest was written two or three years later, in 1880, by Li Hung-chang (fig. 49u). Li severely admonishes someone who had had the audacity to question the authenticity of the painting, and he returns to a theme that runs through the colophons, the essentially didactic purpose of the work:

> When the ancient men made paintings, their primary purpose was moral instruction. Not a single thought or brushstroke was accidental. Theirs was no "art for art's sake," as in the modern world of art. The excellence of brush and ink in this painting can by no means be regarded as spurious. One can enjoy it from morning till night, seeking to discover wherein lies its meaning. Nor can it be said to be without some small assistance in the path of establishing one's life and serving one's parents.

Following other colophons by P'an Yü-jen (fig. 49w), Hsia Li-pang, and Chang Yü (fig. 49x) is a notation by the connoisseur and collector Yang Hsien, who examined the scroll in his studio in the same year, 1880 (fig. 49y). It was later owned by C. C. Wang, whose brief note is the last written (fig. 49z).

APPENDIX 2
The Conservation and Remounting of the *Classic of Filial Piety*

Sondra Castile and Takemitsu Oba

The timing of the conservation of a work of art is critical to its preservation. Asian paintings and calligraphy must maintain a delicate balance between pigment, support, and mounting materials—each of which is usually a single thin layer adhered or joined to another layer in a variety of ways. When the materials themselves become unstable or the equilibrium between them is lost, deterioration begins. This may be the result of inherent vice, the term used to describe the capacity of a work of art to degrade in time, but it may be hastened by a deficiency in the skill of the mounter; by the quality, choice, or use of materials; or by the conditions of storage and handling. Whatever the cause, the conservator hopes to have the opportunity to arrest these deleterious processes before further loss can occur, for although the components of an Asian painting and its mounting may seem fragile individually, when united in a mounting finely executed, they may be expected to survive a very long time.

The conservation and remounting of the Li Kung-lin handscroll the *Classic of Filial Piety* was carried out at the Oka Bokkodo conservation facilities in Kyoto, Japan, and was completed in 1978. The Oka studio has worked on many paintings registered in Japan as National Treasures or Important Cultural Properties, and has remounted other well-known works from collections around the world. It has a reputation for being able to treat paintings in particularly hazardous states of deterioration. It was for this reason that Iwataro Oka, the master of the studio, and his staff were asked to undertake the conservation of this handscroll. When the work was begun, the painting was on loan to Princeton University, and both before and during the process of conservation, Professor Shujiro Shimada, of Princeton's Department of Art and Archaeology, consulted extensively with Mr. Oka.

The frangibility of the handscroll and the various losses that were apparent might not in themselves have been cause for immediate alarm. With infrequent handling and optimum storage conditions, a scroll with what appears to be similar deficiencies may survive for a long time without further appreciable loss. But with the prospect of more frequent handling for study purposes and the anticipation of public exhibition, the need for remounting assumed a certain urgency. This determination was reinforced by the preliminary examination, which revealed that the first backing, the one adhered directly to the painting, was silk rather than paper.

Although there is in China a long history of the use of silk as the first backing, experience has shown that its use causes a particular kind of deterioration. Where losses are sustained and no repairs have been made to the missing portions, a second silk backing would cover all the holes at once. This does not, however, constitute what is referred to as a fill, since where a loss existed there is one layer of silk, whereas where no loss existed there are two layers. This scattered imbalance cannot be entirely compensated for in the mounting processes that follow.

The Li Kung-lin handscroll had silk repairs in addition to the silk backing. The backing therefore constituted a second layer over the entire reverse of the painting support. As the handscroll was rolled and unrolled, the two layers of silk wore against each other, resulting in expanded losses caused by the additional breakage of threads on the outside perimeters of the holes. New losses also resulted where small areas of a few threads were not filled before the silk backing was applied. In general, a silk backing ultimately lacks the long-term flexibility and adhesion of paper, and this was certainly the case in the handscroll under consideration.

The twelfth-century painter and calligrapher Mi Fu, who was himself known as an accomplished mounter, cautioned against the use of silk as a backing. He also noted the damage that could occur from the use of silk for patching by methods in use at the time. Mi Fu's observations remain valid, and the practices he describes have not been abandoned even today. For a variety of reasons, many mounters continue to use methods of silk application in repair or backing that may have been observed to hasten deterioration.

The conservation and remounting of the *Classic of Filial Piety* began with a thorough analysis of the individual elements of the painting and colophons, and of the condition of the pigment surfaces, the silk and paper supports, and the mounting. The mounting included the backings, textiles, rollers, cord, and fittings that adapted the painting to the handscroll format. These findings and the interpretation of them were the basis for determining the procedures for conservation that would be necessary and appropriate. In general, there are three fundamental questions that must be taken into consideration: (1) How will areas of loss in the silk be resolved, and is the appropriate silk for repair available? (2) What material will constitute the first new backing? (3) Will the textiles of the present mounting be repaired and used again, or will they be changed? Without answers to these questions remounting cannot begin; materials must be prepared and the method of their use determined beforehand. Because the mounting provides overall stabilization, the conservator should not dismantle the mounting until assured that steady progress through all phases of the remounting will occur; experimentation is rarely possible.

Paintings and Colophons

Silk thread thins with age, and there was evidence of such thinning of the silk support. Many warp threads were broken, often leaving only weft threads in place. As a result of this breakage, there remained many scattered islands of loosely associated threads. Additional losses had been sustained since the last remounting, and in many areas the silk support was lifting from the backing and in danger of imminent loss. Much of this condition could be ascribed to the adverse effects of the first backing.

The silk of the backing was of heavier thread and a coarser weave than that of the painting. Consequently, it was still quite strong and not disintegrated, though it had adhered unevenly as the paste bond weakened.

At some time in the past, the top and bottom edges of the painting silk had frayed or been damaged and had been replaced with silk to restore height and to even the edges. Repairs within the painting itself had been made with silk and applied with varying degrees of skill. Although the repairs had probably been made during a single remounting, it was evident that the work had been done by more than one person. The repairs were placed in the missing areas and cut on straight lines generally conforming to the shape of the uneven missing areas. The edges of these areas had first been trimmed away to make straight edges, and in this way thread ends had been lost. The silk backing was applied when these repairs were in place. Very small areas of two or three threads, commonly warp threads, had not been filled. The technique of repairing these very small losses is difficult, and the previous mounter did not, or perhaps did not have the expertise to, address the problem.

The ink and slight red pigment of the painting surface were generally stable. No pigments, such as aquamarine or malachite, which tend to weaken silk, had been used. Some small movement of red, which had occurred in the past, was noted.

Several problems had to be dealt with in the planning of the conservation:

- How would the many small, isolated thread clusters and the areas where broken warp threads had left only weft fragments be preserved during the removal of the backing?
- Should any, or all, of the existing repairs be retained?
- How should losses be compensated for, and what repairs should be made where there were broken or lost warp threads? To what extent should repairs be made to preserve the painting from further losses without becoming obtrusive?
- What silk would be compatible for repair?

The dark silk backing had made the repaired areas unobtrusive, but it had at the same time rendered fine lines less distinct and difficult to read. The tone of the new paper backing would be critical in achieving a visual balance and redefining the finest lines.

The silk repairs that filled losses in the area of the painting itself preserved details of the images as the in-painter had imagined them to be originally. Ink lines had been extended on the repairs, and various details had been filled in. By this method, the previous restorer may have intended to avoid distraction to the eye, but they are clearly not by the hand of the artist. Although well painted they contain errors, most notably in a figure near the beginning of the scroll who has acquired a third leg (figs. 51a, b).

It had to be decided whether the existing mounting—that is, the textile portions and other sections not directly used for painting or colophons—would be reused. It is inevitably easier to begin with new materials. (The practice of discarding an existing mounting was, and today remains, prevalent and may be attested to by the frequent and conspicuous loss of parts of seals on Chinese paintings where two sections are joined.) The materials of an existing mounting must be of a quality demanded by the work of art. If they are not, it must be determined whether materials exist to improve

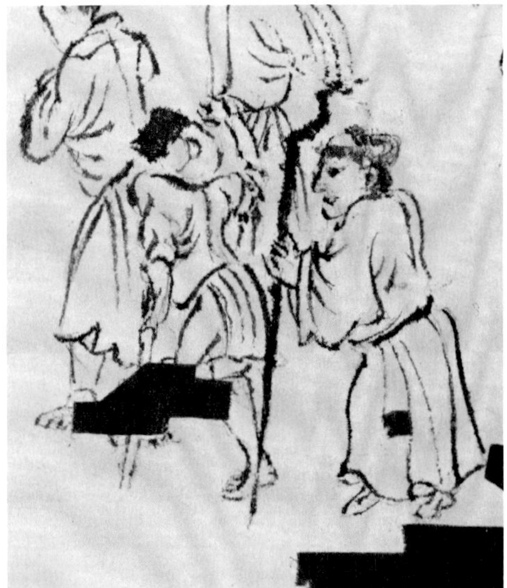

a

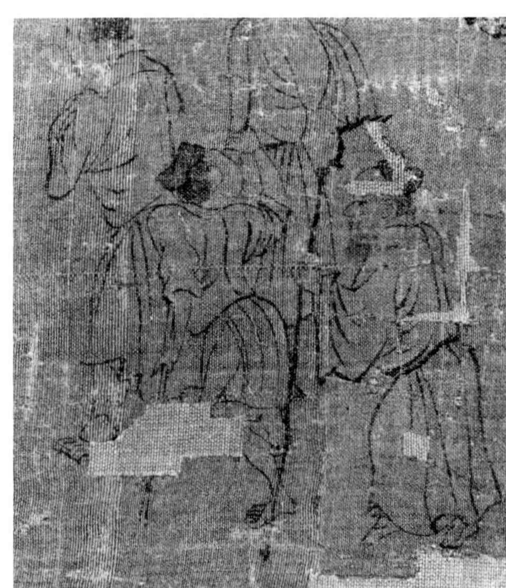

b

Figure 51a. Facsimile, showing detail of figure with third leg drawn on repair

Figure 51b. Detail of same figure after conservation

upon them. The juxtaposition of color and pattern must complement the painting and take into account relevant historical and thematic considerations. The measurements of the mounting not only create an overall balance between the elements of the scroll but also aid in its preservation—that is, the edges must be wide enough and the sections next to the rollers long enough to prevent damage.

It was determined that the following procedures would be adopted. The section of the handscroll that held the title sheet, the painting, and the first colophon by Tung Ch'i-ch'ang would constitute one scroll. Because this colophon was joined by its mounting and by a seal, it could not be permanently separated and joined to the other colophons. The remaining colophons would constitute a second handscroll. All previous repairs would be removed and preserved, pasted in their original position, on a free-hand line copy of the painting. The Ming title slip mounted on the outside textile would be removed and placed next to the earlier title slip inside the scroll. One repair that had seals impressed upon it would be kept in its present position with the painting section. Because the quality of this in-painting was high, it would be preserved and remain also as a record of past conservation.

Procedures

Pigments or ink on a painting must be stable before any treatment can begin. If they are not, stabilization is usually achieved by applying a weak solution of animal glue to each of the pigmented areas individually. It may be necessary to repeat this process many times until the deteriorated binder has been replaced and the pigment again firmly adhered. In the Li Kung-lin scroll only the red pigment, which in one area had bled, may have been unstable. However, as the entire silk support was particularly thin and weakened, it was treated with a 1.5 percent solution of rabbit-skin glue. This served to enliven and strengthen the silk.

We began by removing the outer and inner rollers. First, the paper or silk of the mounting attached to the rollers was dampened slightly, and, when the paste relaxed, the rollers were separated from the scroll.

With a sheet of rayon paper dampened and brushed out on the worktable, a section of the scroll was extended facedown. It was dampened evenly and smoothed out by brushing. When the dampness had penetrated and softened the paste between layers, each of the backings was removed by peeling, until the layer at which the different sections of the handscroll were joined was revealed. Each section was then separated by lifting the edge where the overlap was joined. Measurements of each section were taken.

Because of the extreme weakness of the silk, combined with losses and tears, the first backing next to the painting was not removed at this time.

Removal of the First Backing

A sheet of rayon paper extending an inch beyond the painting support on all four sides was dampened and brushed out smooth on a glass table. The silk was dampened with a fine spray of water. In a few minutes, the water was absorbed and the silk rested on the table in undulations. To remove the slack, the silk was lifted slowly from both ends. Twelve-inch sections of rayon paper, with a one-inch overlap, were applied successively to cover the face of the silk. The dampness retained in the silk made it possible to affix the paper evenly and smoothly. With the use of a soft-haired brush, all creases and air bubbles in the rayon paper were eliminated.

The painting was turned facedown and smoothed out. With the aid of transmitted light, the silk backing was slowly removed. During the time the support was dampened, the paste with which the first backing had been adhered softened, gradually absorbing the moisture. As this bond weakened, the backing silk was carefully drawn back in small sections. Where the silk was more difficult to remove, or where previous repairs or thread islands were tenuously in place, pencil-sized brushes were used to ease the two silks apart. This left the intact section of the silk support, previous repairs, and separated fragments still resting on the rayon paper beneath.

With this technique, once removal of the first backing had begun, the process had to continue—or the same conditions be maintained—until the first new backing had been applied. Because this process could not be completed in one day, the silk was kept damp in a cool environment overnight, until the backing could be entirely removed.

The repairs to the original (fig. 52a) were lifted off to be placed on the facsimile (fig. 52b). At this time, errant threads were realigned. Lines of the painting that were not coherent or that might have shifted slightly during the removal of the backing were eased into their proper position. Single silk threads and islands of loosely joined threads were straightened in the direction of warp and weft. This justification can no longer be accomplished when the first backing is in place. The illustration below (fig. 52c) shows the same section after completion of conservation.

Dyeing of Backing Papers

It was determined that dyeing the backing paper in a very light shade similar to that of the silk support would produce the desired effect of creating an overall balance of tone and of preserving the definition of fine lines. The paper was dyed with an extract of alder cones (*Alnus firma*). A mordant of wood-ash lye was used, and the papers were given a final rinse.

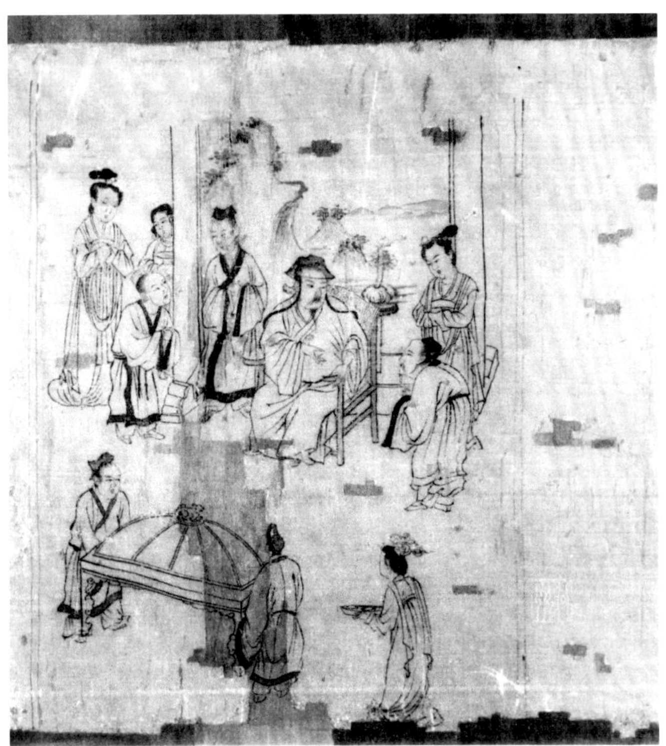
a

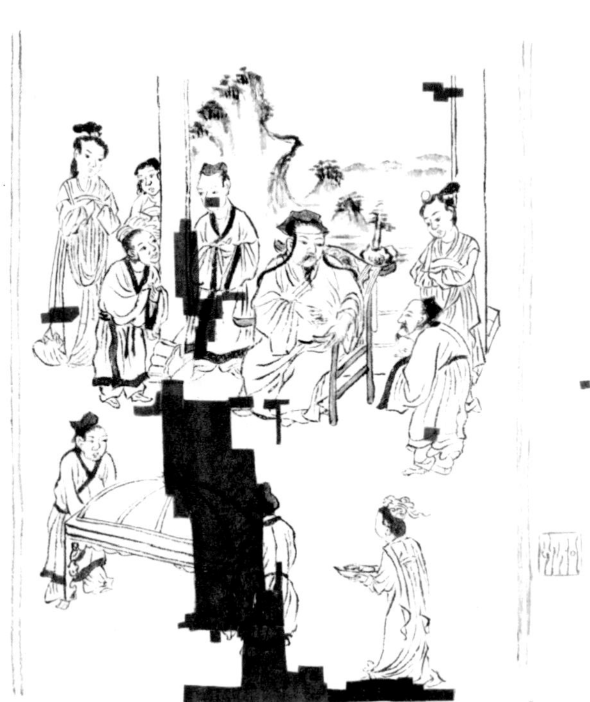
b

Paste

The paste used today is essentially the same as that used on the earliest mountings known. It is a material that, if properly utilized, makes the process completely reversible even after hundreds of years.

Care must be taken in the preparation of paste used for mounting. Paste for mounting is always made rather thick, as it will later be thinned in the mounting process. Wheat starch from which most of the gluten has been removed is first mixed with water and stirred over heat. For part of this process, the heat is high and the liquid boils. The amount of water necessary to make a thick paste and the time it takes for it to pass through the various stages differ as a result of variations in humidity and in the starch. It is normally made within an hour. The person making paste must be alert throughout and the paste stirred constantly for the process to be successful. "Good" and "bad" paste may look exactly the same, but the latter will not have the proper tack.

Flexibility is required in the mounting of scrolls; a strong, stiff bond is not desirable. Wheat starch produces a weak adhesive. The relative strength of the adhesive is further controlled by diluting the paste to various consistencies as needed. In the mounting of old paintings and calligraphy, an even weaker bond is preferable. For this reason, much of the paste used on some parts of an old mounting will have been aged from six to ten years. This paste is made in the same way as regular paste and is stored in a cool place with little fluctuation in temperature. During this period, various bacteria reduce the paste to a more pliable consistency. When used on the last backing, after being strained and diluted, it has the consistency of slightly milky water.

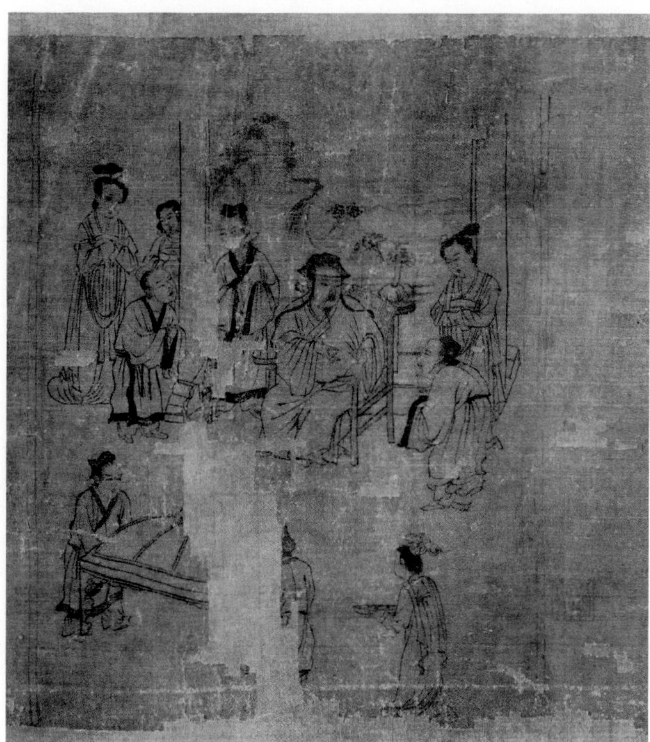

c

Figure 52a. Chapter 13 of the *Classic of Filial Piety* before conservation, showing previous repairs

Figure 52b. Chapter 13, showing repairs on facsimile

Figure 52c. Chapter 13 after conservation

First Backing

When the process of thread alignment was complete and while the silk support was still damp, the first backing was applied. The paste was diluted to a consistency that would flow off the brush in a thin stream. For this backing, the paste was brushed onto the smooth side of the paper, which is directly affixed to the reverse of the painting silk. (The last backing is pasted on the rough side, so that the smooth side of the paper will be facing out.) The paste was applied liberally and the excess removed until the layer was even over the whole sheet. A few minutes later, when the tack had built up with the evaporation of a slight amount of moisture, the backing was smoothed out on the silk by brushing into place. The timing of this procedure is very important. Too much or too little moisture on the silk and/or backing paper will result in poor or uneven adhesion. The effects of this miscalculation may not become evident immediately but may cause premature delamination of layers of the mounting at a later time.

After being backed, the painting was lifted from the table and turned faceup. The protective rayon sheets were then removed one by one and the painting was placed on a fine woolen blanket, the woolen fibers providing just enough support for even drying throughout.

The removal of the backings on the calligraphy and colophon sections followed a similar course. Transmitted light was used to detect particularly thin areas, and, where necessary, layers were removed to achieve an evenness throughout. Necessary repairs were made with paper before backing.

Backings were also removed from the various parts of the mounting. Before backing, warp and weft threads were straightened and repairs made. The illustration below

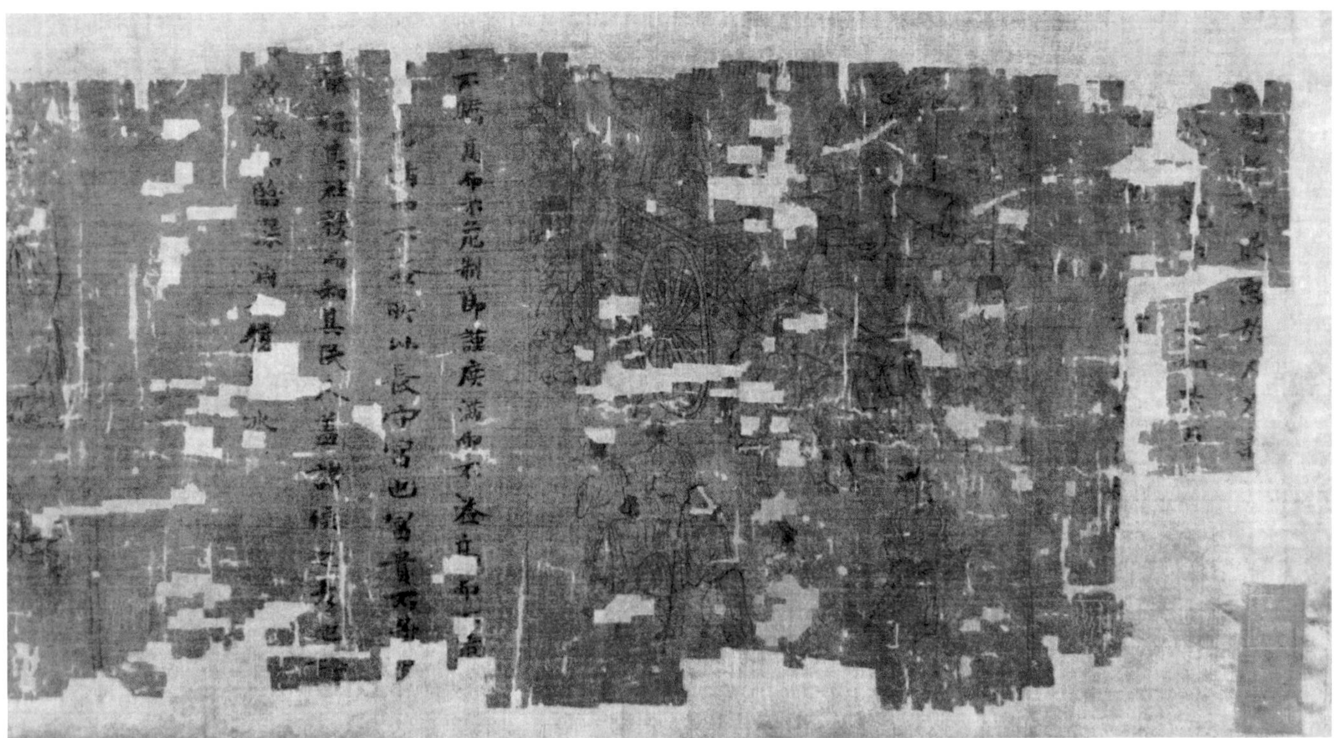

Figure 53. Chapter 3 of the *Classic of Filial Piety* before in-painting

shows a section of the scroll after backing and after repairs were made, but before in-painting (fig. 53).

Drying Boards

The time that the various pieces of mounting and painting spend on the drying boards, and the time spent there after the work is joined, is critical in achieving the final balance between the many disparate parts. The time spent on the boards may be thought of as a time of acclimatization, during which old and new textiles, papers, and paste are united in a single object.

The discrepancies between the various materials as they lie adjacent or joined to one another in a scroll—differences in the weaves, the thickness of the threads, and the direction of use, whether warp or weft—must be individually evened out by the choice of backing, paste consistency, and brushing techniques. While these decisions are usually straightforward with new works of art and new materials, old works of art and old or used materials make the problem much more complex, as deteriorated materials are not of uniform strength and tend to respond unevenly.

During the backing, it is crucial to be able to control the amount of deformity that occurs. Such regulation is possible through a knowledge of the probable limits of this process and the subsequent application of moisture. The tendency of a textile to stretch and to shrink will be minimized by the application of less moisture. Weave distortion may also be controlled or minimized in this way. Based on knowledge of this distortion factor among the materials being used, each piece was dampened to the degree considered necessary, with the aim of having all pieces dry uniformly. Whether the piece is brushed in the direction of the warp, the weft, both ways, or neither way is critical. Too much dampness on a section that expands a great deal will cause excessive shrinkage in drying, and it will not be consistently flat. Achieving the sought-for balance during the times the sections are on the drying boards is accomplished by continuous refinement. After the sections have been joined, this adjustment can no longer be made.

The backed section is pasted to the drying boards along the narrow edges of the backing paper that extend on all four sides.

Silk Repair

With the first backing in place, repair of the losses could begin. The silk used in the repair, though differing in the number of warp threads, was of a similar weave and weight as that of the painting silk. The existing tone was deepened slightly by dyeing with alder-cone extract and ink ground from an ink stick. This added color brought the tone somewhat closer to that of the painting support, which made it easier to achieve the final tone desired by later in-painting.

After dyeing, drying, and rinsing away the dye residue from the repair silk, the threads were aligned and a thin backing sheet was put on with a very diluted paste. With the painting faceup, the edges of the backing paper extending beyond the silk support were pasted to a glass light table. The silk was slightly dampened so that it dried perfectly flat. By means of transmitted light the exact shapes of the losses were clearly visible. The repair silk was aligned facedown with the warp and weft of the painting support. The outlines of the losses were individually traced with pencil on the thin paper backing of the repair silk and then cut out with a fine blade, severing the warp and weft threads one by one to make the edge of the repair mesh with the edges of the loss. Paste was applied to the exposed silk of the repair and set firmly on the backing paper beneath the hole. Moisture applied from the tip of a small brush loosened the paper backing of the silk repair which was then lifted off, leaving the silk repair in place.

Joining of Sections and Reinforcement

All sections were removed from the drying boards. The edges to be joined were made square. Reinforcing strips—narrow strips of very thin paper lightly dyed to the tone of the backing—were applied over the first backing to weakened lines or creases in the painting. These had to provide strength without causing stiffness and without being visible from the front.

If the paper strips are too thick or too wide or are improperly placed, further creasing will occur. Damage to the pigments on the surface may also result. The scroll, with its first backing, was curved gently around a roller and pressed lightly with the thumb and forefinger, revealing a slight rise or peak at weakened places. The length of this incipient crease was then marked with a fine pencil on the backing paper. Other weak places were later detected with transmitted light. After the strips were pasted on the scroll, the entire scroll was checked once again and more strips were added as necessary.

Second Backing

As different thicknesses of paper were used in the first backing of each section to address the problem of balance, the selection of paper thickness for the second backing continued to pursue this balance. Where there was less strength, firmer paper was used. In this way, the discrepancies along the length of the scroll were gradually evened out. A soft paper with a small clay content was used.

Last Backing

Because the folded top and bottom edges of the silk mounting had been worn through, a folded-paper reinforcing border was added over the length of the scroll, extending almost invisibly from the mounting edge. The final backing of Chinese paper was pasted with the smooth side facing away from the scroll. The scroll was then returned to the drying boards, and when it was perfectly flat, the in-painting of the repairs was begun.

In-painting

Although the repair silk had been minimally dyed beforehand, the tone was kept intentionally lighter than the final effect would require. Silk darkens with age, and in-painting must take this into account; even after many years the in-painted areas should never become darker than the surrounding silk. (The ill effects of the initial matching of the color of the in-painting to that of the surrounding silk may be observed in many Asian paintings that have been repaired and remounted. Repairs that were once very close in color to a surrounding pigment have become obtrusive and appear as darker patches on the painting.) The philosophy of in-painting on the Li Kung-lin handscroll was to make the repairs unobtrusive while ensuring, as far as possible, that these areas would not at a later time conspicuously darken. It was also decided that missing lines and other portions of the painting would not be added, following the belief that no attempt should be made to restore the original work but rather to preserve what remained in the best condition for the longest possible time.

Cord

All three scrolls now needed cords. Because there was not sufficient old cord of a single pattern available, new cord was woven, following the pattern of a sample borrowed from another Sung scroll. The pattern was prepared for the weaver at the Oka studio. A thread count was made, and the pattern copied thread for thread on graph paper. The silk thread was also then dyed at the studio. The cord was woven with a technique that reveals the design on one side in white with a beige ground and on the other in beige with a white ground.

Boxes

Three boxes of paulownia wood were made for the scrolls. The two that contain the painting and the colophons are more formal in style than the perfectly plain one that contains the facsimile and repairs. A deep persimmon-colored lacquered box, also of paulownia wood, was made to hold the three scroll boxes. The boxes and the three large-diameter rollers, themselves works of great precision, were made in Kyoto by Yusai Maeda, whose family has a long history in this craft.

A paper cover, coated with persimmon tannin, was made for the outer box to protect the wood from scratches and staining. A woven green cord passes through slots at the bottom of the box and ties over the paper cover.

The conservation and remounting of the Li Kung-lin handscroll took several years. Some processes—such as silk repair and in-painting—were particularly time-consuming, and much time passed while the work was in various stages on the drying boards. Now complete, the conservation and remounting of the handscroll should extend its life several hundred years.

PHOTOGRAPH CREDITS

Chung-kuo mei-shu ch'üan-chi: Shu-fa chuan-k'o pien (The Complete Collection of Chinese Arts: Calligraphy and Seal Carvings). 7 volumes. Shanghai: Shanghai Shu-hua Ch'u-pan-she, 1986–89.

Figure 27: vol. 4, 1986, p. 34
Figure 30b: vol. 4, 1986, pp. 34–35
Figure 31a: vol. 4, 1986, p. 35
Figure 32: vol. 4, 1986, pp. 34–35

Shodō zenshū (Compilation of Calligraphic Works). New series. 26 volumes. Tokyo: Heibonsha, 1954–69.

Figure 20a: vol. 3, 1959, pl. 6–1
Figure 20b: vol. 3, 1959, pl. 127
Figure 21: vol. 3, 1959, pl. 107
Figure 22: vol. 3, 1959, pl. 113
Figure 26: vol. 15, 1954, pls. 8, 9
Figure 29: vol. 15, 1954, pl. 47
Figure 30: vol. 15, 1954, pls. 8, 9, 11

Shoseki meihin sōkan (Series of Masterpieces of Calligraphy). Tokyo: Nigensha, 1958–79.

Figure 11a: vol. 5, 1958, p. 25
Figure 14b: vol. 5, 1958, pp. 29, 34, 77, 76
Figure 15a: vol. 49, 1960, p. 12
Figure 16a: vol. 28, 1960, p. 42
Figure 16b: vol. 7, 1959, p. 7
Figure 17c: vol. 49, 1960, p. 12
Figure 17d: vol. 5, 1958, p. 34
Figure 18a: vol. 49, 1960, p. 38
Figure 18b: vol. 16, 1959, p. 45
Figure 18c: vol. 5, 1958, p. 16
Figure 18d: vol. 49, 1960, p. 25
Figure 19b: vol. 49, 1960, p. 34
Figure 19c: vol. 7, 1959, p. 21
Figure 24: vol. 96, 1962, p. 5; pp. 12, 13
Figure 25: vol. 96, 1962, p. 7
Figure 28: vol. 45, 1960, p. 30
Figure 30c: vol. 45, 1960, pp. 30–32
Figure 31b: vol. 45, 1960, pp. 30, 32, 33
Figure 32b: vol. 45, 1960, pp. 31, 32, 34